PICTURES AND POPERY

Pictures and Popery

Art and Religion in England, 1660–1760

CLARE HAYNES
University of East Anglia, UK

ASHGATE

Published by
Ashgate Publishing Limited
Gower House
Croft Road
Aldershot
Hampshire GU11 3HR
England

Ashgate Publishing Company
Suite 420
101 Cherry Street
Burlington, VT 05401-4405
USA

Ashgate website: http://www.ashgate.com

British Library Cataloguing in Publication Data
Haynes, Clare, 1960–
    Pictures and Popery: Art and Religion in England, 1660–1760
    1. Art and religion – England – History – 17th century. 2. Art and religion –
    England – History – 18th century. 3. Art and society – England - History –
    17th century. 4. Art and society – England – History – 18th century. 5. Christian
    art and symbolism – Modern period, 1500– . I. Title.
    701'.03'0942

Library of Congress Cataloging-in-Publication Data
Haynes, Clare, 1960–
    Pictures and Popery: Art and Religion in England, 1660–1760 / by Clare Haynes.
        p.   cm.
    Includes bibliographical references and index.
    1. Art and religion – England – History – 17th century. 2. Art and religion –
    England – History – 18th century. 3. Art and society – England – History –
    17th century. 4. Art and society – England – History – 18th century. 5. Christian
    art and symbolism – Modern, 1500– . I. Title.
    N72.R4H37 2006
    701'.030942--dc22   2006005222

ISBN-13: 978-0-7546-5506-0
ISBN-10: 0 7546 5506 7

This book is printed on acid-free paper

Printed and bound in Great Britain by MPG Books Ltd, Bodmin, Cornwall.

Contents

List of Illustrations

Pictures and Poetry

Acknowledgements

The book results mainly from research undertaken for my PhD, which was funded by a scholarship from the AHRB. This work was supplemented by research undertaken in the course of a postdoctoral fellowship awarded by the British Academy (another book, provisionally entitled *Idol or Ornament? Art in the Church of England* is the planned outcome of the postdoctoral research).

I am very grateful to the staff of the following libraries and archives: Lambeth Palace Library, Norwich Cathedral Library, Norfolk Record Office, Canterbury Cathedral and Cambridge University Library. The staff at Ashgate Press, especially Tom Gray, have been great. I would like to express my thanks to Dr John Spurr and Dr Margit Thöfner for their readings of the text.

My thanks to Dr Jane Winters and Dr Jason McElligott for their permission to reproduce parts of Chapters 2 and 5 which appeared in different forms in *Historical Research* and in an essay in *Fear, Exclusion and Revolution: Roger Morrice and his Worlds, 1675–1700*.

A grant from the Scouloudi Foundation in association with the Institute of Historical research ensured that publication was possible.

I have always had an aversion to gushy acknowledgements, but faced with the job of writing my own for the first time, I now understand why they frequently appear so. It proves impossible for me not to take this opportunity to write down in a place where they can all read it, just how grateful I am to the following people for all that they have given me.

My doctoral supervisor, Professor Ludmilla Jordanova, challenged and supported me by turns, teaching me with huge generosity from her experience and scholarship. One cannot hope to repay such a debt, only to accept the gift gracefully and do one's best to honour it. Other academic and administrative staff in the School of World Art Studies & Museology at the University of East Anglia also ensured that I benefited from the wonderful education they provide there.

A number of other scholars have been of great help to me – generous with criticism, words of advice and encouragement (whether I had the wisdom to listen to their criticisms is another matter, and they will be able to judge that from what follows). I am thinking of, in particular, Professor Shearer West, Dr Simon Dell, Dr Mark Goldie, Mr Sandy Heslop, Dr Mark Knights, Mr John Mitchell and Dr Stephen Taylor.

Friends, including Alison Drayton, Jonathan Fuller, Christopher Gärtner, Mary Rose Grieve, Sam Jackson, Judith Miller, Sally Parkinson, Sheena Rolph and Susie West, have taught me a great deal (and made me laugh).

My parents, Mary and Peter Haynes, my brother Simon and my sister Frances have shown, repeatedly, that there are some things one does not have to question.

Chapter 1

Introduction: Art and Anti-Catholicism

Sad to consider that the occasional rise of painting, being chiefly from the popish priesthood, the improvement and culture of it (except the vicious part for the cabinets of the grandees etc.) has turned wholly on the nourishment and support of superstition (chiefly too in ugly forms), and exaltation of that vile shrivelling passion of beggarly modern devotion ... Witness the best picture in the world, Domenichino's *St Jerome*. [Plate 1][1]

In eighteenth-century England, at a time when the nation prided itself on its stalwart defence of the Reformation, the works of art that were most prized were Roman Catholic in subject matter and provenance. Raphael's *Cartoons* [Plates 12–14], whilst they were recognized as works of Catholic apologetics, were considered the foremost works of art existing in England and Domenichino's *Last Communion of St Jerome* [Plate 1] was widely accepted by the English as one of the greatest works of art in the world, and simultaneously, as a work of 'beggarly modern devotion'. This is the first of two apparent paradoxes addressed in this book. The second relates to the Church of England. Despite having strongly worded doctrinal statements against the use of images and a long history of periodic iconoclasm, paintings of the Last Supper, paired 'portraits' of Moses and Aaron, sculpted doves, pelicans and angels and a host of other imagery were to be found in churches during the period. These two paradoxes are not distinct because both result from the same historical phenomenon: the nature of English Protestantism. This book attempts to describe and explain how these paradoxes were dealt with, and contends that religious concerns were very important to how art was viewed and made in England. In addition, it shows how these concerns were mobilized in ongoing debates within the Church of England over the proper forms for the worship of God. Thus, it aims to contribute to two still

---

1   Shaftesbury (1969), p. 119. This passage is taken from Shaftesbury's essay *Plastics* which was unpublished at his death. Domenichino's *Last Communion of St Jerome* was widely appreciated as one of the best paintings in Rome, often appearing in lists of the best three, five or ten pictures (see, for example, Samber (1722), p. 163 and Wright (1764), p. 251).

largely distinct strands of the historiography of the period: the history of art and the history of religion.

Religion mattered in eighteenth-century England. Even for those few with no religious faith, it still mattered a great deal. The country had been through a bitter civil war, and was to depose another Stuart king, over questions of religion. Religious beliefs, ideas and prejudices (most notably, but not exclusively, anti-Catholicism) were discussed in public, frequently and with vigour. It was the stuff of politics in ways that it is perhaps hard for us to grasp. It also shaped people's lives in more intimate ways. Most believed they would one day have to face judgement, and most understood the natural world as working according to God's design. Providence still had a prominent role in explaining events. Even for those few who had set aside conventional religion, religion still shaped the questions they asked of the world, determined the focus of their interests and frequently fired the arguments they had.[2]

The experience of the historian Edward Gibbon (1737–94) illustrates this well. As a young man Gibbon had an eclectic religious life: brought up in a nonjuring family, he converted to Catholicism while he was at Oxford, causing his father to send him to Lausanne to have good Protestant principles instilled in him.[3] Ten years later, on an autumn day in 1764, when he sat listening to vespers being sung in Santa Maria d'Aracoeli on the Capitol, in Rome, and apparently decided on the work that would occupy almost all of the rest of his life, Gibbon may not have believed in God at all. Nevertheless, the book he determined to write that day was formed by Christianity. I am not arguing merely that Gibbon's *History of the Decline and Fall of the Roman Empire* is a book about religion, which it certainly is, but more than that it is a book that was written from a religious viewpoint, however sceptical a one it was.[4] Gibbon engaged with theology and religious history all his life: it mattered to him and his contemporaries.[5] To ignore religion was hardly possible, either for the intellectual or the uneducated.[6]

---

2   See Porter (2000), esp. Chapter 5, and Young (1998b).

3   A Nonjuror was someone who was unable to take the Oaths of Allegiance and Supremacy to William and Mary and their successors after James II had been deposed from the throne in 1688. They believed that to do so would be to break their previous oaths to James. Nonjurors were therefore excluded from the Church of England. See Cross and Livingstone (eds) (1997), Broxap (1924) and Goldie (1982) for Nonjurors and Vallance (2004) for Nonjurors and oaths.

4   Young (1998c).

5   For Gibbon's life see Gibbon (1990) and Porter (1995). See also Gibbon (1961), Bowersock, Clive and Graubard (eds) (1977) and Womersley (ed.) (1997) for a variety of approaches to Edward Gibbon.

6   See Porter (1981) and (2000), Walsh and Taylor (1993) and Wright (ed.) (1988).

Art could hardly matter to the same degree, but it still mattered more than we might imagine. This was for two principal reasons. Firstly art, as a signal of cultural and social superiority, took on new import in what was a period of tremendous social and economic change. As Iain Pears has shown, the number of pictures imported and bought and sold in England increased dramatically after the Restoration in 1660, and art was enmeshed in prominent debates about taste, education and morality.[7] Secondly, the arts were called upon to support the developing sense of England as the great nation of Europe. However, it was troublingly clear that English art did not reign supreme in Europe. When Edward Gibbon acknowledged this ironically in his account of Paris in his *Memoirs,* he observed that:

> an Englishman may hear without reluctance that … Paris is superior to London, since the opulence of the French capital arises from the defects of its government and religion … All superfluous ornament is rejected by the cold frugality of the Protestants; but the Catholic superstition, which is always the enemy of reason, is often the parent of taste.[8]

Gibbon was not the first to observe that Catholicism seemed more fertile ground for art than Protestantism, nor would he be the last. However, his tone of blithe detachment was rarely matched elsewhere, and much effort, both intellectual and practical, was put into encouraging the arts as a patriotic endeavour. Accompanying these efforts was the anxiety as to whether England was actually capable of producing great art at all. If England was a great nation, as most believed it to be, it should be capable of producing great art that would in turn demonstrate its success, as had the great nations of the past.

In terms of the contemporary discourses of art, great art meant only one thing – history painting.[9] Raphael's *Cartoons* and Domenichino's *Last Communion of St Jerome* are history paintings, large-scale narrative paintings of authoritative, and morally or religiously edifying, subject matter. The European canon of art, which the English assented to, was dominated by works, such as those by Raphael and Domenichino, which drew on the Bible, the history and literature of ancient Greece and Rome, the doctrines of the Roman Catholic Church and the lives of the saints. History painting was seen as the summit of artistic achievement, the genre through which artists displayed supreme creative and intellectual skills. It demanded learning, intellectual discernment, as well as masterly skills and a considerable amount of an artist's time. It thus demanded a special kind of attention from the spectator. Often discussed as having a public purpose of moral

---

7   Pears (1988).

8   Gibbon (1990), pp. 134–5.

9   Sculpture, also valued, was rarely considered in English theoretical writings about art.

improvement, history painting was frequently compared to portraiture, which could be perceived as a more private art with the essentially private purpose of remembrance. Thus history painting was the genre in which public virtues were advocated and in which a suitably public system of virtue and excellence was felt to reside and be demonstrated.

However, English patrons were conspicuously unwilling to commission history paintings from English artists; instead, portraiture dominated the market. Ambitious artists had almost insuperable difficulties in earning a living from history painting in England during the eighteenth century, and, perhaps with the exceptions of John Singleton Copley (1738–1815) and Benjamin West (1738–1820), none did.[10] How could an English school of art, worthy of the name, ever develop in these circumstances? The lack of encouragement for home-produced history painting during the eighteenth century has been felt so strongly that subsequently it has been described as the 'tragedy' of British painting. Historians have diagnosed three main causes for it: lack of court patronage, the impracticality of large pictures in contemporary interiors and the antipathy of the Church of England to religious art.[11] The lack of court patronage is well attested, especially in the period after William III and before George III's patronage of Benjamin West. The question of interiors is slightly less clear-cut, as we will see – foreign history paintings were collected and displayed, sometimes even in decorative schemes designed around them. As for the Church of England, it is certain that there were not the extensive opportunities Roman Catholic churches could provide, with an intact tradition of church decoration and the extensive use of side altars.

This latter reason was the one stressed most frequently by contemporaries. For example, it is the only specific reason given by Richard Steele for the lack of history painting in England, in an essay on the English School of painting that appeared in *The Spectator* in 1712. Steele suggested provocatively that rather than founding the English School on history painting, it should be based on portraiture, arguing that England's greatness at portraiture was a national achievement and the result of the nation's particular character and 'climate'. The Italians could not fail to be the best at history painting, he argued, with their store of antique statues and bas-reliefs as 'helps', while England was supreme in portraiture because the country abounded with 'beautiful and noble faces'. In addition, 'no nation in the world delights so much in having their own, or friends' or relations' pictures; whether from their *national* good-nature, or having a love to painting' [my emphasis]. This meant that:

---

10   For J.S. Copley's career in England see Neff (1995). For George III's patronage of Benjamin West see Meyer (1976) and, for West's career, von Erffa and Staley (1986).

11   See Butlin (1991), p. 7 for a summary of this position.

instead of going to Italy, or elsewhere, one that designs for portrait painting ought to study in England. Hither such should come from Holland, France, Italy, Germany &c. as he that intends to practise any other kinds of painting, should go to those parts where 'tis in greatest perfection. 'Tis said that the Blessed Virgin descended from heaven to sit to St. Luke; I dare venture to affirm, that if she should desire another Madonna to be painted by the life, she would come to England.[12]

This playful argument, while it deploys the stuff of anti-Catholic rhetoric, suggests too how profoundly entangled art was with Popery in the English imagination. We will see how this influenced the ways in which the English engaged with art, affecting not just their reception of foreign Catholic art, but the expectations for art as a whole. Steele was quite clear that the popularity of portraiture was due to the fact that patrons were:

not ... encouraged in that great article of religious pictures which the purity of our worship refuses the *free* use of, or from whatever other cause (my emphasis).[13]

His phrase 'free use' is a telling one. Steele does not suggest that the Church of England had a complete antipathy to art, which is now a popular perception of the period. His comment also shows how the identity of history painting was bound up with religious subjects. Portraiture was simply safer.

Similar comments about the lack of encouragement from the Church of England made by William Hogarth (1697–1764), Benjamin Ralph and André Rouquet have been interpreted as suggesting that there were no opportunities for such work. Hogarth, for example, noted rather cryptically in his *Apology for Painters* that 'our religion forbids nay doth not require Images for worship or pictures to work up enthusiasm'. It is undoubtedly significant that, in each case, the context for the remarks was a plea for more patronage of history painting by individual patrons.[14] Artists could not rely on the institutions of church and state for a regular flow of commissions as Catholic painters might be able to. So, if English painters were going to become great artists, the only way this could happen would be through English collectors commissioning history paintings from English artists, rather than buying foreign works. This work of encouraging patrons to commission history paintings appeared

---

12 *The Spectator*, No. 555, 6 December 1712.

13 Ibid.

14 Hogarth, (ed.) Kitson (1968) p. 89 and Rouquet (1755), p. 22. Ralph suggested that ''Tis my opinion, that holy and devout pictures are no fault in themselves, and 'tis certain they have a very fine effect in making the face of religion gay and beautiful' (quoted in Paulson (1993), vol. II, p. 81). In the recent *World of Art* volume on British painting by William Vaughan, the chapter on history paintings is called 'The Tragedy of British History Painting' and the arguments advanced by Ralph are discussed briefly. Historians have argued that the Church's Protestant antipathy to painting 'was at the base of the lack of British history painting' (Vaughan (1999), p. 111).

urgent to many contemporaries exercised by England's apparent failure to develop a great school of art, and these men deployed a rather emphatic rhetoric, which should not be read too literally.

Hogarth repeatedly argued for the elevation of subjects more apt to the current English moment, suggesting that 'modern moral subjects' should take the place of outdated and alien subject matter. In a letter published in the *St James Evening Post* in 1737, he criticized the 'shiploads of dead Christs, Holy Families and Madonnas, and other dismal dark subjects, neither entertaining or ornamental', which dealers were importing (and what is more, Hogarth argued, they were frequently copies passed off on an uneducated public as original works).[15] Pictures like these can be seen to be attacking his own works in his *Battle of the Pictures* [Plate 2], which Hogarth made as an advertisement, in the form of a bidder's ticket, for the auction of his paintings that he organized in 1745. Hogarth's war with what he saw as the twinned corruptions of the subject matter of much European art and the operations of the market was a theme of his life, played out in his writings and his art.[16] Hogarth painted only one work for a church – the large and highly unusual triptych for St Mary's Redcliffe, Bristol, of *The Ascension of Christ* with *The Sealing of the Sepulchre* and *The Three Marys Visiting the Sepulchre*. However, there were other opportunities for religious painting in England. Hogarth, for example, painted a staircase at St Bartholomew's hospital based on the parable of the Good Samaritan; the subject of *Moses before Pharaoh's Daughter* for the Foundling Hospital and *Paul before Felix* for Lincoln's Inn. In addition, and contrary to common perception, there was actually a good deal of figurative and narrative art deployed in many churches in this period. Once we begin to take this body of material into account, our understanding of the possibilities for art in eighteenth-century England will be refined. This will be discussed in Chapter 5.

Chapters 2, 3 and 4 deal with the reception of art in England. Chapter 2 is set in Italy, though. A visit to Rome was considered highly desirable for the education of elite young men as part of a European grand tour. Besides treading in the footsteps of the heroes of the classical literature they had been taught to model themselves on, they also went to see and learn to appreciate all the best of ancient and modern art. This was, as we shall see, considered an important means of training the individual's taste and judgement. When Joshua Reynolds (1723–92) arrived in Rome in 1750 he wrote home to one of

---

15   Quoted in Uglow (1997), p. 323.

16   His only attempt at 'grand manner' history painting, *Sigismunda*, made in response to the sale of a dubious Correggio in the Luke Schaub sale of 1758, for the enormous sum of £404, 5s (the painting has subsequently been attributed to the less prestigious artist Francesco Furini). Hogarth's painting met only with derision. See Uglow (1997), esp. pp. 622–40 and Paulson (1993), vol. 3, pp. 224–35.

his patrons, Lord Edgcumbe (1716–61), expressing succinctly his gratitude and enthusiasm:

> I am now (thanks to your lordship) at the height of my wishes, in the midst of the greatest works of art that the world has produced. I had a very long passage, though a very pleasant one. I am at last in Rome.[17]

The grand tour was the single most important way in which experience and knowledge of art was gathered by artists and the English elite in this period. We will explore, in particular, how tourists experienced the contemporary Catholicism of Rome alongside its ancient past, and on what terms they engaged with the art that they went to see in churches. The knowledge and experience that tourists gained filtered through to a wider audience through reproductions, and discussions of painting in newspapers, books on art and travel, and in poetry.

At the time, the most famous and most reproduced works of art in England were the *Raphael Cartoons*, which were owned by the crown. The *Cartoons* were known across Europe, recognized as major works by Raphael, who was almost universally acknowledged to be the greatest modern artist (together with Michelangelo). In Chapter 3, we will explore how the Catholic content of the *Cartoons* was attended to, while their status as the most important works outside Rome by Raphael was celebrated and used to support arguments for England's cultural superiority. We will see that these works of art were transposed into an English Protestant register, becoming simultaneously works of spiritual edification and objects of national pride. In Chapter 4 we discuss the role of Catholic pictures in English homes. After a discussion of the extent to which such pictures were collected, the chapter addresses the question of what English Protestants thought about the pictures on their walls which showed subject matter that was not just alien to them, but to which they were positively antagonistic.

Chapter 5 deals with the use of art in the Church of England. Much of the discussion of the previous chapters begs one question: what was a properly orthodox position for a member of the Church of England to take in relation to the depiction of religious subjects? This chapter explores the ongoing debates in the Church of England about the possibility that there was a safe and justifiable role for art to play in reformed religion. It reveals that the questions that an English tourist might have asked himself in a church in Rome, or in a picture gallery, went beyond being about art, going to the heart of what it meant to be English and a Protestant.

The chronological span of the book, from 1660 to 1760 was chosen for several reasons. The end date was picked for the pragmatic reason that one simply has to stop somewhere (rather than the year George III succeeded to

---

17 Reynolds to Lord Edgcumbe after May 1750 in Ingamells and Edgcumbe (eds) (2000), p. 9.

the throne being of any significance to the story told here). By contrast, the
start date for the study, 1660, saw the restoration of the Stuart monarchy. This
event and the re-establishment of the Church of England in 1660–62 are often
used by historians to mark the beginning of the eighteenth century, thereby
suggesting, however unintentionally, that what went before was different
from what came after. 1660–62 is the start date for this study because the
Church of England is very important to the story the book tells. However,
there is a great deal to be said for seeing the events of 1660–62 in the context
of a much longer history of the Reformation in England: the restoration
certainly did not settle any of the disputes over religious difference that had
been at the heart of the civil war, and in many ways it fired further disputes,
which would continue on into the eighteenth and nineteenth centuries.
It is also true that the central dilemmas faced by English Protestants in
regard to images in the eighteenth century had existed since the beginning
of the Reformation. However, the restoration settlement, the rise of a very
substantial market for art and the new political and social charges that
taste took on in the eighteenth century, did mean that these problems were
approached differently. This study will therefore attend to continuities as
well as changes.

The Reformation in England was part of a Europe-wide movement that
sought to refigure the relationship of the individual and his God. It involved,
as John Bossy expressed it, 'a devaluation of the image and symbol in favour
of the audible or visible word; it was also a devaluation of the collective
existence represented by sacraments, saints, and the "unwritten" tradition of
the Church, in favour of a naked confrontation with the scriptures'.[18] Every
aspect of religious practice and tradition was questioned, and a shared past
was collectively rejected in those places where Protestantism was embraced.
The revolutionary aspect of the Reformation is perhaps most visible to us
in the campaigns of iconoclasm which marked its arrival in many places.
However, the Reformation was not a single seismic event, for the questions
to be solved were large and all-embracing: if the past was devalued, what
should stand in its place, and could anything be safely salvaged from it? The
Reformation was not completed in the sixteenth century; it was still being
worked on and fought over in the late eighteenth century, as we will discuss
in Chapter 5.

There is not space to review the religious conflicts of the sixteenth and
early seventeenth centuries here, but there was nothing inevitable about the
settlement that was reached in 1662, and it was a fragile one. Puritanism had
not won the hearts and minds of the English, but neither had Laudianism.

---

18   Bossy (1985), p. 97. Bossy is making a general point about the Reformation as
a pan-European movement, but it is possible to apply it more specifically to the case
of England. For the national characteristics and shared culture of the Reformation
Scribner, Porter and Teich (eds) (1994) is very useful.

A middle way between Popery and Dissent was sought, but it must suffice to say here that the Church that was re-established in 1662 was one whose doctrines were ambiguous and 'full of anomalies and compromises'.[19] The *Book of Common Prayer* and the *Book of Homilies*, the two key books of doctrine of the Church of England, were inconsistent and capable of multiple interpretations. It has been claimed by more than one historian that it was this very ambiguity, which was a kind of pragmatism, that allowed the Church to survive.[20] Nevertheless the *Act of Uniformity* which re-established the Church officially in 1662, by imposing the exclusive use of the *Book of Common Prayer* in public worship, revealed immediately a major fracture in the potential polity of the church. Ministers who refused to be episcopally ordained or refused to take oaths against armed rebellion and the National Covenant were excluded from the Church. It was a purge designed to rid the Church of England of Presbyterians and of republican radicals among the clergy. It was an attempt to end finally the influence of what had been known as Puritanism. In all around 2,000 ministers left or were forced from their posts. Politics and religion were inseparable.

The *Act of Uniformity* was a measure designed to reintegrate church and state under the jurisdiction of monarch and parliament and to enforce civil peace by imposing a single model of religious practice. Many will have hoped that those ejected from the Church would find their way back to it. Although Charles II had promised comprehension and toleration, measures such as the *Conventicle Act* (1664) and the cancellation of his *Declaration of Indulgence* in 1673 ensured that those Protestants who had been excluded from the Church were subject to increasing legal constraint and, sometimes, harassment. Threats from abroad and fears that the country might yet slide back into civil war were felt vividly. The intense political battles, which ensued between Whigs and Tories over the threat of Catholicism, which we will discuss further in Chapter 5, meant that it proved impossible to gather all consciences within one church.

Nevertheless, the Church was a communion of diverse beliefs: for example, some conformed to the Church of England merely in order to satisfy the confessional qualification for public office, while they continued to maintain beliefs contrary to the Church's doctrines. But it was not just those with Dissenting sympathies who felt uncomfortable, for the revised *Book of Common Prayer* still contained some aspects of Calvinist doctrine, such as Article 17 on Predestination. The *Act of Uniformity* did not deliver orthodoxy and thus, the Church was a heterogeneous body under enormous tensions and parishes could include members ill at ease with one another. Among all the advocacy of particular positions, there was a widespread view that different views of the liturgy and identity of the Church had

---

19 MacCulloch (1991), p. 5.
20 MacCulloch (1991) and Spurr (1991).

somehow to be accommodated because the cost of a further schism would be the breakdown of order in the state as a whole – a return to the chaos of the 1640s. Thus, the necessity for the existence of an established Church was widely perceived, even among some Dissenters; hence the attempts made to find a comprehensive formulation for the national church both by those inside and outside the Church. Its role as part of the political settlement, as the bastion against the re-emergence of civil conflict and Popery, was considered essential.

When, in 1685, Charles II died and his brother James II succeeded to the throne, many in the nation felt considerable foreboding. James II was a Roman Catholic. After just three years of rule, he was deposed from the throne by his people, having given them sufficient signs to make them believe that he intended to reintroduce absolutism and Roman Catholicism. When, in the summer of 1688, his wife, the ardently Catholic Mary of Modena, gave birth to a healthy male heir, the possibility of a Roman Catholic successor to James became real. A formal invitation by just seven fairly senior politicians was all the excuse that the Dutchman, William of Orange, needed to invade, and on the arrival of William's troops and many desertions from his own army, James II fled to France. William and his wife Mary, who was James's eldest daughter, were both staunchly Protestant. Never again would a Catholic be allowed to ascend the throne. The deposition of James was nothing less than a revolution, although very little blood was spilled in the process of it. However, it did require many to wrestle with their consciences because fundamental principles, of non-resistance and the belief in James's divine right to rule, had to be set aside in order that the 'Popery' of this Catholic ruler could be resisted. Some could not find peace because of the oaths they had made to James II and they found themselves unable to make oaths to William and Mary. Again, the Church of England excluded some of the nation's Protestants. Four hundred ministers and bishops were deprived in 1689, and had to leave the Church, as did some prominent laymen. A parallel Church of England was set up by these Nonjurors, which survived until the late eighteenth century.

Much more significant than the Nonjurors for British politics was the movement that developed in support of James II. Exiled in France, and establishing a shadow court just outside Paris, the deposed king attracted a loose association of Nonjurors, Protestants, some Catholics and the simply disaffected, who supported his claim to the throne, which developed into a movement known as Jacobitism. Support from the French government meant that the fears of an armed invasion to take back the throne were well founded, and indeed twice in the next 60 years, two of James's successors led major, if, in the end, unsuccessful, invasions. The Battle at Culloden in 1746 marked the end of these ambitions and the fear of the restoration of Roman Catholicism as a political force in the nation consequently receded. However, the war against Popery did not end there.

Opposition to Catholicism was maintained on two grounds: even after the Council of Trent curbed some of the worst abuses, the Catholic Church was still viewed as a corruption of Christ's church on earth. It is worth making clear here that anti-Catholicism was maintained with very little reference to the actual doctrines of the Church of Rome. The break with Rome was final and the Church of England aimed to be a 'true' church: true to the apostolic principles of the New Testament. Just what this 'true' church should consist of was a matter of vigorous debate. However, it must be kept in mind that anti-Catholicism was a religious conviction of a quite fundamental sort, a set of ideas which was formative of people's own religious beliefs. The second reason for resisting Popery was political. It was coupled with corrupt governance in English minds, with the reputation of Louis XIV, for example, which James's short reign merely reinforced. Thus anti-Catholicism was a religious and a political position. This essential fact of anti-Catholicism was the idea that held the Church of England together, as it held the nation together. For all its ambiguity, the Church of England had to remain clearly and simply that which the Church of Rome was not and if there was one thing all Protestants could agree about, it was a clear need to distance themselves from Popery.

Anti-Catholicism has been much discussed in recent years, as it has become clear that it was the most important aspect of British identity. The work of Colin Haydon and Linda Colley, together with a number of subsequent studies, has demonstrated just how fundamental it was to the experience of nationality in the eighteenth century.[21] 'No Popery' became the British shibboleth, but it had long served the Protestants of the four nations. Anti-Catholicism was also institutionalized. There were many legal sanctions against Catholics, which were, from time to time, viciously enacted, and the national calendar was dominated by remembrance of events in which the triumph over Catholicism could be celebrated, and the procession and burning of effigies of the pope was frequently a feature of such celebrations. It is worth stressing that individuals were imprisoned for practising their religion, they were subject to double land taxes, were not entitled to own weapons or horses, nor could they play a role in public life. Although the application of the penal code against Catholics depended on the opinion of the local aristocracy and other local leaders towards the Catholics in their communities, punitive taxation remained in force throughout the eighteenth century, raids on suspected mass houses were still being instigated in

---

21 I am prevented from using the term 'British' because the intimate connections between the reception of art and the Church of England is an important part of the story I want to tell. I hope readers will treat this book as a case study in respect of the wider British history of which it is a part. For a discussion of the overlapping identities of Englishness and Britishness see Colley (1992a), esp. pp. 13 and 162.

the 1760s and in times of crisis, Catholics were the first to be targeted as suspicious.

Once the threat of Jacobitism faded in 1746, toleration grew up among some sections of the governing elite, although the extent of it is still open to question. Political events in America eventually prompted the first easing of the disabilities Catholics were under in 1778, but the recognition by the papacy of George III as King in 1766, and the suppression of the Jesuits by Clement XIV in 1773, were key events, suggesting to many that Catholicism was changing. However, as late as the 1760s there were scares about a rise in Popery, which were widely believed, even among the elite, and in 1780 the worst riots ever known in London took place, because of the moves to alleviate some of the legal sanctions against Catholics. Again, cries of 'No Popery' resounded through the streets, prisons were raided, the Bank of England was attacked and Catholic houses were set on fire, as were those of Sir George Savile (1726–84), who introduced the bill that became the Catholic Relief Act of 1778, and the Lord Chief Justice, Sir James Mansfield (c.1734–1821). Other causes contributed to the ferocity of the riots besides a fear of Popery, but the riots demonstrated how anti-Catholicism was still a potent force in the national psyche. This has not evaporated completely today.

It may not need rehearsing, but anti-Catholicism was sustained because of the fundamental fact that the Reformation involved a negation of Catholicism – Protestantism was inescapably anti-Catholic. It was not just that there were aspects of Catholic doctrine (both perceived and actual) that Protestants did not believe (principally: transubstantiation, the use of images, the intercession of the saints and the powers assumed by priests and especially the pope). Catholicism was not a separate 'other', whose alien beliefs could safely be disregarded. For example, some have suggested that the Catholic content of some pictures was ignored or neutralized by English spectators.[22] In fact, just as they worked out what their religious practice was by being very aware of the 'heresies' of Catholicism, English Protestants developed ways of approaching Catholic art, which allowed its undoubted prestige to accrue to the nation and to the individual spectator, while they policed very carefully the ideas it expressed and their responses to it. There could be no simple formula for doing this, and this book will not untie the paradoxes that were discussed at the beginning of the Introduction. It will describe instead how contemporaries managed their responses to Catholic culture, and how religious concerns were mobilized frequently in art theory and practice. As we shall see, much of this rested on the judgement of an individual and his own religious aesthetic. Take for example two men who had, in many ways, very similar outlooks. Both Thomas Newton (1704–82) and Richard Terrick (1710–77) were bishops of the Church of England and both had prosecuted Catholic mass houses in the Popery scare of the mid

---

22   See Llewellyn (1999), p. 77 and Pears (1988), p. 43.

1760s. However, in 1773 they were lined up on opposing sides over plans for the installation of some religious paintings by leading members of the Royal Academy, including Sir Joshua Reynolds, Benjamin West and others in St Paul's Cathedral. Thomas Newton, who was Bishop of Bristol, was also Dean of St Paul's and was in support of the scheme, but Terrick, the Bishop of London, was opposed to it and would not let it proceed even though there were many influential figures, including George III, known to support it. Terrick's position was straightforward: the introduction of paintings into the cathedral would encourage Popery. At the heart of this dispute was one simple question – just how reformed was the English nation?

Chapter 2

The Grand Tour: Art in the Maintenance of the Cultural Hegemony of the Gentleman

Samuel Johnson (1709–84), who never visited Italy, remarked that 'a man who has not been in Italy, is always conscious of an inferiority, from his not having seen what it is expected a man should see'. These remarks are quoted frequently to demonstrate the cultural and social power of the grand tour. Less frequently discussed is the amplification Johnson made of his remarks:

> The grand object of travelling is to see the shores of the Mediterranean. On those shores were the four great Empires of the world; the Assyrian, the Persian, the Grecian, and the Roman. All our religion, almost all our law, almost all our arts, almost all that sets us above savages, has come to us from the shores of Mediterranean.[1]

Johnson's recognition of Italy as the main artery of culture, through which the influences of past civilizations had passed, gives a different cast to the first section of his remarks, suggesting something of the complex hold the peninsula had, not just on the English, but on the pan-European imagination.[2] His amplification demonstrates too the richly historicized nature of the tour, and the intellectual as well as cultural status it carried. Scholars have, on the whole, settled for providing accounts of the journeys, experiences, sights and sounds and souvenirs of the grand tour, rather than discussing the complexities of the political and cultural project which lay at its heart.[3] I want to argue that by thinking about the tour in terms of the visual and historical education it provided, we should see more clearly why looking at art, and the tour itself, was thought to be so important.

---

1   Boswell (1980), p. 742.

2   His stress of the other areas of the Mediterranean, as places to travel to, was less usual. Certainly in the first half of the century extended tours would have been rare, before, for example, Stuart and Revett's *Antiquities of Athens* (1762).

3   The exceptions are Chloe Chard whose work on the grand tour has invigorated discussion, esp. Chard (1999), and Jeremy Black who has offered some insightful and properly historicized comments in Black (1990) and Black (1997b). See also Cohen (1996) for a very useful discussion of gender, education and the tour.

Just how should we think about an English Protestant walking into a Catholic church in Rome to see and admire works of art? On what basis did tourists engage with the art they had come to see? How was the encounter with Popery, the sights, sounds and smells of contemporary Catholicism, managed in relation to these works of art? A perhaps unique visual record of this almost commonplace event in the life of a tourist is the extraordinary drawing commissioned by Thomas Coke, First Earl of Leicester, from Bartoli, of his tutor Dr Hobart and himself being shown the chapel of St Ignatius Loyola, the founder of the Jesuits, in the Gesù [Plate 3]. It is suggestive that the figures are dwarfed by the depiction of the opulently ornamented architecture, which is prioritized by a subtle exaggeration of proportion and an unrealistic perspective. Unfortunately we have no textual record of what passed through these particular tourists' minds as they viewed the chapel, but we do have other sources which can help us to build up a sense of the terms on which the English looked at pictures and other works of art. This is a theme which has received surprisingly little attention in the literature on the grand tour.[4] In the course of establishing a history of looking in modern Rome, we will also discuss the associations that were established between the contemporary experience of modern Rome and the Rome of the grand tourist's imagination – the Rome whose ancient ruins he came to walk among.

Italy's past, as the conduit of the mixed inheritance referred to by Johnson, and Rome's past, more especially, acted as a web of significance which enmeshed European culture: ancient Rome, its history, politics, philosophy and arts had unrivalled authority during this period.[5] Classical poetry and sculpture, for example, stood in such high esteem that imitation of the ancients in these fields was given a very high priority in cultural practice.[6] Rome was, as an identification, ubiquitous: London was sometimes described as the new Rome (with both positive and negative connotations), politicians employed images of themselves as republican senators, and widespread use was made of classical allusions which depended on an intimate association of 'Ancient' Rome and 'Modern' England.[7] This association was manifest in, and reinforced by, elite education. After learning to read and write and making a start on their religious education, students progressed to the study of a curriculum loosely based on the *trivium* and *quadrivium*, supplemented by history and geography. This form of education, as Joseph Levine has argued,

---

4   However, see Black (1997b) for a brief discussion pp. 268–74.

5   This also included the acknowledgement of Rome's inheritance from the Greeks, whose achievements were similarly celebrated, but perhaps not so ubiquitously. Debate over the relative merits of the Ancients and Moderns was vigorous and continuous during our period. In some spheres, such as religion and science, put simply, the moderns felt themselves to be ascendant. See Levine (1991).

6   See Levine (1987), Erskine-Hill (1983) and Haskell and Penny (1981).

7   See Ayres (1997).

was almost 'perfectly continuous from Thomas Elyot under Henry VIII to Horace Walpole and the Earl of Chesterfield under George III'.[8] It was a system that operated across Europe and provided a common frame of reference and stock of intellectual resources that was the basis of cosmopolitan culture. The grand tour was intended to supplement this education in two particular ways: firstly, by allowing the tourist to see significant sites of antiquity. As Richard Steele put it, in his essay on the tour in *The Spectator*:

> nother end of travelling, which deserves to be considered, is the improving our taste of the best authors of antiquity, by seeing the places where they lived, and of which they wrote; to compare the natural face of the country with the descriptions they have given us, and observe how well the picture agrees with the original.[9]

Secondly, travelling itself was perceived to be a beneficial experience:

> Certainly the true End of visiting Foreign Parts, is to look into their Customs and Policies, and observe in what Particulars they excel or come short of our own; to unlearn some odd Peculiarities in our Manners, and wear off such awkward Stiffnesses and Affectations in our Behaviour, as may possibly have been contracted from constantly associating with one Nation of men, by a more free, general, and mixed Conversation.[10]

While it is true that for some the tour functioned more as an adventurous rite of passage than a sober learning experience, these two aspects of the tour were widely assented to, which explains why nearly all tours had the journey to Rome as their main axis.[11]

There was considerable debate about the value of the tour and at what age the traveller might accrue most benefit from it.[12] The 'polishing' of a

---

8   Levine (1987), p. 74. As Levine points out, the education of dissenters would have been slightly different. In addition, as the century progressed, new initiatives prompted by the thinking of Rousseau, by educational innovators such as Joseph Priestley and the growing concern that the old system was not suitable for fitting children for the new world of trade, gradually changed the type of education thought apt for all groups, including the elite. See Langford (1989), pp. 79–90 on middle-class schooling and Brauer (1959) for elite education. See Porter (2000), pp. 339–63 for a broad overview of theories of education during this period, particularly the period of active change in the second half of the long eighteenth century. Also useful is Ogilvie (1964) regarding the place of Latin and Greek in education.

9   *The Spectator*, no. 364, 28 April 1712.

10   *The Spectator*, no. 364, 28 April 1712.

11   Many secondary accounts of the grand tour describe, and are shaped by, this itinerary: for example, Hibbert (1987) and Wilton and Bignamini (eds) (1996). Black (1997b), pp. 14–83 provides a useful summary of the broadening of itineraries during the century.

12   See Black (1990), pp. 287–305 for a secondary account of this debate. The essays of George Turnbull (1971) and Richard Hurd (1764) provide the most philosophically

young man was a widely discussed aim and, in practice, most of the tourists in the first half of the century were young. 'Polish' was a rather vague holistic concept based on the idea that social grace was significant as the outward sign of a well-stocked mind and some experience of the world.[13] Young men were often accompanied on their tour by an older man as guardian, who might also act as tutor to supervise studies and guide the tourist in the social interactions, which were a key part of the experience. Besides learning languages (particularly French, which was still used at court in England and was the European language of diplomacy) and taking fencing and dancing lessons, the tourist usually undertook a course of guided reading in history and geography, particularly of the areas through which he passed. The tourist was meant to supplement these studies by close observation of the customs, manners, laws, agriculture and manufactures of each region, a stock of knowledge intended to fit him for governing, for running an estate and administering justice when he returned home. In addition it was expected that the young man would be civilized by his experience of French manners, conversation with the elites of the cities he visited and that his judgement, a crucial faculty (as we shall see), would be tuned, and his taste refined, by viewing Italian art and architecture.

However, the journey to Italy was undertaken by a diverse group of men, not all of whom were young, and certainly the details of their programme could vary considerably from the broad outline I have laid out.[14] A rough survey of a substantial number of the entries in the *Dictionary of British and Irish Travellers in Italy, 1701–1800* provides some evidence.[15] Amongst the large number of aristocrats we find men who were, or were to become, lawyers, physicians and artists. A large percentage of them were elected as members of parliament, many became members of learned societies and many of them had been to Oxford or Cambridge. None of these categories is of much analytical help when we consider the remark made by the Professor of English at Oxford, Joseph Spence (1699–1768) during his second trip to Italy (1739–41), when he accompanied, as tutor, Henry, Ninth Earl of Lincoln (1720–94):

> One of the greatest advantages in travelling, for a little man like me, is to make acquaintances with several persons of a higher rank than one could well get at in

---

systematic discussion of the benefits of travel. However, almost every text includes a discussion of the benefits and the best methods for gaining them.

13   The scandal Lord Chesterfield's letters caused is only the most famous example of the heavy reliance that was placed on this principle. See Solkin (1992a), pp. 1–105, esp. 1–49.

14   The grand tour became more popular, especially after the end of the Seven Years War in 1763 and it was increasingly undertaken by women accompanied by male relatives (see Black (1997b), Bohls (1995) and Dolan (2001)).

15   Ingamells (1997).

England, and to converse with them on a foot, and with greater familiarity than one ever could have done, had one stayed always at home.[16]

Spence suggests that he was able to accrue social advantage from his travels. This transformative aspect of the tour means that looking for a class/ professional basis to identify this group of travellers may not be fruitful and, indeed, that to think of the tour solely as the preserve of the rich and young is mistaken. I propose something less tidy as an approach, which is to establish a small set of concepts which I believe each of these tourists would have known about, understood and depended upon. This will enable us to establish how tourists as a group might have looked at pictures in the general terms necessary for this project. It is only by doing this that we can be alive to the complex patterns of significance to be found in the records of the tourists' encounters with Italian religious art during this period. An advantage of this approach is its inclusivity, so that while a philosopher–tourist might hold an idea in its most worked-through form, the youngest or least-educated tourist might grasp it in an attenuated way. This method also acknowledges the different balances in which ideas, complementary and contradicting, are held by individuals. The disadvantage is that it can function just like a least common denominator and hardly do justice to the elaborate positions of each individual. Therefore, where it seems interesting or significant I will discuss some individual positions. However, I hope it will become clear that this set of ideas would have been held at a fairly sophisticated level by almost all these men because of the effects of the dominant system of education (which we have discussed) and the vigorous shared culture of the periodical during this period.[17] There are three attitudes or understandings, in addition to the anti-Catholicism that we discussed in Chapter 1, which I think most tourists would have held, to varying degrees, and we will discuss each of them in turn. They are: 'politeness'; the desirability of a fairly substantial knowledge of ancient Rome (and an appreciation of it providing lessons for contemporary politics and society); and lastly, an acceptance of taste and works of art as indicators of social eminence.

The first of these concepts, 'politeness', was a politically charged cognate of 'polish'. The tour was imagined in terms of the morally charged discourses of politeness that were actively employed in the period covered in this book and which, for example, Addison and Steele were influential in promoting through their periodicals *The Tatler*, *Spectator* and *Guardian*. The tour can be thought of as a 'polite' project; it was meant to engender politeness, an outlook and a demeanour which can be best understood, in Lawrence Klein's formulation, as 'gentlemanly, worldly and graceful'.[18]

---

16 Letter dated 25 April 1741 in Spence (1975), p. 356.

17 See Porter (2000), pp. 72–95 and Downie and Corns (eds) (1993) for the culture of the periodical.

18 Klein (1984–85), p. 203.

Politeness in the hands of Addison, Steele and Shaftesbury was a model of sociability deployed to ease the increasingly anxious relations between different ranks in a period of considerable upheaval in the social order.[19] The fundamental political problem that politeness was aimed at addressing was the identity and recognition of the gentleman in civic society. Fairly rapid changes in economic wealth and structures made the management of political identities and demands of the ranks much less easy.[20] As Paul Langford has observed, 'the debasement of gentility is one of the clearest signs of social change in the eighteenth century, the mark of a fundamental transformation'.[21] In this unstable situation, a potentially inclusive model of social eminence was developed which reinforced the connection of moral virtue to culture, making taste a sign for virtue. Politeness was conceived of as a way of being in the world, as a culture-centred set of practices and a set of moral values, the one standing as the visible guarantee of the other's safe keeping in the polite. The frailty and circularity of such a model is evident at first glance: for example, Shaftesbury never intended that politeness should offer a challenge to aristocratic leadership of the nation and the essentially visual or performative qualities of politeness meant that the system could easily be subverted or adapted by those with no claims to be placed among the polite.[22] Nevertheless, politeness did operate broadly as a social goal, mediating sociability among previously more dispersed social ranks and thus zones for polite activities and interaction proliferated during this period.[23]

The tour operated, as Joseph Spence's comments demonstrate, as one of these zones. The journey to Rome was essentially a journey to gentlemanly political virtue.[24] The intense debate over the identity of the gentleman in society was shaped by the legacy of antiquity and in the field of politics and public life the ancients led, indisputably, over the moderns.[25] Ancient writers on citizenship and the connected concepts of virtue, luxury and the structure

---

19 Corfield (1991) and Earle (1989). See Phillipson (1993) on Addison and Steele and politeness.

20 One of the crucial and most troubling distinctions was made between wealth held in the form of land or 'paper'. See Berry (1994), Pocock (1985) and Phillipson (1993).

21 Langford (1989), p. 66. See also Langford (1991) for this generally and Whyman (1999) for a fascinating account of the tensions of this situation in one gentry family.

22 See Klein (1995a) for 'plebeian' politeness and Phillipson (1993), p. 227 for a discussion of the perceived dangers of hypocrisy.

23 See Brewer (1997), Langford (1991) and several of the essays in Bermingham and Brewer (1995) are useful here. Pears (1982) provides a brief but useful examination of the role of the arts in negotiating social distinctions during this period.

24 I do not mean virtue in a specifically moral sense. It was widely accepted that sexual experimentation was also an aim of many tourists. See Brewer (1997), p. 261 and Chard (1999).

25 See Levine (1981) and (1999), pp. 5–6.

of the polity were given prominence in philosophical thought. The central virtues of *humanitas* elaborated by ancient Roman philosophers (particularly Cicero (143–106 BC)), which had been revived in the Renaissance, were vigorously espoused by intellectuals of the Enlightenment and can be seen to have flourished during this period in attenuated forms among a wider circle than that. This set of qualities which defined the civilized man included active and passive virtues: open-mindedness in religious matters, belief in the brotherhood of all men, the cultivation of reason, an education in the liberal arts, responsibility for the management of justice and the defence of the constitution against tyranny.[26] We can explore how the journey functioned in relation to these ideas of personal and political virtue by returning to Steele's essay on travel, which we discussed earlier. Steele suggested that one of the benefits of seeing ancient sites was that it would improve 'our taste of the best authors of antiquity'. He went on to claim something much more substantial:

> This must certainly be a most charming exercise to the mind that is rightly turned for it; besides, that it may in a good measure be made subservient to morality, if the person is capable of drawing just conclusions concerning the uncertainty of humane things, from the ruinous alterations time and barbarity have brought upon so many palaces, cities, and whole countries, which make the most illustrious figures in history. And this hint may be not a little improved by examining every spot of ground that we find celebrated as the scene of some famous action, or retaining any footsteps of a Cato, Cicero or Brutus, or some such great vertuous man. A nearer view of any such particular, though really little and trifling in its self, may serve the more powerfully to warm a generous mind to an emulation of their virtues, and a greater ardency of ambition to imitate their bright examples.[27]

Steele's essay demonstrates how highly charged the tour was as a cultural phenomenon and how intimate the connections were between English virtue and Italian tourism. The semantic proximity of the words 'virtue', 'virtuoso' and '*vertu*', meaning moral rectitude, a person of learning and judgement and objects of artistic or connoisseurial interest, respectively, underlines this connection and explains why, for example, Horace Walpole (1717–97) could describe Italy as 'virtu-land' in a letter to Horace Mann (1701–86) in 1764.[28] Among objects of '*vertu*', antique sculpture was highly prized by tourists and finding, repairing (and forging) classical remains for sale to tourists was an increasingly lucrative business in Italy.[29] These works were considered embodiments of the ideas and associations we have been discussing, and

---

26 This account of *humanitas* depends heavily on that given in Lentin et al. (1979), pp. 17–22.

27 *The Spectator*, no. 364, 28 April 1712.

28 Quoted in Sloan (1996), p. 75. On the virtuoso, see Houghton (1942).

29 See Haskell and Penny (1981).

spaces especially designed to house them when they were brought home emphasized these associations.[30] A similar process of generating and attaching virtuous associations was at work in English sculpted and painted portraiture of the period, as antique schema were used associatively in a number of different ways.[31]

Steele's comments also demonstrate how alive the relationship of contemporary Italy to its ancient past was, as a locus for meditation and of moral significance. This is the second of the shared concepts in the tourist's travel kit that we are exploring. We can observe how sophisticated and historicized was the imaginative repertoire on which the tourist could call, either directly for himself or through the work of writers of tours, such as Addison's very successful *Remarks on Several Parts of Italy* (first published 1705) which concentrated almost entirely on locations and works of classical significance.[32] During his tour (1700–04), Addison wrote a poem addressed to Lord Halifax (1661–1715), *A Letter from Italy*, which is an extended meditation on the contrast between ancient and modern Rome:

> Immortal glories in my mind revive,
> And in my soul a thousand passions strive,
> When Rome's exalted beauties I descry
> Magnificent in piles of ruine lie
> An ampitheater's amazing height
> Here fills my eye with terror and delight,
> ... Here pillars rough with sculpture pierce the skies
> And here the proud triumphal arches rise,
> Where the old Romans deathless acts display'd,
> Their base degenerate progeny upbraid ...

Addison continues by describing the magnificence of ancient sculpture and the 'heavenly figures' of Raphael and then moves on to describe Italy in its contemporary condition:

> How has kind heav'n adorn'd the happy land,
> And scatter'd blessings with a wasteful hand!
> But what avail her unexhausted stores,
> Her blooming mountains, and her sunny shores,
> ... While proud oppression in her valleys reigns,
> And tyranny usurps her happy plains?

The connection between the landscape and liberty was a long established trope in writings about England, as well as of Italy, and Addison's argument moves

---

30 See Ayres (1997), pp. 132–42 and Coatu (1997) and (2000) for sculpture galleries.

31 Solkin (1986), Baker (1995), Coltman (1999).

32 For which he was criticized by Henry Fielding and Horace Walpole (see 'Joseph Addison' in Ingamells (1997)).

swiftly to argue that, although the sun may not shine so brightly over Britain, "'Tis Liberty that crowns Britannia's Isle'.[33] Such arguments as Addison's appear frequently in the literature and it appears that this trope functioned to bolster English national pride in the face of historical Italian cultural superiority. As Jeremy Black demonstrates, it was not just Italy that was subject to this kind of criticism by tourists; the countryside of France and the misery of its inhabitants were described in similar terms, the reasons offered in both cases being the same: the arbitrariness of the governments and the superstition of their religion.[34] However, the Roman Campagna was a particularly powerful stimulus to these kinds of political meditations. Most, if not all, tourists approached Rome with a sense of awe, and the appearance of the countryside on their approach to the city seems to have struck them frequently. As Richard Creed recorded:

> The country or Campania of Rome turns to very little account; there not being people to manage it, it is naturally low, but for want of care is all boggy; and so produces a very ill unwholesome air; the Roman government depopulates and ruins all the country; here it ruins the soil as well as the body.[35]

The appearance of Rome, its topography of ancient ruins and modern churches which jostled for the tourist's attention, seems to have presented a considerable challenge to the tourist which was worked out through historical comparisons between the two ages of the city.[36] In genres such as the *capriccio* [Plate 4] or in *vedute* [Plates 5 and 7], these comparisons were represented and explored frequently. Paired views of ancient and modern Rome, fantastic views which belied the modern appearance of the city and which brought together widely spread buildings into an imagined landscape, demonstrate the play that was alive in the imagining of Rome. Of course, there was no escape from the Catholicism of modern Rome for the English tourist, even if he wanted to avoid it, and as we will discuss, a great deal of what the tourist came to see were modern works of art which hung in Catholic churches.

These comparisons of ancient and modern Rome were actually contrasts, stressing the stark distinctions between the two ages of Rome's history. The contrast between them was felt most acutely by tourists on visiting ancient sites such as the Pantheon and the Colosseum, which were being used as

---

33   Addison (1753b edition), pp. 51, 53. See also Addison's *Remarks*, pp. 113–15 for similar comments in prose. See Mainwaring (1965, first published 1925) for the reputation of the Italian landscape in England. Williamson (1995), Barrell (1984) and Everett (1994) deal with the intersecting ideas of the English landscape in different ways.

34   Black also shows how this was quite sensitive to the foreign political climate. Black (1997b), pp. 222–35.

35   Creed quoted in Black (1997b), p. 222.

36   See, for example, John Dyer's *The Ruins of Rome* (1971, first published 1761) or George Keate's *Ancient and Modern Rome* (1760).

Catholic churches, and, to an extent, as continuing propaganda for the Church of Rome. The claims of the ancient and the modern collided and English anti-Catholicism had to confront Popery head on in those ancient buildings that the Roman Church had put to its own use. During this period the Papacy continued to use the restoration of ancient buildings to assert that the Roman church was the *Ecclesia Triumphans*. Clement XI (1700–21), for example, ordered major renovations of, and alterations to, many of the key palaeo-Christian sites during his papacy (for example, the statues of the Apostles and paintings of the Prophets which he commissioned for the nave of Saint John Lateran, and the repairs and new high altar for the Pantheon, which had been a church since AD 609). Benedict XIV (1740–58) undertook similar projects, including the erection of a large cross and chapels in the Colosseum [Plate 5]. Benedict declared, in a bull of 1749, that:

> Here [at Rome] we see the former rule of superstition buried in oblivion ... we see the sanctuaries of false gods razed to the ground ... how the monuments of tyrants lie prostrate in the dust ... how the precious works intended for the honouring of Roman pride are used for the embellishment of churches: how the memorials erected in thanksgiving to heathen deities for the subjugation of provinces, now, purged of their godless superstition, bear on their summits ... the victorious symbol of the unconquerable cross.[37]

Whether Benedict's words met with any direct comment from Englishmen I have been unable to discover, but their sentiments regarding this practice, in general, are recorded in books, diaries and letters and images [Plate 6]. Joseph Spence wrote of his encounter with antiquity in this way:

> All these places I have often seen with pleasure, but there's one thing that mortifies one – that they turn these old Roman things into modern popish ones ... To a lover of antiquities this is a great fault to see these old things and customs turned into modern ones. The great amphitheatre is daubed over with pictures of saints in fifty places, and the Rotonda (the finest temple left of the ancients) which was dedicated to Jupiter and all the gods, is now dedicated to the Virgin and all the saints.[38]

Spence was not alone in his distaste. Conyers Middleton (1683–1750), famous for his later essay on miracles, also wrote an influential *Letter from Rome, Shewing an Exact Conformity between Popery and Paganism* (1729), which is of considerable use to us.[39] Middleton describes, in conventional terms, his joy at having the opportunity to visit:

---

37 Quoted in Johns (2000), p. 28. For the work of Clement XI see Johns (1993) and for one of his predecessors, Alexander VII (1655–67), see Krautheimer (1985).

38 Letter dated 2/8/1732 in Spence (1975), p. 115.

39 See Stephen (1902), vol. 1, pp. 253–73 and Harrison (1990), p. 144 for Middleton's 'pagano-Papism'.

the authentick monuments of Antiquity that demonstrate the certainty of those histories, which ... have ever since been the chief employment of the learned and polite world; in treading that ground, where at every step we stumble on the ruins of some fabrick described by the Ancients, and cannot help setting a foot on the memorial of some celebrated action, in which the great heroes of antiquity had been personally engaged.[40]

He explains that, by contrast:

my zeal was not that of visiting the holy thresholds of the Apostles, or kissing the feet of their successor. I knew that the ecclesiastical antiquities were most fabulous and legendary; supported by fictions and impostures, too gross to employ the attention of a man of sense. For should we allow them that St Peter had been at Rome (which some learned men, however, have doubted of) yet they had not, I knew, any authentick monuments remaining of him; any visible footsteps subsisting to demonstrate his residence among them.[41]

Having suggested that the apostolic succession, as claimed by the Roman Catholic Church, is a Popish 'fiction' (notice his emphasis on the 'certainty of those histories' in the previous passage), Middleton argues that a rather different succession is more in evidence:

[Nothing] so much helped my imagination to fancy myself wandering about in old heathen Rome, as to observe and attend to their religious worship; all whose ceremonies appeared plainly to have been copied from the rituals of primitive paganism, as if handed down by an uninterrupted succession from the priests of old to the priests of new Rome ...

Nowhere did Middleton sense this more clearly than at the Pantheon [Plate 7], which as the most intact, and architecturally accomplished, ancient building remaining in Rome had a very high status among tourists. Witnessing Popish worship there seems to have raised these feelings very acutely for the English visitor.[42] Middleton argues that worship at the Pantheon was no different from what it had been in the superstitious era when it was erected:

---

40 Middleton (1729), p. 11.
41 Middleton (1729), pp. 9–10.
42 Gibbon's famous resolution to write the *Decline and Fall* took place in much the same circumstances. He recorded it in his Memoirs: on 'the fifteenth of October 1764, in the close of evening, as I sat musing in the Church of the Zoccolanti or Franciscan friars, while they were singing Vespers in the Temple of Jupiter on the ruins of the Capitol'. Gibbon (1990), p. 143. It has been suggested, by Melvyn New, that this was a trope that Gibbon had borrowed from Middleton. New quotes another revealing example of this from Middleton's *History of the Life of ... Cicero*, in which he described the use of Cicero's villa as a Dominican monastery in these terms:

For as in the old temple every one might find the god of his country, and address himself to that deity, whose religion he was most devoted to; 'tis just the same thing now; every one chuses the patron he likes best; and one may see here different services going on at the same time at different altars, with distinct congregations around them, just as the inclinations of the people lead them to the worship of this or that particular saint.[43]

Middleton, like everyone on the tour, could not avoid encountering Roman Catholicism; the challenge was how one managed that encounter. Much of the reason for coming to Rome was to see great 'modern' works of art, many of which were to be found in Catholic churches for, as Thomas Nugent put it in his widely used guide *The Grand Tour*:

Rome is the great school of painters, abounding with a larger quantity of excellent pictures than any other city of the universe. These paintings are all by modern hands, that is, since the restoration of learning and the polite arts; the antient paintings having perished through the injury of time.[44]

So before we consider how the English did handle looking at art in Rome, we need to understand just what the investment was that the British had in looking so attentively at art, which was often in settings and depicting ideas to which they were politically and religiously antagonistic. This is the last of the three 'concepts' that we will explore, before turning to consider how English tourists looked at Catholic art. It is significant that the spectatorship of Catholic art in Rome has not been explored in any depth before and this is probably partly due to the fact that the Renaissance art the British admired was, and remains, so canonical that it can appear a facile question – it is, self-evidently as it were, the best art.[45] However, once we acknowledge that

---

Strange revolution! to see Cicero's portico's converted to Monkish cloisters! The seat of the most refined reason, wit, and learning, to a nursery of superstition, bigotry, and enthusiasm!

Quoted in New (1978), p. 51.

43   Middleton (1729), p. 32. We will discuss English Protestant opposition to Catholic practice in more depth in Chapter 4. Middleton also muses on the turning of ancient statues into images of saints. As does Edward Wright (Wright (1764), p. 208). Both writers wonder about which it would be better to worship and both conclude that the modern worship of images is more superstitious than the ancient.

44   Nugent (1756), vol. III, p. 258. Nugent does acknowledge three exceptions to this statement including the very famous *Aldobrandini Wedding*, but the small amount of painting left made its status rather uncertain because there was no way of judging it in comparison with the claims made for classical painting in texts, nor of knowing whether these remaining examples were excellent or poor examples. Thus comparisons of ancient and modern painting were limited, in ways that comparisons of sculpture were not.

45   For scholarship that does acknowledge these issues briefly see Pears (1988), principally, pp. 42–3 and Llewellyn (1999).

there were potential difficulties involved, attention must be given to both the reasons the British accepted this hierarchy and the strategies they developed to manage any conflict that arose.

One quickly gains the impression from tour writers that their experience of the continent had served only to reinforce the idea that the English were lagging behind in matters of high culture.[46] In his *Essay towards the Preventing the Ruin of Great Britain*, written on his return from one of the most extensive tours of the period (as tutor to St George Ashe (*c*.1698–1721)), the philosopher and classicist George Berkeley DD (1685–1753) argued, as many others did, that the arts should be at the heart of public life:

> Those noble arts of architecture, sculpture, and painting do not only adorn the public, but have also an influence on the minds and manners of men, filling them with great ideas, and spiriting them up to an emulation of worthy actions. For this cause they were cultivated and encouraged by the Greek cities, who vied with each other in building and adorning their temples, theaters [*sic*], porticos and the like public works, at the same time that they discouraged private luxury: the very reverse of our conduct.[47]

Berkeley considered all the arts together and it is worth mentioning that while this book addresses painting almost exclusively because the problems of religious identity were discussed most urgently in relation to that art form, the same questions were asked about architecture, sculpture and music. The idea that a great state manifested its virtue and superiority in its cultural production and that the arts had real political effectiveness were fundamental historical ideas. However, such a perspective was accompanied by an uneasiness over the recent or contemporary artistic excellence manifest in France and Italy, which could not be explained by this model. However, attitudes to other countries were rarely so crude that the more admirable aspects of their cultures could not be appreciated and the lessons learnt, as Steele acknowledged in his essay on travel. Consequently a great many books on painting and sculpture begin with a plea for greater noble and gentry patronage of, and participation in, the arts in England.[48]

---

46   Ventures such as the Anti-Gallicans, the Society for the Encouragement of Arts, Manufactures and Commerce and the Royal Academy can be seen to be the most prominent examples of action over the seriousness with which this problem was viewed, and the broad scope of the effect a flourishing artistic life was viewed as having during this period. In addition, see Shaftesbury's *Letter Concerning Design* in Shaftesbury (1969).

47   Berkeley (1721), pp. 19–20.

48   See, for example, Buckridge's translation and adaptation of de Piles's *L'art de peinture* (first published 1706). The purpose of the work is to advocate the idea that an English school did already exist (although this involves him drafting Rubens and Van Dyck into its ranks). In his dedication to Robert Child he suggests that: the world admires your goût, and are surprised to see so many rare things together in a country

William Aglionby articulated the political nature of these comparisons that underpinned the tour most clearly in his influential *Painting Illustrated in Three Dialogues* (first published 1685). Aglionby's dialogues are between the Traveller and the Friend, whom he seeks to encourage in an appreciation of art as being a pursuit worthy and indicative of his gentlemanly status. The Traveller argues that it was travel that had generated the 'extream delight' he has in pictures. In the second of the dialogues Aglionby makes the complex of ideas implicit in the polite project of the tour rather clearer:

> **Traveller**: [Painting] has been the admiration of antiquity, and is still the greatest charm of the most polite part of mankind.
>
> **Friend**: Pray who do you mean by that glorious epithet?
>
> **Traveller**: I mean chiefly the Italians, to whom none can deny the privilege of having been the civilisers of Europe ... and I mean, besides all those in France, Spain, Germany, Low-countries, and England, who are lovers of those arts, and endeavour to promote them in their own nation.[49]

The fact that travel was needed to develop a taste for art is of great importance because it gives us a further hint of how the appreciation of art was constructed strongly in national terms. Aglionby could be confident that his English readers felt themselves to be superior to, for example, the French and Spanish (with whom the English were frequently at war) and that therefore his point would strike home.[50] As Jonathan Richardson put it in describing the project of his *Discourse on the Dignity, Certainty, Pleasure and Advantage of the Science of a Connoisseur* (1719):

> It is remarkable that in a country as ours, rich, and abounding with gentlemen of a just and delicate taste in music, poetry and all kinds of literature: such fine writers! such solid reasoners! such able statesmen! gallant solders! excellent divines, lawyers, physicians, mathematicians, and mechanics! and yet so few! so very few lovers, and connoisseurs in painting!

Tainted by associations with Catholicism, painting was, as a burgeoning field, more currently problematic than other visual art forms for the English. There was an active market for sculpture in England (which was considered more dangerous in terms of potential idolatrous significance), but it was

---

where painting, and the politer arts, are not so much encouraged as in those places, where, perhaps, the nobility and gentry are not so well qualified to judge of merit, nor so well able to reward it as in England.

We will discuss the qualities to which Buckridge refers in Chapter 4. See also Berkeley (1721) and Anon (1736) for the national and personal advantages to be gained from patronage of the arts.

49 Aglionby (1972), p. 34.
50 For attitudes to particular foreign nationalities, see Duffy (1986).

almost only for the production of tomb and other forms of commemorative figure sculpture.[51] Sculpture received very little attention in accounts of the tour. Discussions of painting frequently included an account of the art which traced it back to the Greeks and Romans, stressing, as Berkeley did, the high status it had in these 'ideal' societies and the necessity of patronage to the encouragement of the arts.[52] Richardson argued:

> Since the best times of the ancient Greeks and Romans, when this art was in its greatest esteem, and perfection, such a national magnanimity as seems to be the characteristic of our nation has been lost in the world; and yet the love, and knowledge of painting ... bears no proportion to what is to be found not only in Italy ... but in France, Holland and Flanders.[53]

Thus, the 'national magnanimity' of contemporary England was the proper soil for a resurrection of the arts. Furthermore, Richardson suggested in the conclusion of the essay that the English had one more important and fundamental advantage over other nations. In an unusual step, Richardson argued, perhaps for the first time, that the Church of England could act as a guarantor for a new rise of the arts:

> It is the glory of the Protestant church, and especially of the church of England, [which is] the best national church in the world. I say it is the glory of the reformation, that thereby men are set at liberty to judge for themselves. We are thus a body of free men; not the major part in subjection to the rest. Here we are all connoisseurs as we are Protestants; though (as it must needs happen) some are abler connoisseurs than others. And we have abundantly experienced the

---

51 See Coatu (2000) for a discussion of the contents of the sculpture gallery of Charles Lennox, Third Duke of Richmond (1735–1806), which opened in 1758 for the use of artists. Among the antique casts were others from the modern period, together representing, as it were, a history of sculpture. The modern works, including those by Ghiberti (*c*.1378–1455), Sansovino (1486–1570), Michelangelo and Giambologna (1529–1608), were all of secular subjects. Works by Bernini and Legros, which were of religious subjects, were represented only by fragments of the hands from the sculptures (the hands of the figures of Charity and Fortitude from Bernini's tomb of Urban VIII in St Peter's and those from the statue of St Ignatius at the Gesù by Legros (1666–1719)). The single exception to this was a cast of Duquesnoy's (1597–1643) *Saint Susanna*, which one may observe is classical both in the style of its drapery and the restraint of expression. The choices made for the Duke's sculpture gallery are, I believe, very suggestive and worthy of further consideration in the context of the issues being discussed here.

52 See, for example: Samber's translation of Castiglione's *The Courtier* (1724), Book I, pp. 85–6; the preface to an anonymous *Historical and Chronological Series of the Most Eminent Painters* (1739) and Breval's *Remarks on Several Parts of Europe* (1738).

53 Richardson (1792), p. 172. See the similar remarks made by Richardson in his earlier *Essay on the Theory of Painting*: Richardson (1792 edition), pp. 93–5.

advantages of this, since we have thus resumed our natural rights as rational creatures ...

A man that thinks boldly, freely, and thoroughly; that stands upon his own legs, and sees with his own eyes, has a firmness, and serenity of mind, which he that is dependent upon others has not, or cannot reasonably have.[54]

Richardson declares that rational judgement guarantees personal liberty and that in turn this liberty is secure in England because of the religious settlement. This is a significant move in reorientating the discourses of art and taste to fit English circumstances. Images were still intimately associated with superstition and this was perceived to be the major stumbling block for the development of painting and sculpture. If they were to work effectively in this culture, Protestantism had somehow to be brought to work within a model of the operation of the fine arts and the arts within Protestantism. Richardson achieves this, in his argument, by two manoeuvres: first, he asserts that Protestantism is the only true motor of fine judgement and second, that the exercise and improvement of judgement (calling on the rest of his argument in the essay) is the major benefit ascribed to a committed engagement with painting (what Richardson calls 'connoisseurship'). We noted earlier how judgement and virtue were constructed politically, at this time, in the concept of politeness and we can see this operating in justifications for painting as an art. Richardson had already argued that, in a very similar way to Steele:

Not only such ideas are conveyed to us by the help of this art as merely give us pleasure, but such as enlighten the understanding, and put the soul in motion.[55]

George Turnbull argued at length, in his *Treatise on Ancient Painting* (1740), for the benefits of the arts, in similar terms, using a different strategy:

The best ancient philosophers entertained ... [these] sentiments concerning [sculpture and painting]: their fitness in particular, to teach human nature; to display the beauties of virtue and the turpitude of vice; and to convey the most profitable instructions into the mind in the most agreeable manner ... Some moderns of our own country, who are owned to have come nearest to the best ancients in agreeable as well as useful writing, have earnestly inculcated the like notion of the polite arts, and recommended them together with the manly exercises as necessary to complete a truly liberal education.[56]

---

54 Ibid., pp. 259–60.
55 Ibid., p. 178.
56 Turnbull (1971), p. xxi.

Turnbull goes on to argue that 'good taste of nature, of art, and of life, is the same'.[57] Thus painting, as a mode of expression, is integrated, by Richardson and Turnbull, into the model of a polite gentleman in a seamless way: painting is effectively freed from any negative associations with Popish idolatry by the emphasis of antique precedents, the operation of reason and Protestantism.

However, with little or no painting known from the classical period, attention to the art of painting focused on the whole in England on the works of Raphael and his near contemporaries. Antique sculpture, of which much more remained, and modern painting, were tied together as authoritative, in the belief that, along with the other arts of poetry and rhetoric, painting and sculpture had flourished together in antiquity, declined, and that painting, in particular, had begun to revive in Italy in the thirteenth century, reaching its apogee in the work of Raphael and Michelangelo (1475–1564).[58] This chronology was widely accepted and had been promoted most influentially by Giorgio Vasari in his *Lives of the Most Eminent Painters* (1550), and it went unchallenged in England until the nineteenth century. Vasari's work had been read in Britain in the originals and in abridged adaptations from 1622 when Peacham included some of the lives in his *Compleat Gentleman*.[59] Vasari's Florentine/Roman model (both directly and indirectly, through other writers such as Lomazzo (1538–1600) and Bellori (1615–96)) can be said to be the major influence in English understandings of high renaissance art.[60] In Alexander Pope's (1688–1744) *Essay on Criticism* (1711), which advocates the primacy of the ancients over the moderns in poetry, there is a usefully concise summary of this historical view. Having asserted the qualities of a number of ancient critics, including Longinus (*fl.* third century BC) and Quintilian (AD *c*.35–*c*.100), Pope argues:

Thus long succeeding critics justly reigned,
Licence repressed, and useful laws ordained.
Learning and Rome alike in empire grew;
And arts still followed where her eagles flew;
From the same foes, at last, both felt their doom,
And the same age saw learning fall, and Rome.
With tyranny, then superstition joined,
As that the body, this enslaved the mind;

---

57   Ibid., p. xxiii.

58   See Hale (1996), esp. pp. 55–81, and Levine (1999), esp. pp. 101–4, for an interesting discussion of Dryden and Kneller and the parallel of painting and poetry which was a very popular theme during this period.

59   See Gent (1981) for art books in late sixteenth-century and early seventeenth-century libraries.

60   See, for example, Henry Bell's chapter 'On the Rise and Emergency Again of this Art in Italy' in his *An Historical Essay on the Original*[sic] *of Painting* (1728).

Much was believed, but little understood,
And to be dull was construed to be good;
A second deluge learning thus o'er run,
And the monks finished what the Goths begun.
At length Erasmus, that great, injured name,
(The glory of the priesthood, and the shame!)
Stemmed the wild torrent of a barborous age,
And drove those holy vandals off the stage.

But see! each Muse, in Leo's golden days,
Starts from her trance, and trims her withered bays!
Rome's ancient Genius, o'er its ruins spread,
Shakes off the dust, and rears his reverend head.
Then sculpture and her sister-arts revive;
Stones leaped to form, and rocks begin to live;
With sweeter notes each rising temple rung;
A Raphael painted and a Vida sung.[61]

Thus 'modern' painting (and poetry) carried with it the authority of a revival of the excellence of the ancients.[62] As Turnbull put it:

> The analogy between those two ages of painting [of Apelles and of Raphael] in many circumstances is indeed surprising; but it is well vouched and not imagined.[63]

Such a parallel was widely observed and various explanations offered of it.[64] It is worth drawing attention to the way in which the authority of the ancients appears to guarantee that of the moderns in these accounts, so that the modern rise of the arts is conceived of on the same chronological trajectory. Indeed, without acknowledgement of this strong link with antiquity, the British taste for modern art is, I believe, much less easy to understand. The Europe-wide, cosmopolitan taste for sixteenth and early seventeenth century Italian art and the long history of aristocratic collecting of such works in England served to reinforce its ascendancy, but cannot completely explain the hold it

---

61 Pope, *Essay on Criticism*, II, 681–704 in Rogers (ed.) (1993), pp. 37–8. See Hale (1996) pp. 36–41.

62 It is worth noticing how frequently the single name of Raphael is made to carry the weight of this idea, something we will discuss in the next chapter. Addison used the same technique in his *Letter from Italy* (1753b) quoted above.

63 Turnbull (1971), p. xxii. Turnbull's argument is lengthy but is usefully summarized in one of his footnotes: p. 48, fn. 117.

64 See, for example, Richardson's *An Essay on the Theory of Painting*, (1792 edition), pp. 93–5 or George Keate's poem *Ancient and Modern Rome* (1760).

maintained through England's long Reformation.[65] We will explore different aspects of this relationship further in the next chapter.

Although it carried similar connotations for gentlemanly discernment, the spectatorship for modern art was much more hedged round with unease. Whereas looking at a piece of classical sculpture or tracing the steps of Cicero offered relatively safe, long-established and rather direct opportunities for generating meditative associations for the tourist, it is by no means clear that such straightforward transactions were involved when he looked at the art of the moderns. This is not to say that tourists' responses to classical remains were always the same. It is important to remember that political life in England was fraught and that both Whigs and Tories turned to antiquity, and often to the same sources, for comfort and example.[66] Much of the modern painting tourists engaged with was challenging in a different, much more direct way. The *oeuvres* of many of the most-admired artists were dominated by religious works and many of these were to be found in Catholic churches in Papal Rome.

In order to discuss how tourists looked at these works, I will use a small group of grand tour journals and guidebooks, a mix of both relatively well-known and unexplored texts. This resource is rarely used beyond the field of grand tour studies to discuss issues of broader significance, so it may be useful to describe briefly its scope and some of the characteristics of the genre. The published texts used here were all successful, going into at least two editions in the period and some, many more. Books on the tour vary from very expensive large-format texts, often including engravings, to small pocket-sized guides. Most travel accounts describe modern as well as classical art and architecture, amongst descriptions of the topography, commerce, agriculture, laws and histories of the places visited.[67] Addison's account of his tour, discussed earlier, is therefore rare in its concentration on the antique.

Accounts of the grand tour are strikingly interdependent. While a tourist might quote works by writers such as Addison, Keyssler and Bellori in their private journals and correspondence, published writers did so too. Often writers will resist describing certain things they have seen, referring the reader instead to an existing, authoritative account. Sometimes a writer might enter into a dialogue with another, in which supplementary information

---

65 This aspect of my argument will be reinforced by consideration of the use of religious imagery in the Church of England in Chapter 5. For the idea of a 'Long Reformation' see Tyacke (ed.) (1998).

66 See Ayres (1997).

67 Misson's *A New Voyage of Italy* (1695), Nugent's *The Grand Tour* (1756) and Keyssler's *Travels through Germany...* (1756) are three very successful examples of this genre. Unpublished accounts follow this pattern too. For two local examples see the journals of Hamon L'Estrange (1713) (NRO: NF2) and Edmund Rolfe (1759–62) (NRO: MS21GUN3 362X5).

is provided or errors identified. This suggests that there was a sense of this literature as a collective, authoritative, reflexive genre of description. Edward Wright (*c.*1695–*c.*1758), who was particularly interested in painting, and whose tour went into two editions, provides us with a good example of this in his account of his tour:

> We are now come to those noble apartments, generally called the Apartments of Raphael: all the principal paintings in them having been either done by his hand, or at least design'd by him. I shall not pretend to give any description of these admirable performances; 'twould be but *actum agere*; they have been so largely and fully described by Bellori and others formerly, and by Mr Richardson of late, that to these I refer the reader.[68]

Jeremy Black has argued that 'there was a major difference between writing for a small and intimate circle, and producing a work for a large anonymous market ... the conventions expected by the market and the reviewers had to be respected.'[69] While this distinction can be seen to be operative in terms of the intimacy of language and the prominence of the author–subject, it is very noticeable how normative different kinds of accounts of the tour are.[70] Given the shared agenda I have discussed and the interdependence of accounts, this is not surprising. It is worth adding that for many tourists, knowing how to respond well in strange and potentially difficult situations, and demonstrating that this had been achieved, was very important. Hence the advice offered frequently by writers on how to behave inside a Roman Catholic church during a service:

> ... At the exaltation of the host, when they are all upon their knees, many of them thumping their breasts and kissing the ground, and so remaining in that lowest inclination, till the exaltation is over, 'tis sufficient for strangers to incline their bodies a little, without directly kneeling down; and if they omit even that, they stand indeed the gaze of the congregation, as distinguishing themselves for heretics, but receive no personal affront. They will perhaps have it said of them, *Non Sono Christiani*, [they are not Christians;] for they account none to be such, but those that are directly of their own communion.[71]

Religious paintings, while not such doctrinally significant things as the moment when the transubstantiated host is shown to the congregation for

---

68 Wright (1764, first published 1730), p. 262. For Wright, see Connor (1998).

69 Black (1990), p. 188. See Wilton and Bignamini (eds) (1996), pp. 95–103 for other examples of this literature (including a short commentary by Edward Chaney).

70 See Batten (1978) for a discussion of the standards of decorum applying to travel literature during this period.

71 Wright (1764), p. 204. A similar commentary is to be found in Keyssler (1756), vol. II, p. 38. Reports of Roman Catholic services are frequent in tour journals. See Black (1997b), pp. 238–51 for an introduction to religious aspects of the tour.

veneration, were, nevertheless, potentially dangerous as well. As we will discuss in Chapter 5, religious art had not lost its negative associations with idolatry and Popish superstitions for the English. Looking at such works in Roman Catholic churches was therefore likely to be a complex activity.

It is confounding, therefore, to notice that the most obvious characteristic of writing about religious pictures is its general straightforwardness. Paintings are often commented on in the most basic way through the use of single epithets such as 'fine' or 'capital', which might suggest the possession of neither a large critical vocabulary nor much interest. Some tourists used these single terms to describe whole groups of pictures and many journals and published accounts include only checklists of paintings and their locations.[72] In his excellent edition of Sir Joshua Reynolds' tours to Flanders and Holland Harry Mount describes the use of such phrases as expressing 'dumbfounded' admiration. I hope that it will become clear that this is probably not a correct assessment.[73] Hamon l'Estrange, who set off on tour from Hunstanton, Norfolk in 1713, wrote of one of the high points of his tour thus:

> Florence is a beautiful town. The houses being large, and well built. The streets paved with broad smooth stones, here the churches are numerous, and finely painted. The gentlemen let out their coaches to strangers by the day.

Edmund Rolfe, another Norfolk tourist, wrote of the gallery at Parma:

> In the Gallery, is the famous picture of Corregio [sic], which is esteemed one of the best in Italy, and the finest that ever was done by this master, the subject is the Virgin with the infant in her arms, the Magdalene kissing his feet, and St Jerome, and an angel on the other side.

At Bologna he commented:

> At the church of St Giesu & Maria is a picture of the circumcision of our Saviour by Guercino. There is a very tender concern expressed in the face of the Virgin. St Joseph is a fine character.[74]

For writers with a particular interest in painting, descriptions, even of very famous works, are scarcely more elaborate, and in the most sophisticated discussions of pictures there is rarely to be found any mention of idolatry, very little argument with the subject matter of the works, and certainly little sense of them as acts of faith in an alien religious setting. One could compare Rolfe's descriptions to those of Edward Gibbon, for example, who described

---

72 See, for example. Thomas Nugent's list of paintings to be seen in Rome, (1756), vol. 3, pp. 259–68.

73 See Mount (ed.) (1996), p. xxv.

74 L'Estrange, NRO: NF2; Rolfe, NRO: MS21GUN3 362X5, unpaginated.

Domenichino's *Last Communion of St Jerome* in this way in his journal of his journey in 1764:

> [it is] esteemed the second and most faultless picture in Rome [presumably, after Raphael's *Transfiguration*]. The expression is admirable & entirely directed to the Saint, who[se] weakness struggling with his devotion is finely painted. One could scarce conceive that this venerable figure and the sweet innocent boy who is kneeling could be by the same hand.[75]

I want to suggest that the simplicity and uncontentiousness of these descriptions of canonical pictures is entirely *à propos*, that they are part of a modulated pattern of responses to art, which must be considered as a whole. In order to absorb famous, even canonical works into the English sphere of taste, they had to be cut free, to some extent, from the negative connotations of Roman Catholicism. Of course, such connotations could not be done away with completely because they were essential elements in anti-Catholic discourse, entirely necessary to the English patriotic view of its superiority over Catholic Europe. I hope to demonstrate that canonical works of art were allowed to transcend the circumstances in which they were viewed.

To understand this complex situation we must acknowledge the elaborate and often extensive anti-Catholic rhetoric that was also carried in these texts. Much of this rhetoric was, in fact, directed towards anxieties over images and religious enthusiasm, so painting, as a form, was not cut free from the problem of idolatry completely. Extended discussions of idolatry and superstition were, on the whole, kept separate from the discussion of canonical pictures. There were very few ventures made into the doctrinal significance of such works whereas the superstitions attached to, and doctrinal content of, non-canonical works were frequently discussed. Damning criticism of Roman Catholic priests (particularly their duping their congregations through manipulative preaching techniques or the encouragement of superstitious practices), of papal power (often in relation to the wealth of church decoration) and of the practices of votive pictures and offerings (often made in comparison with pagan rituals) were some of the main strategies used by writers about art to discuss the specifically Popish *use* of religious painting that they encountered.

Edward Wright's *Some Observations* ... (1730) is a useful and authoritative text for us because it offers us one of the most substantial accounts of Italian painting made during the period. Wright's work was well known and went into a second edition in 1764.[76] In it the demarcation of canonical from non-canonical is very clearly to be seen at work. In Wright's Preface the division of superstition from canonical works in his descriptive strategy is to be discovered almost immediately:

---

75 Gibbon (1961), p. 244.
76 See Connor (1998), pp. 29–30.

I have here and there interspersed some little stories, as they came in my way, relating to celebrated pieces of painting or other arts ... Some of another kind, I could not forbear inserting, only as a taste, or specimen, of multitudes of others of the like nature, current among them, which may serve to shew the strange superstitious absurdities which are swallowed in gross by the common people, and seem to be even a part of *their* religion: they are laughed at indeed by men of sense, even there; but as they have their effect upon the weaker minds, in subjugating them still more to the power of the priests; the gentlemen are not only suffered, but encouraged to carry on the *pious fraud* and catch the people with whatever bait will serve best to take them.[77]

The clear separation of 'celebrated pieces of painting' from 'superstitious absurdities' is repeated in all of his descriptions of the churches of Rome. Each description of a church follows the same pattern: having described its setting, history and exterior, he proceeds to describe the interior, discussing the best pictures and statues first, and then often finishes it with an account of a superstition associated with the church. Wright discusses only those churches with a work by a canonical artist or at which some particular practice can be brought to the reader's attention as another example of Popish superstition. For example, when Wright discusses the church of S Girolamo della Carità he describes Domenichino's *Last Communion of St Jerome* as one of the 'three pictures esteemed the most capital in Rome, that are not of Raphael's painting'.[78] This painting was described as 'the best picture in the world' by Shaftesbury, and the second best in Rome by Edward Gibbon. In Wright's discussion of the painting, by contrast, he tells a story about the artist:

Domenichino, after having been absent from Rome some time, coming into this church, perhaps to take a view of his own celebrated performance, found a painter at work copying it, and looking over him, pointed out some particulars, which he told him he thought might be mended. The copyer, who possibly might be one of some account, not knowing who it was that directed him, rose up in a sort of disdain, put the pencils in to his hand, and desired him to mend it himself. Domenichino, who was remarkable for the mildness of his temper, silently accepted the offer, turned his back to the original, and not only mended the faults he had named, but ran over all the whole picture, with a wonderful facility and freedom. The other needed not now to be told who Domenichino was; nor was he wanting in making suitable acknowledgements for the specimen of his skill, and the unexpected civility of his behaviour.[79]

77　Wright (1764), pp. ix–x.

78　Ibid., p. 251. The others are Daniele da Volterra's (1509–66) *Descent from the Cross* and Andrea Sacchi's (1599–1661) picture of *S. Romoaldo*.

79　Wright (1764), pp. 250–51. See the comparable description of the work in Samber's *Roma Illustrata* (1722), pp. 82–3.

The painting is described here as an object of artistic authority and as the work of a great painter, who manifests his greatness in his 'civility'.[80] This description should be contrasted with that of the church of SS Vicenzo and Anastasio which is reasonably typical of Wright's accounts of those churches with less celebrated artistic treasures:

> In the church of S Vicenzo and Anastasio, without the walls, are the twelve apostles painted in fresco after the designs of Raphael, and executed, as say some virtuosi, by his hand; but that did not at all appear to me. If they are of his hand, it seem'd to differ much from what we see of his in other places. There is a picture of S Anastasius, said to be nine hundred years old, which frights away devils, and cures diseases, as in the inscription, *Imago S. Anastasi monachi & martyris, cujus aspectu fugari daemones* ['tis enough, indeed to fright the devil] *mobosque curari, acta secundi concilii Niceni testantur* – As this is expressed, it is not clear whether the miracle is ascribed to the saint or to the picture; I should apply it to the saint, but the people there apply it to the picture; perhaps it may be equally true of either ...
>
> I should not trouble the reader, or indeed myself, with such stories as these, but that I think they shew a good deal of the genius and temper of the people, one part of whom is so ready to impose, and the other to receive them.[81]

The arch tone of irony of the phrase 'it may be equally true of either' is representative of the manner in which such 'lesser' pictures as these are discussed by tourists and it is only these for which some idolatrous purposes are acknowledged by tourists.[82] It is worth reiterating the form Wright's commentary on art is taking: works by 'great' artists, such as Domenichino's *St Jerome*, or the frescoes of the apostles, are treated with the language of art criticism, while less conventionally prestigious works are engaged to further an argument against Popish superstition. While pictures of the Apostles are not necessarily contentious subjects, we will see that even where the doctrinal or affective content of works is obviously challenging to the Protestant spectator, such as the *St Jerome* this is nearly always sidestepped in some way for works of the canon. Other paintings, such as the old painting of Saint Anastasius, can be seen to be made to bear the weight of the Roman Catholic

---

80   This should be compared to the similar ways in which Richardson discusses the qualities of Raphael which we will consider briefly in Chapter 3. See Richardson's *Theory of Painting* for the qualities necessary for an artist (*Works*, (1792), pp. 15–19, 90–91, 94–5). These kinds of narrative strategies have a long history in the history of art. See Kriz and Kurz (1979).

81   Wright (1764), pp. 242–3.

82   For example, see Russel (1750), p. 15 and Harvey (NRO: MS20677, T140B).

doctrinal context, so that the canonical works can stand free to be admired by the Protestant tourist.[83]

The creation of a 'safe' zone in which pictures could be admired was made particularly difficult when Popish practices impacted very closely on the spectatorship of a picture:

> I wish the modern devotees would spare one thing in their churches, which the mistaken zeal puts there for ornament, I mean a plate of silver (or sometimes perhaps baser metal), which we see often fix'd upon the picture about the head of the Blessed Virgin, intended for a glory, but looks just like a horseshoe. Sometimes the plate is in the form of a crown, and it is always attended with another of the same sort, but smaller, about the head of Christ. Another way of dressing up the Madonna, much of the same taste, but I think rather more rarely used, is sticking a huge amber necklace upon the picture, across the neck; and covering the painted drapery with a real one of some rich stuff, spread over like an apron. 'Tis well when this zeal lights upon a bad picture; as (to speak truth) it generally does; but, to my great vexation, I have sometimes seen a good one thus mauled and disguised.[84]

Wright's position, as spectator, is revealed in his deployment of a distinction between 'good' and 'bad' pictures. It affirms the idea that we have developed of different standards being deployed. What is clear here is that this practice of extra-ornamenting a picture renders it incapable of being considered as a work of art. By using the words 'mauled' and 'disguised' he suggests that these paintings are transformed, that they are made into something transgressive. The language of English art spectatorship, which as we have seen, did not acknowledge the religious functions this art was made to fulfil, is confronted here by pictures as 'images', as objects with a function, a continuing religious significance.[85] Thus, Wright argues, pictures that might otherwise have merited his attention, which in other circumstances the English tourist might have attended to, must be passed over because the accretions of Popish superstition cannot be ignored. The idea of these works as Popish cannot be evacuated or pushed aside from the tourist's experience of them. Jonathan Richardson discussed the same practice of extra-ornamentation from a slightly different angle:

---

83   We will discuss the terms on which such pictures were approached in more detail in Chapters 3 and 4.

84   Wright (1764), pp. 201–2. Wright also discusses the decoration of sculptures such as that of S Maria de Carmine, at the church of San Chrysogonus in Rome, which was 'dressed out in a perfect modern hoop-petticoat, with a world of other ornaments, which they had hung upon the statue against one of her holidays. She was mightily set out with candles, and had great adoration paid to her' (p. 240).

85   See Chapter 4 for further discussion.

generally speaking the monks, as they know very little of pictures, they are exceedingly careless of them, so that those that are in monasteries are for the most part horridly ill used. Another piece of *Gothicism* I must not omit, which is, that 'tis very common in Italy to see a fine picture of the Blessed Virgin cut to let in a glaring, tinsel crown over her head to attract the eyes of the silly people, even though a crown had been already painted. Thus I have seen the arms of a God the Father, and a Christ that were crowning the Virgin half cut off, to make room for a vast great crown of this foolish kind.[86]

Here, too, no safe space for Protestant appreciation could be cleared around such works, however 'fine' they were, the word 'Gothicism' raising immediately associations of unreason, or lack of judgement. We will consider the term 'Gothicism' further when we discuss descriptions of Raphael's work in the Vatican. We should also notice how Richardson's criticism of the care of 'pictures' serves to suggest a rather complex relationship between art and its setting. Richardson argues that if they had been better cared for, these objects might have received the rightful attention of a spectator such as himself. However, they cannot be, because the monks, who Richardson implies have no judgement, have allowed the pictures to deteriorate through carelessness. The same lack of judgement has allowed pictures to be made into objects 'to attract the eyes of the silly people'.[87] In other words, such paintings have been transformed into images, with all the negative associations that this term implies for the English spectator. Here the proximity of idolatry and painted image is too close for comfort, and both writers assert the superiority of the Protestant gaze by refusing to acknowledge the cultural circumstances in which all these works, whether of greater or lesser significance to the Protestant tourist, were made – to occupy the Catholic gaze.

There are a number of threads here which need unravelling and investigating further. For example, it is unlikely that distinguishing between the two categories of religious art that Richardson and Wright delineate was as straightforward as they suggest. It is by no means obvious how this might be achieved securely in practice, with so few explicit criteria (although of course it was one of the functions of these guidebooks to offer a secure way by which works could be readily identified). How did Protestant tourists respond when they witnessed the Catholics praying in front of the good pictures? A significant aspect of the difficulties that Richardson and Wright were responding to was that, surprisingly, there was no firm idea within the Church of England of the right use of art in relation to religious practice. The image was an object of uncertain status and therefore so was the reputation of the art of painting (hence the efforts of Richardson which we discussed at

---

86 Richardson (1722), p. 37.

87 Richardson's choice of subject matter may not be coincidental for pictures of the Virgin and, especially, of God the Father were the most intensely criticized by Protestants as unacceptably Popish. See below for Samber's account of idolatry.

the beginning of the chapter to integrate painting and Protestant judgement).
English tourists could not base their spectatorship on a fixed position of their
own. In his translation of the widely read *Art of Painting* by the prominent
French theorist Roger de Piles (1635–1709), John Savage (1673–1747) had to
contend with this particular aspect of the problem head on. In Chapter VIII,
de Piles considers the question of truth in relation to painting in which he
argues:

> If [St Austin] ... had had a true idea of painting, as it is only an imitation of
> truth, and had reflected that by the imitation the souls of the righteous may be
> a thousand ways raised up to divine love, he would have written a panegyric
> on this fine art with so much the more warmth by how much the more he was
> himself sensible of everything that might carry a man to heaven.

So uncomfortable did this make Savage that in the margin is printed the
comment: ''Tis a Roman Catholick that said it'.[88] Again, in Chapter XXIII,
de Piles argues that it is permissible to represent divine things by human
allegorical figures:

> There is a fine description of God, under the form of an old man, in the seventh
> chapter of Daniel, and the ninth verse. The same Holy Writ informs us of
> several apparitions of angels under human forms. For this reason, the church
> in the Council of Nice [*sic*], made no scruple to allow painters to represent God
> the Father, under the figure of a venerable old man, and angels under human
> figures...

Savage intervenes in the text again, this time into its body, asserting himself
more boldly this time:

> The reader will easily perceive 'tis a Papist that argues thus for the idolatrous
> custom of representing the Holy Trinity, and the angels under human figures; the
> argument is so mean it deserves no answer, and the poison so weak, it needs no
> antidote, or we might quote against him, the 7th verse of the 97th Psalm, the same
> he has quoted above, where are those words:

> Confounded be all they that serve graven images, that boast themselves of idols,
> worship him all ye Gods.[89]

The same problem was confronted by Robert Samber (*fl.*1706–31) in his
translation of another French text, Raguenet's *Les Monuments de Rome*, which
consists of very short chapters, each dealing with a single antique or modern

---

88   Buckridge (1969), p. 24.

89   Ibid., pp. 40–44. Other examples of this kind of mediation of continental theory
are to be found in Haydocke's translation of Lomazzo (1598), and in the preface to the
English translation of the *Groot Schilderbook* by Gerard de Lairesse ((1778), p. iii). For
Haydocke's translation of Lomazzo see Höltgen (1984), pp. 138–45.

work of art. Samber, however, adopted a different solution from Savage. In the preface to the text, he states:

> I have purposely omitted the description of the picture of the Trinity, in the Church of the Trinity of the Pilgrims, painted by Guido Reni, and one of the finest pieces in Rome, because I would give no offence to Protestant ears. For tho' the Roman Catholicks make no scruple to paint the Trinity ... yet with the Reformed, it is look'd upon little less than a species of idolatry. I have for that reason omitted it, because I would offend no body.[90]

In the rest of his Preface, Samber deals ironically with Roman arguments for the use of images by describing a rather absurd discussion which he says took place between himself and an English priest one day, while visiting St Peter's in Rome. Although he pretends to be a little nonplussed by the priest's rhetoric, the ridiculousness of the Papist's claims are allowed to speak for themselves. Placing this discussion of idolatry at the beginning of his text can be seen, perhaps, as a strategic clearing of an intellectual space in which the subsequent discussion of the works of art can be understood, all possible objections on the grounds of idolatry having been pre-empted. This may have appeared essential because when he translates Raguenet's description of Reni's *Christ Crowned With Thorns*, he has to present the argument:

> In a languishing complexion, livid with wounds, and on the blood, which almost covers the face of Christ, and where it seems to have been a while coagulated, Guido has made appear such shining strokes of majesty, such an elevated air of grandeur, so sensible an image of divinity, that nothing but a God could thus be formed, and that never a man in the world, in the flower of his youth, and the most happy fortune, had an air so grand as this Christ, in the most deplorable condition a person could ever be reduced to.[91]

To suggest that Christ's spirit, his divinity, could be represented accurately was to come very close to suggesting that God's divinity could be imbued into a man-made object, which was one definition of idolatry. Richardson was well aware of this and argued stridently:

> I plead for the art, not its abuses ... if when I see a madonna though painted by Rafaelle, I be enticed and drawn away to idolatry; or if the subject of a picture, though painted by Annibale Caracci pollutes my mind with impure images, and transforms me into a brute; or if any other, though never so excellent, rob me of my innocence, and virtue, may my tongue cleave to the roof of my mouth, and my right hand forget its cunning if I am its advocate as it is instrumental to such detested purposes.[92]

---

90   Samber (1722), Preface, unpaginated. In his description of this painting, Edward Gibbon writes 'what a satyre of the doctrine is a picture of it' (1961), p. 244.

91   Samber (1722), pp. 37–8.

92   Richardson, *The Science of a Connoisseur*, (1792 edition), p. 189.

But when he discusses a drawing by Raphael of the figure of God the Father, Richardson is seen to stumble, if only slightly, on the hurdle of great art (notice the phrase 'though never so excellent' in the passage above which suggests that the greater the art, the more it has the capacity to elicit idolatrous glances):

> A man cannot look upon, and consider this admirable drawing without secretly adoring, and loving the Supreme Being, and particularly for endowing one of our own species with a capacity such as that of Rafaelle.[93]

Careful consideration of this passage reveals that Richardson is arguing that such a drawing brings him properly to a greater love of God. It is daring not least because it discusses a depiction of God the Father, widely seen in England as an idolatrous practice. Richardson's appreciation of such a depiction, and his assertion of its capacity to encourage proper religious feelings, is very unusual indeed. However, it allows him to demonstrate the possibility of looking with decorum on such a drawing: he is clear that the 'adoration' and 'love' is directed at God, not at the drawing, and by underlining Raphael's power as an artist in the last part of the passage, he asserts the artist's skill as God-given. Thus Richardson articulates the orthodox Roman Catholic view, not that he nor any of his contemporary Protestants would have said as much. It is worth taking this opportunity to reiterate the point because it is illustrated well here, that it was English Protestant perceptions and propaganda about Popery, not orthodox Roman Catholic doctrine or practice, that was important to the production of art and the use of imagery in religious practice in England.

To return to our discussion of the grand tour, tourists had always to manage the manner of their gaze, but they also, often, had to handle subject matter which was unequivocally Papist in doctrine. A very prominent example of this was experienced in the midst of one of the high-points of any tourist's journey: Raphael's fresco known in English as *The Disputation over the Sacrament* in the Stanza della Segnatura in the Vatican [Plate 8]. How could the English manage this complex meditation on the Roman Catholic sacrament in which they did not believe and, moreover, which they thought was idolatrous? John Breval (1680?–1738), a writer whose book *Remarks on Several Parts of Europe* was well used as a guidebook during the century, omitted the painting in an admittedly sketchy account of the Vatican. He did notice Raphael's *School of Athens* painted on the opposite wall to *The Disputation*, which may help us to understand the comments that he did make about the Stanza:

---

93 Richardson, *An essay on the Theory of Painting*, (1792 edition), pp. 26–7. See Chapter 4 for a similar argument presented by Horace Walpole in his *Sermon on Painting* (1752).

A description of the rest of the pieces of that incomparable master in the apartments of the Vatican ... would carry me too great a length. I shall therefore only remark this of them in general, that 'tho they have infinite beauties, as every thing had that came from Rafael's pencil, yet he appears in some instances to have been cramped by the nature of his subject, which was the choice in all likelihood of the pope that employed him; and where the redundancy of his invention had not room to shew and exert itself, in like manner as in the Battle [of Constantine] I have mention'd, in our Cartoons of Hampton Court, the Transfiguration of St Pietro Montorio, and the School of Athens, which is another of the prodigies of the Vatican.[94]

The fact that Breval does not mention the painting, which was among the most famous works of Raphael, seems suggestive. It may be that the subject matter of *The Disputation* is exactly the sort of thing Breval had in mind when he wrote the phrase 'cramp'd by the nature of his subject'. By contrast, Richardson, characteristically, tackles the problem head on. In a description of the fresco covering more than seven pages, he offers criticism of it on a number of counts, two of which we need to examine here.[95] He starts by disputing with Vasari, quoting Bellori in support, arguing that this painting was not made after *The School of Athens*, but before it:

For there is an apparent difference in the style, and manner of painting of this, ... the glory, and ornaments are heighten'd with gold, which was the way of the old painters; and there is a regularity, and stiffness in the disposition of the figures, and which also savours of *Gothicism*, and is more than is to be found in any of the other pictures, as indeed the whole is a style inferior to what he did afterwards.[96]

The word 'gothicism' would have raised a number of associations, as we have already noted, one of which was Popish superstition. It is also a word that suggests an over-elaborated, anti-naturalistic (and anti-classical) style linked, as a chronological term, to indicate a period before the rise of 'great' art. Richardson does recognise that this fresco is part of a scheme, but subdues the therefore probable close succession of the works in Raphael's output (in fact they were made within a year of each other). This manoeuvre is, I believe, closely connected with his justification of Raphael's portrayal of such a contentious subject as the doctrine of transubstantiation. Having acknowledged that the picture describes a 'kind of local system of the Christian religion', he puts this into a historical perspective, arguing that the picture does not detail a dispute at all, for at the time it was painted ('before the reformation was begun by Luther'), there would have been no dispute

---

94 Breval (1738), p. 278.

95 For example, he comments on the lack of attention paid by the other figures to God the Father. He quibbles with the prominent position of St John the Baptist and criticizes Raphael's 'management of the light' (Richardson (1722), pp. 202–7).

96 Ibid., p. 202.

over what he nevertheless calls 'the greatest stretch that ever was made by Man in the affair of religion'. By using this phrase, Richardson emphatically declares his reformed position, maintaining a distance from the beliefs the picture serves, by suggesting that it represents a far-fetched piece of Popish doctrine. Nevertheless, he can still argue that:

> The business of this picture is to set forth the great articles and mysteries of religion; and to excite sentiments of piety, and devotion; and this it does by clear, noble and lively representations, and by expressions just and strong; and all with that grace and nobleness of style peculiar to Raffaele, but in what degree I have observed already.

The Dispute is praised and admired by Richardson for its capacity to raise feelings of 'piety and devotion', the appropriate feelings that all great history paintings of religious subjects were meant to suggest to the spectator. Thus, by emphasizing the painting's qualities as painting, he keeps one of Raphael's works in its position in the hierarchy, but, significantly, he weakens this by arguing that it is not one of his greatest works, that it is a 'gothic', an immature work.

The critical function of this chronological deception becomes clearer when Richardson suggests that 'it might have been the noblest of all those [pictures] in the Vatican, if it had not been done 'till about the time he painted the Cartoons which are at Hampton Court'. This comparison is a hugely significant one for Richardson's argument here, his other work and for us. We will consider it again in the next chapter. When we read, in the closing passage of Richardson's description of the Vatican apartments, that 'I believe there is a palace where one may receive a higher, a juster, and a more complete idea of him [that is, Raphael] than here, or any where else, and that is Hampton Court', we witness an important example of how the English spectator might translate his experience of Catholic art in Italy into something that was usable and manageable at home. Richardson is surely arguing for an idea of Raphael, which can transcend the 'local', with all that that implies, and thereby makes him available for the complete possession of the English. In the next chapter we will consider just how the English did engage with the 'higher, juster, and more complete idea of Raphael' as they looked at, and celebrated, the Raphael Cartoons. We will consider in greater depth how the hurdles of doctrinal content were tackled and how English ownership of these works, which had strong Catholic associations, became a matter of national pride.

When the gentleman came home from the tour he brought with him an education in looking. His gaze was complex, a channel that had become used to mediating and managing competing associations and relations between art and religion. We have seen that tourists developed a number of strategies for handling Catholicism and the dangers of idolatry. For example, art works were divided into the two categories of 'image' and those 'capital' or 'fine' paintings worthy of their glance. Descriptions of paintings tended to exclude discussions of their subject matter, emphasizing qualities of invention and expression (which we will explore in the next chapter). In addition, canonical works of art were imagined historically as existing in a chronology, which tied them into ways of thinking about great works of antiquity – they became universal statements of artistic excellence. Even when, as in the case of Raphael's *Disputation*, the content of such a work could not be passed over by someone as conscientious as Richardson, the placing of the work in amongst his early performances means that Raphael's late phase, acknowledged as the period of his greatness, is celebrated. Such manoeuvres seem fragile, perhaps even hypocritical or simplistic. However, this was urgent work and the variety of these strategies and their ubiquity demonstrate that an investment was made in mediating the inherent contradictions in looking at Italian art. By allying modern art with the antique or by seeing canonical art in one way, and lesser works in another, the English were able to participate in this highly valued culture and reorientate it so that it could serve to support a vision of English social and political life.

Chapter 3

Raphael's Religion: The Interpretation of Catholic Pictures in England

By the 1720s, the Raphael Cartoons had become almost iconic images to the English, considered close to perfect works by a near perfect artist.[1] The seven paintings had enjoyed a very high reputation throughout Europe since Raphael (1483–1520) had painted them and they were known both in the form of tapestries and by the famous engravings by Marcantonio Raimondi (c.1480–c.1534), among others.[2] However, it was not until the very end of the seventeenth century that their status as works of art became a matter of national pride in England and this happened despite the fact that the Cartoons were conceived of, and recognized as, works of Catholic apologetics. In this chapter we will explore how this was achieved. In addition to discovering how these specific works were approached, we will be able to see how alien subject matter was managed in practice by spectators of Catholic pictures, particularly in relation to questions of national identity. John Shearman was, I believe, the first to note the status of the Cartoons in English culture, happily describing Raphael as having being made an 'honorary Englishman' during this period.[3] It is the 'Englishing' of Raphael that this chapter discusses.

The Cartoons were influential in England as works of art, but they also functioned, surprisingly, as religious images and as a symbol of the cultural, and therefore, to some extent, the political health of the nation.[4] During this period, despite fashions for chinoiserie, for example, and for looking with wonder at objects of natural and 'artificial' curiosity, the model of excellence in the visual arts was very narrow.[5] Therefore, in the context of a country seeking to assert its political supremacy, the ownership of such major works of the pan-European canon was likely to become invested with deep

---

1   During this period there was no consensus of the spelling of the artist's name or the word 'cartoon' – it is sometimes spelt 'carton'. To facilitate the reader, I have silently edited quotations to read 'Raphael' and 'cartoon'.

2   See Griffiths (ed.) (1996), pp. 17, 51 for Raimondi's reputation.

3   Shearman (1972), p. 151.

4   This distinction between 'works of art' and 'religious images' has been explored a little in the previous chapter and will be discussed again in Chapters 4 and 5.

5   See Altick (1978) for a broad overview of the visual culture of London during this period and Impey (1977) and Jacobson (1993) for chinoiserie.

significance. Indeed, the Cartoons had a life outside the narrow circle of the virtuosi, which was due, however, to the authority with which the Cartoons were invested by this group. This status was multifaceted: they were used to decorate homes, to ornament Bibles and to embellish ephemeral objects such as this sheet [Plate 9], which was intended as a model to copy from to develop writing skills. So significant were the Cartoons that they can be seen as a nexus through which ideas about society, religion, art and history were mediated. The complex contradictions that existed during this period between cultural priorities and those of religion, and the tools that were developed to deal with them, are exposed here. In this chapter we will explore what was a process of transformation, by which a piece of Catholic apologia was made available for use as, as one eighteenth-century politician put it, an 'invaluable national treasure'.[6] By examining the strategies writers used in developing interpretations of the Cartoons, I hope to show that an uneasy balance was reached, and held, in the reputation of Raphael and his works, between the reception of art and English Protestantism.

This balance is significant in a further way because it can be seen to have guided the reception of the whole of the category that we can call 'high art'. The Cartoons were at the heart of English art, a touchstone of excellence, a resource of example, but this position was not unproblematic, even though the force of the reputation of the works was so compelling. By looking at the hurdles to their unequivocal acceptance and the ways that were found to get over them, we will reveal how formative this engagement with Catholic art was on English attitudes to art.

The Cartoons, which now hang in the Victoria and Albert Museum (on loan from HM the Queen), were commissioned by Pope Leo X (1475–1521) in 1515 for a set of tapestries to add to the already magnificent decoration of the Sistine Chapel. The tapestries were intended for the lower portions of the side walls below the two ranks of late fifteenth-century frescoes. The lower rank of frescoes consists of scenes from the lives of Christ and Moses, including those painted by Perugino (c.1445/50–1523) and Botticelli (c.1445–1510), and above these is a series of portraits of the popes. Dominating the Chapel by the time Raphael started work on the tapestry scheme was the complex programme of frescoes by Michelangelo (1475–1574), commissioned by Julius II (1443–1513), which occupied the upper walls and ceiling (the Last Judgement scene on the altar wall was not commissioned until c.1535). Even though the Cartoons were made for a pragmatic purpose, they have always been seen as very important examples of the period, just before his death, when Raphael was working at the height of his powers. The Cartoons are very impressive objects not least in terms of their size, with many of the figures drawn substantially larger than life. They are striking too because

---

6   John Wilkes, in a speech to the House of Commons 1777. Quoted in Shearman (1972), p. 152. For Wilkes and 'High Art' see Conlin (2001).

of their apparent simplicity of composition, subtle colouring and moving expressiveness.

There is still considerable doubt about the exact nature of the contribution the tapestries were to make to the iconographical programme of the Chapel because of uncertainty over the number of tapestries intended and the order in which they might have been meant to hang.[7] However, the broad theme of the scheme is clear enough: the lineage of authority over Christ's church, derived from St Peter and St Paul through succession, in the office of pope. The primacy of St Peter over the other Apostles was one of the principal messages of the programme together with an elaborate exposition of the pope's dual succession from St Paul and St Peter, as scenes from each life are paralleled with one another and with the scenes from the lives of Christ and Moses in the frescoes above. Raphael's scheme, as Shearman has shown, is erudite and multilayered. There is no doubt that in the context of the Chapel these meanings were intensified and made more explicit by iconographical connections it was intended the spectator should make between the tapestries and the fresco schemes above and by the echoes set up between scenes set opposite and next to one another.[8] Outside of the Sistine Chapel, recreating the same interpretation was impossible, for they were designed to work for that space.

Within thirty years of the commission several heads of state owned sets of tapestries made from the Cartoons, or from copies of them.[9] Among these sets was one purchased by Henry VIII in the 1540s.[10] In 1623, Charles I (1600–49), then Prince of Wales, bought seven of the ten Cartoons for use at the Mortlake works, where at least a dozen sets of tapestries were made from copies of the Cartoons by Francis Cleyn (?1582–1657) (who also designed new borders for them) and Thomas de Critz (?–1654). A number of painted copies were also made.[11] It was not until the reign of William III (1650–1702), however, that the Cartoons seem to have been seen as works worthy of display in themselves and it is said that, until then, they had been kept, in the strips necessary for weaving, in wooden boxes in the Banqueting Hall during the Commonwealth and reigns of Charles II and James II. In 1699, however, the newly restored and reassembled Cartoons were hung in a specially designed gallery at Hampton Court Palace [Plate 10]. By 1701, six of a set of copies by Cleyn were displayed in the Long Gallery at Knole [Plate 11] and by the middle of the eighteenth century painted and tapestry

---

7   See Fermor (1996), pp. 10–12 and Shearman (1972), pp. 21–44.

8   Shearman's account is still the most authoritative: Shearman (1972).

9   Fermor (1996), pp. 19–20.

10   This set remained in the Royal Collection until 1650 when it was sold in the Commonwealth sales.

11   See Croft-Murray (1962–70), vol. I, p. 247 and Whinney and Millar (1957), pp. 125–7 for copies made during this period.

versions were to be found in country houses across England.[12] Not only did the public want copies of the Cartoons, but artists wanted to copy them as exercises since they had become works of supreme technical and aesthetic authority.[13]

In addition, many sets of engravings of the Cartoons were produced which, by the 1750s, included woodcuts sold by Dicey for one shilling as well as the very fine prints of Dorigny (1658–1746) [Plate 12] and Gribelin (1661–1733).[14] There were at least a dozen different sets produced between 1709 and 1755, which suggests, taking into account the range of prices as well (from five guineas to one shilling), that the Cartoons did have a powerful presence in the national culture and that it was wide-reaching. There was indeed a broad audience for the Cartoons. We have seen already a writing sheet and the use of the Cartoons to illustrate Newbury's *The New Testament Adapted to the Capacities of Children* (1755) suggests how 'naturalized' they must have been for these quite sensitive projects aimed at children.[15] The Cartoons were also discussed and referred to in poems, sermons and newspapers and were so well known that the phrase 'the Cartoons' sufficed to identify them. Their status was such that they also served as authoritative material for various experimental ventures, apparently lending weight to what might appear flighty projects, such as the colour prints of Elisha Kirkhall (?1682–1742) or J.C. Le Blon's (1670–1741) experiments with tapestry manufacture at Chelsea or colour reproduction at the Picture Office.[16] It is, I think, indicative of their force that the Cartoons were used for such different ends. We are now well used to popular reproductions of works of art in diverse zones (the use of 'high art' in advertising, on Christmas cards, as well as the sophisticated marketing of museum collections are just a few examples), but the conspicuous presence of the Cartoons was, I suspect, unprecedented in England and certainly they enjoyed the highest reputation of any work of art in England during this period.

The precise ways in which appreciation of the Cartoons was expressed is revealing. As we would expect of such major works of history painting, their capacity to raise the thoughts of the spectator is the praise most frequently

---

12 John Loveday (1711–89) noted a number of painted copies and tapestry sets made from the Cartoons on his travels round England (see Markham (1984), *passim*).

13 For further information on artists making drawn and painted copies see Meyer (1996), pp. 31–45 and Wood (1999).

14 See Clayton (1997), pp. 49–53, O'Connell (1999), pp. 152–4 and Miller (1995).

15 See Herbert (ed.) (1968) for illustrated bibles. Boase mentions in his brief survey of illustrated bibles that engravings after Raphael's loggia frescoes and cartoons 'pervade all Biblical illustration' (Boase (1963), p. 160).

16 Shearman (1972), p. 50 fn. 36; Meyer (1996), p. 21. See Lambert, *The Image Multiplied*, (1987), p. 87 for Le Blon. Kirkhall published sets of coloured engravings of the Cartoons in red, green and yellow.

expressed of them. In an article in *The Spectator* written to encourage subscriptions for a set of engravings of the Cartoons, Richard Steele described the work as:

> Impossible for a man of sense to behold, without being warmed with the noblest sentiments that can be inspired by love, admiration, compassion, contempt of this world, and expectation of a better.[17]

George Turnbull in his *Treatise on Ancient Painting* (1740) argues that works, such as the Raphael Cartoons or Poussin's Sacraments, are possessed of 'extraordinary sublimity of genius' and that:

> There is a force and energy [in their pieces] which wonderfully erects and ennobles the mind, inflames the imagination, and lights up the understanding, calling up great and elevated conceptions, which make so much the more forcible impression on the mind, because the spectator really imagines them entirely his own product ... only hinted to him occasionally by the pictures he admires. Let any one reflect on what it is that so highly pleases, and transports him. ... and he will immediately resolve it principally into this surprising art of affording an inexhaustible source of true and great thoughts to the spectator, in which the mind exults as its own, more being suggested by these sublime, divine pieces than is fully expressed.[18]

For both writers the Cartoons are so valuable as works of art because they engage spectators in an encounter, which is transformative, causing them to be moved to contemplate moral and religious ideas in an elevated and special way. Indeed this transcendent instrumentality was widely seen as the principal virtue of the works. I want to emphasize two fundamental assumptions made by both writers. Firstly, they imply that Raphael's depictions are truthful and secondly, each claims them to be 'religious works' (elsewhere in his article, Steele declares that Raphael has represented 'in the most exquisite degree ... the beauty of holiness').[19] We noted in the previous chapter how tourists

---

17　*The Spectator*, No. 226, 19 November 1711. Steele wrote the piece in support of the scheme proposed by Nicholas Dorigny who had been encouraged to come to England from Rome to engrave the Cartoons by a group of aristocratic virtuosi. It was proposed that the engravings should be paid for by Queen Anne and distributed as gifts as an expression of British cultural prestige in emulation of French schemes such as the *Cabinet du Roi*. However Dorigny's price was considered too high and he had to undertake the work at his own risk. The engravings were published in 1719 as the *Pinacotecha Hamptoniana* and were highly esteemed. See Clayton (1997), p. 49 and Meyer (1996), pp. 27–30.

18　Turnbull (1971), p. 27.

19　*The Spectator*, No. 226, 19 November 1711. Two years later Steele used the same phrase when arguing that works like Raphael's could help in the encouragement of religion. Interestingly he argues that the works of secular men, like Raphael, 'and all men not called to the altar, are collateral helps not to be despised by the ministers

denied the ongoing religious function of much canonical work they looked at in Italy, while accepting that non-canonical painting was often being used in contemporary Catholic practice, in other words, in superstitious ways. Here Steele and Turnbull intend their readers to understand that they are deploying an entirely safe category of religious image, one that is properly Protestant. Turnbull's phrase 'these sublime, divine pieces' is matched in Steele's account when he argues that the Cartoons are:

> An exercise of the highest piety in the painter; and all the touches of a religious mind are expressed in a manner much more forcible than can possibly be performed by the most moving eloquence.[20]

The truth and power (notice how both writers use the word 'forcible') of Raphael's depictions are not straightforward. Steele and Turnbull value the interpretations they can construct from the picture surface, not unmediated responses to it. They do not expect to read them simply, but to work at them, creating and enlarging meaning, thereby raising 'noble sentiments'. Raphael's pictures as history paintings were meant to be turned into thoughts, even into 'true and great thoughts'. Such an identity implies the existence of a hermeneutic space between the picture and the spectator, in which the spectator is at liberty to think. The spectator is not granted complete interpretative autonomy, however. He can be seen to enter into a kind of contract with the painter through the picture surface to which interpretations had to be pinned. Notice how both writers depend on the idea, which was a principle of the theory of painting as a liberal art, that Raphael's ideas, his intention and his 'religious' mind were the motors of the paintings and that his ideas were recoverable from observation of the pictures. This suggests that there are complex notions of authority at work in this 'space'. Given the Roman Catholic nature of these works, Protestant spectators had to find ways of establishing their authority in negotiation, as it were, with the picture surface.

We need to explore further how commentators discussed the pictures, to open out the rhetorical mechanisms by which the Cartoons could function so successfully as Protestant images. By the time that Steele was writing, and increasingly during this period, there were a substantial number of works of art theory available to the English, written in French, Italian and English, which offered varied accounts of a, nevertheless fairly conventionalized,

---

of the Gospel ... All the arts and sciences ought to be employed in one confederacy against the prevailing torrent of vice and impiety and it will be no small step in the progress of religion, if it was as evident as it ought to be, that he wants the best taste and best sense a man can have, who is cold to the *beauty of holiness*' (my emphasis). *The Guardian*, No. 21, 4 April 1713.

20 *The Spectator*, No. 226, 19 November 1711.

way of engaging with pictures.[21] I am not arguing that such conventions fixed the ways in which spectators looked at the Cartoons, or any other pictures, but that such conventions do seem to have guided the terms in which they were discussed. Of considerable interest to us, in this respect, is Jonathan Richardson's *Theory of Painting* (1715), which can be seen as the first substantial theoretical work on painting in English.[22] The Cartoons lie at the heart of Richardson's project, providing a stock of exemplary models that he calls upon frequently and the first edition even had a separate index through which every mention of the Cartoons could be traced by the reader.[23] This strategy affirms Raphael's status and the consequent importance of the Cartoons for the English, it can also be interpreted as a patriotic gesture. Richardson's theory of art is fairly conventional in European terms (he borrowed from Junius, Du Bos, Dufresnoy, Bellori among others), but the attention he paid to the Cartoons was new and designed for his English audience.

In his *Theory of Painting*, Richardson divided painting into seven constituent elements: invention, expression, composition, design, colouring, handling and 'grace and greatness'.[24] Richardson treats them in turn, frequently looking to the Cartoons to exemplify his argument. Terms approximating to his categories of invention and expression are those deployed most frequently by commentators on the Cartoons. Thus, Richardson can provide us with authoritative working definitions of these two ideas, which will help us to consider the rhetorical devices that were used by others to deal with the Roman Catholic aspects of the works.

Richardson carefully delineates the stages of development of the idea that is the key component of any history painting, and he describes a number of stages that a history painter must go through before he puts brush to canvas. The first of these is to choose an appropriate narrative as the subject. He must then master the story through study, pick the most telling moment of the narrative, and then 'improve it within the bounds of probability'.[25] Such improvements are termed invention and are justified by reference to the authority of ancient writers:

---

21 For brief accounts of the literature available in English during the seventeenth century see Gent (1981), Ogden and Ogden (1947) and Salerno (1951) and for the eighteenth century, Draper (1931).

22 It was also quite successful, being enlarged in a second edition in 1725 and appearing as part of Richardson's works published in 1773 and 1792.

23 See Gibson-Wood (2000), p. 152. The only other special index, as Gibson-Wood points out, directed the reader to comments on portraiture, the most popular genre in England during this period and the one in which the English saw themselves as leading Europe.

24 Ibid., pp. 149–50 for a discussion of this division in relation to European treatises. In fact Richardson's categories do overlap considerably.

25 Richardson (1792), p. 21.

No body can imagine (for example) that Livy, or Thucydides, had direct, express authorities for all the speeches they have given us at length, or even for all the incidents they have delivered to us as facts; but they have made their stories as beautiful, and considerable as they could; and this with very good reason, for not only it makes the reading of them more pleasant, but their relations with such additions are sometimes more probably the truth, than when nothing more is supposed to have happened than what they might have had express warrant for.[26]

In Richardson's definition of invention there are two key terms: improvement and probability. By improvement Richardson means those devices of narration the artist uses to 'enrich' or 'heighten' his works for which he has not 'express' authority from the text. Such improvements are, however, not to exceed probability: '... nothing more is supposed to have happened than what they might have had express warrant for'.[27] Invention encompasses basic things, such as the position in which a figure stands, as well as more significant deviations from the story, such as the number of people shown present and so on. Probability was a highly significant term in hermeneutics and it was particularly so during this period (for reasons we will discuss).

In his *Poetics* Aristotle (384–322 BC) had argued influentially that the poet had, when writing epic poetry, the 'licence to describe "the kinds of thing that might happen, that is, that could happen because they are, in the circumstances, either probable or necessary"'.[28] Richardson uses the Aristotelian formula when he argues that the artist can go so far as to 'depart even from natural, and historical truth', a point he illustrates with a pair of descriptions. Describing first a departure from 'natural truth', Richardson claims:

Thus in the cartoon of the draught of fishes, Raphael has made a boat too little to hold the figures he has placed in it ... the truth is, had he made the boat large enough for those figures, his picture would have been all boat, which would have had a disagreeable effect; and to have made his figures small enough for a vessel of that size, would have rendered them unsuitable to the rest of the set, and have made those figures less considerable ...[29]

---

26 Ibid., p. 21.

27 Ibid., p. 22.

28 Aristotle quoted in Shearman (1972), p. 128. Shearman uses this quotation to make a slightly different point about Raphael's design process. See Chapter 4 for a discussion of Charles Lamotte's essay on licence in poetry and painting which can be seen to be a rebuttal of Richardson's sanction of certain types of licence which Lamotte found 'unwarrantable' (for example, artists placing figures who were non-contemporaries together in a picture).

29 See Plates 5 or 9.

Then, using the example of the cartoon of the *Lame Man Healed*, he argues that that Raphael:

> Has departed from historical truth in the pillars that are at the beautiful gate of the temple; the imagery is by no means agreeable to the superstition of the Jews at that time, and all along after the captivity. Nor were those kind of pillars known even in antique architecture in any nation; but they are so nobly invented by Raphael, and so prodigiously magnificent, that it would have been a pity if he had not indulged himself in this piece of licentiousness, which undoubtedly he knew to be such.

Richardson deploys contemporary understanding of ancient architecture to illustrate the strategies a painter must knowingly adopt to communicate the narrative and its meanings, departing through 'invention' from strict 'historical truth'. However, Richardson warns that these things must not go too far:

> History must not be corrupted ... every person, and thing must be made to sustain its proper character ... the circumstances must [also] be observed, the scene of action, the country, or place, the habits ... proportions and the like, must correspond. This is called observing the *Costûme*.[30]

The painter's management of probability within the bounds of decorum is thus the test of the artist's judgement.

This reintroduces the idea of a contingent relationship between the spectator and the work of art we noticed in the comments of Steele and Turnbull. Indeed, Richardson goes on to argue that the painter should 'far ... from inserting any thing superfluous, ... he ought to leave something to the imagination. He must not say all he can on his subject, and so seem to distrust his reader.'[31] Indeed, probability can be conceived of as a test, which the spectator makes of a work of art, matching his standard of reality with that constructed by the artist. Such tests are guided not just by the spectator's reality but also by decorum in the form of a standard of naturalism thought appropriate to a particular genre. Richardson grants Raphael his licences against *Costûme* because he is able to justify, convincingly, the idea that they allow the artist to work more effectively to fulfil the main task of revealing and 'heightening' the more important truths of the narrative. He does criticize Raphael for offending one of the principal rules of painting that there 'must be one principal action in a picture'.[32] Richardson argues:

---

30   Richardson (1792), p. 25.

31   Ibid., p. 31. Richardson's use of the word 'reader' betrays the extensive dependence art theory had throughout this period on poetic criticism. Indeed one of the most prominent themes in the literature is the relationship between the two forms. See Rensselaer Lee (1940).

32   Richardson (1792), p. 28.

> O divine Raphael, forgive me, if I take the liberty to say, I cannot approve in ... that amazing picture of the Transfiguration, where the incidental action of the man's bringing his son possessed with the dumb devil to the disciples ... is made at least as conspicuous, and as much a principal action as that of the Transfiguration.

But he does go on to describe other paintings (including the cartoon of the *Death of Ananias*) in which, he argues, Raphael has handled episode with better effect. The offences against theological 'truth' that are our main concern were less easy to facilitate.

Expression, the second Richardsonian category, is the idea that every aspect of the painting must contribute to the telling of the narrative:

> Whatever the general character of the story is, the picture must discover it throughout, whether it be joyous, melancholy, grave, terrible, &c.[33]

But Richardson means more than the mere mood setting that this passage appears to suggest. Clothes, buildings, gestures, facial expressions, colouring, composition must each share in communicating the story in its fullest sense. In order to do this, the painter has to make a series of decisions, which he can only do well if he has good judgement based not just on knowledge of the history but of the 'ways of men' and a strong sense of social decorum:

> In that admirable cartoon of St Paul preaching, the expressions are very just, and delicate throughout. Even the background is not without its meaning: it is expressive of the superstition St Paul was preaching against. But no historian, or orator can possibly give me so great an idea of that eloquent, and zealous apostle as that figure of his does. All the fine things related as said, or wrote by him cannot, for there I see a person, face, air, and action, which no words can sufficiently describe, but which assure me as much as those can, that that man must speak good sense, and to the purpose. And the different sentiments of his auditors are as finely expressed; some appear to be angry, and malicious, others to be attentive, and reasoning upon the matter within themselves, or with one another ... [34]

Richardson claims that Raphael helps him see, to understand, St Paul in a clearer way than he can by any other means. Making such a substantial claim for the capacity of the Cartoons to raise proper religious feelings was not unusual and indeed Steele had expressed almost the same sentiments of this cartoon four years earlier:

> When St Paul is preaching to the Athenians, with what wonderful art are almost all the different tempers of mankind represented in that elegant audience? You see one credulous of all that is said, another wrapt up in deep suspense, another saying there is some reason in what he says, another angry that the Apostle

---

33 Ibid., p. 39.
34 Ibid., pp. 42–3.

destroys a favourite opinion which he is unwilling to give up, another wholly convinced and holding out his hands in rapture; while the generality attend, and wait for the opinion of those who are of leading character in the assembly.[35]

There is no evidence to suggest that Richardson drew upon Steele for his commentary, and indeed such a dependence would be rather beside the point, because the ideas that they express were the kinds of things that were said about this cartoon.[36] When Steele and Richardson argue that the Cartoons are better than any eloquence (we noted above that Steele described them as giving impressions 'more forcible than can possibly be performed by the most moving eloquence'), we must see this not as a rather elaborate compliment to the artist (in the tradition of *ut pictura poesis*), but as something much more substantial.[37] Indeed, Richardson went so far as to claim, in another essay:

> I conceive as highly of St Paul, by once walking through the gallery of Raphael at Hampton-court, as by reading the whole book of the Acts of the Apostles, though written by Divine Inspiration.[38]

Such confidence in painting is perhaps unexpected in a Protestant setting. In order to understand what lay behind Richardson's advocacy of image over word, we need to widen our focus.

During this period interpretation was an extraordinarily fraught area of activity, politically and religiously.[39] Protestantism put a great deal of weight on the individual's unmediated relationship to God, with God's will revealed principally in the Scriptures.[40] Therefore the act of interpretation, not dogma,

---

35   The Spectator, No. 226, 19 November 1711.

36   See, for example, Blackmore (1718) and Ralph (1759). We will discuss each of these texts shortly.

37   Steele also described the cartoon of St Peter receiving the Keys (to which, as we will discuss, he gave a different title) in the following way: 'I cannot but think the just disposition of that piece has in it the force of many volumes on the subject.' *The Guardian*, No. 21, 4 April 1713.

38   Richardson, *A Discourse on the ... Science of a Connoisseur* (1719) reprinted in Richardson (1792), p. 179.

39   In every area of human activity, Enlightenment ideas questioned old mechanisms of interpretation, for example, in history, science, religion, the law, taste and the arts. See Weinsheimer (1993) for a very useful discussion of hermeneutics during this period.

40   A good deal of debate between Protestantism and Catholicism during this period was built on exactly this point. Catholic apologists argued that reason alone was insufficient to interpret the Scriptures and that tradition was as important (affirmed in the Council of Trent) to the sure running of Christ's church according to God's will (on this point see 'Tradition' in Cross and Livingstone (eds) (1977)). Protestants held a wide variety of positions: from those who believed in the literal interpretation of the text of the Scriptures, to those who were guided by 'inner

was placed at the heart of faith. A crucial problem for Protestantism was where, and how, an individual might find and recognize truth. The strongly contested nature of the identity of the Church of England during this period demonstrates just how unstable interpretation was and how intimately connected these questions were with wider political and social issues.[41] For example, how should one deal properly (that is, in moral, doctrinal and legal terms) in the religious, political and social spheres, in a nation made up of people who held markedly different beliefs about such fundamental ideas as the nature of God and Christ, and the right relationship of monarch to people and church to state.[42] No area of experience and human endeavour was remote from these difficulties. The Reformation had raised the fundamental question of how to seek and know truth through the Word without the authority of doctrinal tradition claimed by Roman Catholicism.

John Locke (1632–1704) argued influentially, but certainly not unproblematically, that truth was to be found only through the deployment of the individual's reason, without prejudice. The understandings of others were irrelevant and sometimes even unhelpful. Thus Locke argued in his unpublished *Letter on Infallibility* that authority could not be granted by an individual to another for his beliefs. Freethinkers such as Collins (1676–1729), Tindal (1657–1733) and Toland (1670–1722) took Locke's ideas further, developing ideas which met, however, with strong and influential rebuttal by Law (1686–1761), Butler (1692–1752) and others, who argued that it was the responsibility of some to guide others.[43] These were not debates that can be portrayed simply as between two sides, one inside the Church and the other outside it, between the orthodox and the Deist, or the High

---

light' and those who argued for a historical relativism in interpretation. For some a distinction was sufficient between the central tenets of faith and those inessential things (*adiaphora*) which did not offend against God's will as clearly revealed and for which there was no clear position in the text, but which contributed to worship or morality (this nevertheless led to considerable differences in position). We will explore this in relation to images in Chapter 5. See Cragg (1964), Patey (1984), Porter (2000), Shapiro (1983), Weinsheimer (1993).

41 See Chapter 5 and Young (1998a). See also Holmes (1973) and Holmes (1976) on the Sacheverell Crisis and Rupp (1986), pp. 88–101 on the Bangorian controversy, the two key disputes which had these issues at their heart. For a selection of essays showing the complex interrelations of politics and religion in this period see Harris, Seaward and Goldie (eds) (1990) and for a broader, more philosophical approach see Harrison (1990).

42 Locke, for example, argued both for suppression of difference and for toleration. See Weinsheimer (1993), p. 24 who reminds us that toleration could be a partisan position during this period.

43 For elaboration of reason's part in religious understanding according to Locke and Toland see Weinsheimer (1993), pp. 23–71.

Churchman and the Latitudinarian.[44] The competing authorities of reason and revelation, Scripture and the Church Fathers, the argument from design and the teachings of the Church were weighed, often in shifting balances, by individuals. At the heart of these questions lay the authority of the Word, but also, increasingly, the authority of any words. The difficulties of deriving meaning led the philosopher George Berkeley to suggest momentarily 'the abandonment of language'.[45]

In this context the Cartoons can be seen to be doing an impressive and necessary job for Steele and Richardson by bypassing words to communicate truth. This rather rare ability is for Richardson the unique contribution that history painting has to give to culture:

> Words paint to the imagination but every man forms the thing to himself in his own way; language is very imperfect. There are innumerable colours and figures for which we have no name, and an infinity of other ideas which have no certain words universally agreed upon as denoting them. Whereas a painter can convey his ideas of these things clearly, and without ambiguity; and what he says every one understands in the sense he intends it.

> And this is a language that is universal; men of all nations hear the poet, moralist, historian, divine, or whatever other character the painter assumes, speaking to them in their own mother tongue.[46]

Richardson's claim for history painting is to be taken seriously, not because we recognize it to be, or to have been, true, but because it offers a clear sense of the power history painting was deemed as having. History painting had to be universal; it was a form in which universal truths, and only those, were meant to be spoken.[47] This is the node around which the contradictions involved in the Cartoons being the supreme English examples of history painting pile up.

Not everyone was willing to grant the Cartoons universal status in every respect, although as a set, and in general, they had this reputation. Whereas Steele and Richardson saw Raphael's painting of *St Paul Preaching* [Plate 13] as an utterance of universal truths, Steele's colleague Joseph Addison offered a different view of it in an essay on preaching. In the course of his remarks,

---

44   See Spurr (1988) for a reconsideration of the term Latitudinarianism, which considers the positions of those who have been called Latitudinarians in relation to Dissent and Deism.

45   Quoted in Cragg (1964), p. 102. On the argument from design see Brooke (1991) and Porter (1981) for a particularly concise and cogent description of the relations of religion and science in the English Enlightenment. His very recent book is also useful here (Porter (2000)). On Providence see Spurr (1990a).

46   Richardson (1792), p. 6.

47   Hence the debate later in the century over the status of contemporary-dress history paintings made by Copley and West.

in which he suggests that English preachers would do well to adopt some rhetorical gestures to 'set off the best sermons in the world', he offers a comparison:

> I have heard it observed more than once by those who have seen Italy, that an untravelled Englishman cannot relish all the beauties of Italian pictures, because the postures which are expressed in them are often such as are peculiar to that country. One who has not seen an Italian in the pulpit, will not know what to make of that noble gesture in Raphael's picture of St Paul preaching at Athens, where the apostle is represented as lifting up both his arms, and pouring out the thunder of his rhetoric amidst an audience of pagan philosophers.
>
> If nonsense, when accompanied with such an emotion of voice and body, has such an influence on men's minds, what might we not expect from many of those admirable discourses which are printed in our tongue, were they delivered with a becoming fervour, and with the most agreeable graces of voice and gesture?[48]

Addison suggests by his use of the word 'peculiar' and the description of Italian preaching as 'nonsense' that Raphael has represented St Paul as a Catholic priest. The word 'peculiar' is akin to the phrase 'local system of religion' used by Richardson in his description of Raphael's *Disputation* that we considered in the previous chapter. These two works do not function for Addison and Richardson, in this respect at least, as universal statements. In other words, this cartoon was to Addison, as the *Disputation* was to Richardson, recognizably Catholic. By contrast, we saw that in their comments about the cartoon of *St Paul Preaching*, Richardson and Steele did not see the disposition of St Paul's figure as an obstacle to their claiming the cartoon as an acceptable depiction of the Biblical text. In other words it was amenable to Protestant interpretation.

By contrast, the cartoon of *Christ's Charge to St Peter* [Plate 14] seems to have presented a difficulty to every spectator, although this is not always made explicit in commentaries. By considering the strategies used to describe the cartoon, it becomes clear that it was the one that signalled its Catholic origins most obviously, and problematically, to the Protestant spectator. Raphael based his composition for the cartoon on two texts, an infrequent manoeuvre in history painting but, as Shearman has shown, common in Roman Catholic arguments for the idea of *Primatus Petri*, the primacy of Peter among the other Apostles.[49] By using these two texts together (Matthew 16:18–19 and John 21:15–17), an unambiguous statement of Peter's primacy was developed in Catholicism to support the validity of the Church as the true church on

---

48   Addison, *The Spectator*, No. 407, 17 June 1712.
49   Shearman (1972), p. 65 but see pp. 45–90 for the meanings of each cartoon.

earth in succession from Christ through Peter.[50] In the first Gospel passage, Matthew describes Christ's charge to St Peter:

> And I say ... unto thee, that thou art Peter, and upon this rock I will build my church; and the gates of hell shall not prevail against it. And I will give unto thee the keys of the kingdom of heaven: and whatsoever thou shalt bind on earth shall be bound in heaven: and whatsoever thou shalt loose on earth shall be loosed in heaven.

The second passage, from John's Gospel, describes Christ's appearance to the disciples after his resurrection when the second miraculous draught of fishes takes place. Christ asks Peter three times 'Lovest thou me?' and after the Apostle's three affirmative responses, Christ charges him to 'Feed my sheep'. The boat and fishing gear at the right of the cartoon illustrate the text but also provide an iconographical and interpretative link to the cartoon which was always assumed to have preceded it in the series [Plate 15], which depicts the first miraculous draught of fishes where Christ preached from Peter's boat and ordered him to go out into deeper water (Luke 5: 3–10). This incident had also long been interpreted as demonstrating Peter's primacy.[51] There is a great deal more to these pictures, in terms of sixteenth-century theology, than could be discussed here. However, it is these essentials, the main points of Raphael's programme, which are of importance for, although we cannot assume a particular level of theological sophistication in the audience of the Cartoons in this period, we can be sure that very little of this would have been lost on the English Protestant spectator. Extensive knowledge of the text of the Bible was very general during this period and Raphael's conflation of the texts would have been recognized immediately. The meaning of the conflation is likely to have been understood just as easily. The papacy's claim to inheritance of Christ's mission was widely discussed in anti-Catholic literature and it is clear that each of the commentators on the Cartoons recognized the Popish significance of this cartoon.

Richardson goes straight to the point in the course of his discussion of invention in *The Theory of Painting*. In a passage worth quoting at length, Richardson refers to the cartoon in support of his case that painters must make improvements because a judicious painter will make those that are 'more probably the truth ... than what they might have had express warrant for':

> Such an improvement Raphael has made in the story of our Saviour's directing St Peter to feed his flock commonly called the Giving him the Keys. Our Lord seems, by the relation of the Evangelist (*at least a Roman Catholic, as Raphael was, must be supposed to understand it so*) to commit the care of his church to that Apostle

---

50　We will discuss the idea of the true church in Chapter 5.
51　See Shearman (1972), p. 63.

preferably to the rest, upon the supposition of his loving him better than any of them. Now, though the history be silent, it is exceeding probable that St John, as he was the beloved disciple, would have expected this honour, and be piqued at his being thought to love his master less than Peter. Raphael, therefore, in that cartoon, makes him address himself to our Lord with extreme ardour, as if he was entreating him to believe he loved him no less than St Peter, or any of the other Apostles. And this puts one upon imagining some fine speeches, that it may be supposed, were made on this occasion, whereby Raphael has given a hint for every man to make a farther improvement to himself of this story. [my emphasis][52]

Richardson's efforts to interpret the painting seem fragile, even facile, but we can see that his engagement with the cartoon clearly acknowledges Raphael's Catholic meaning and by his description of the figure of St John suggests another area of the painting for the attention of the Protestant spectator. We can say that Richardson transposes the picture into a Protestant register by choosing a different interpretative key to make it acceptable. By focusing the spectator's gaze on a vivid aspect of Raphael's depiction – the disposition of the figure of St John at the centre of the picture, with its strongly expressive profile directed towards Christ – Richardson subtly modulates its meaning, opening up the possibility for reading the picture as a depiction of the Protestant understanding of Christ's charge to Peter. By drawing attention to the figure of St John, Richardson directs attention to an aspect of the painting that is open to reinterpretation within both Raphael's vision and his own. Raphael's invention is invoked by Richardson who uses the idea of probability to facilitate an opening out of the picture's meaning and allowing the possibility of, as he hints in the final line, the spectator improving the story.[53] Thus, the spectator might improve it into a Protestant interpretation of Christ's commission to St Peter, as the representative of the other Apostles.

Other writers adopt a less transparent strategy in getting over Raphael's intentions. Richard Steele, for example, describes the Apostles this way:

The figures of the eleven [are drawn] according to their characters. Peter receives his master's orders on his knees with an admiration with a more particular attention. The two next with a more open extasie, though still constrained by the awe of the divine presence. The beloved disciple, who I take to be right of the two first figures, has in his countenance wonder drowned in love; and the last personage, whose back is towards the spectator and his side towards the Presence, one would fancy to be St Thomas, as abashed by the conscience of his

---

52   Richardson (1792), p. 22.

53   This aspect of the painting was praised by the Comte de Caylus in one of his lectures to the Academie Royale, but he did not draw the same conclusions from it, merely observing the movement encouraged in the eye by the disposition of the two figures. See Rosenberg (1995), p. 106.

former diffidence; which perplexed concern it is possible Raphael thought too hard a task to draw, but by this acknowledgement of the difficulty, to describe it.[54]

Steele describes the cartoon in terms of expression arguing in the first sentence that Raphael has achieved the goal of describing the internal man by external depiction. More important to us is that Steele uses this to elide Peter's mission with that of the other Apostles, refusing to acknowledge the 'Popish' message of the work. The third sentence carries the weight of meaning as its construction implies that the next two Apostles also receive Christ's orders, just as Peter did, implying further that the rest do too. In the article in *The Guardian* published in 1713 already discussed, Steele again resisted acknowledging the subject matter of the picture, but this time he used a different strategy. He described the cartoon as 'Raphael's picture of Our Saviour appearing to his Disciples after the Resurrection', not as the 'Giving of the Keys' or 'Christ's Charge to St Peter' by which it was more commonly known in England.[55] Again he comments on the expressions, this time distinguishing two groups:

> I cannot but think the just disposition of that piece has in it the force of many volumes on the subject: the Evangelists are easily distinguished from the rest by a passionate zeal and love which the painter has thrown in their faces; the huddle group of those who stand most distant are admirable representations of men abashed with their late unbelief and hardness of heart.[56]

Here Steele ignores Peter altogether. A strategic resignifying of the painting was thus a common device. In the *School of Raphael* published by Boydell in 1759, the Cartoons are described in turn and each description begins with the biblical text on which the cartoon is based. This cartoon is described as 'Christ's charge to St Peter; commonly called the Delivery of the Keys' but only the text from John is quoted. In the description, reference to the keys or Peter's special mission is omitted:

> The time chosen is the moment of our Lord's having just spoken; and that in consequence of our Saviour's interrogating Peter, "Lovest thou me more than these?" the rest of the apostles were eager to reply to that question, by assuring their Lord, that their love for him was at least equal to Peter's; and this solicitude is finely expressed in every character.[57]

---

54 *The Spectator*, No. 226, 19 November 1711.

55 For the title Christ's charge to St Peter, see the writing sheet [Plate 9]. Richardson calls it the 'Giving of the Keys', the title by which the cartoon had been known since at least 1517 (Shearman (1972), p. 55).

56 *The Guardian*, No. 21, 4 April 1713.

57 *The School of Raphael* reproduced in Meyer (1996), p. 5.

It is perhaps worthwhile reiterating that the omission of the Giving of the Keys from the description would have been observable. We should expect that a great many of the readers of these texts would have recognized it, would have known the alternative names for the cartoon (indeed the title given in the Boydell text for the cartoon mentions this) and that, therefore, the cartoon's status as a Catholic work could not be suppressed or disguised by such manoeuvres. Thus the strategies deployed in these descriptions can be seen not as offering a substitute meaning but an additional one, which allowed the Protestant spectator scope for engaging with this most prominent, but problematic, work of art.

One of the most complex strategies employed to describe this cartoon appears in a poetic description of the Cartoons written in 1703 by Sir Richard Blackmore MD FRCP (*c.*1655–1729), a leading London physician who attended both William III and Queen Anne (1665–1714).[58] Blackmore published his *Short Description of the Cartons of Raphael Urbin* with his long poem *A Hymn to the Light of the World*, which is suggestive of the status the Cartoons had already achieved as works of religious significance. The poem on the Cartoons is divided up into sections, each describing a single cartoon. Rearranging the Cartoons from the order in which they are normally dealt with (starting with *The Miraculous Draught of Fishes*, that is, in chronological order, starting with the Gospel texts, before those drawn from Acts), Blackmore deals with the problematic cartoon of *Christ's Charge to St Peter* last. He had licence to do this from the order in which they were hung in the Gallery (see Plate 9), but this was not the order chosen for the Boydell text, which also treats the Cartoons individually, and it may have appeared odd to those reading the poem away from the Gallery. In each section of the poem, Blackmore praises, explicitly and implicitly, Raphael's expression of both the substance of the sacred narratives and the feelings and characters of those involved. For example, the poem begins with a description of the overall effect of Raphael's works:

> Stay, Stranger, here in this apartment stand
> And view the wonders of great Raphael's hand;
> Whose skill does all the sons of art control,
> They only paint the body, he the soul.
> Such admiration will thy eyes possess,
> As none but Raphael's pencil can express.

The last section of the poem is called 'Our Saviour and his Twelve Apostles', an erroneous title, for Raphael only shows eleven Apostles in the painting because the cartoon depicts Christ after the Resurrection (indicated by the marks of his crucifixion and the change in his clothing), and therefore after the betrayal of Judas. The description of this cartoon is the shortest and it

---

58 For Blackmore see Rosenberg (1953).

contains the only criticism of Raphael in the poem. We can usefully consider the whole of the second and final stanza of the section (and the poem):

> See, holy Peter, on his bended knee,
> From his great master's hand received the key,
> that opens wide high Heaven's immortal gate
> To all pure souls, that for admission wait,
> But locks it fast against the impious train
> Doomed to the seats of Death and endless pain.
> Thus the Redeemer did the saint invest
> With power divine, but not above the rest.
> For all the sacred tribe, as well as he,
> Have power to bind, and set a sinner free.
> Much less this grant did sovereign right convey,
> Obliging all the Apostles to obey
> Their monarch Peter's universal sway.
> But do not ask what Raphael's notions were,
> His judgement might, his pencil cannot err.[59]

Blackmore's argument is quite different from those we have considered because he states explicitly what no one else seemed to have been prepared to: that Raphael was wrong. Blackmore acknowledges the conflation of texts and the full implications of this in the phrase 'sovereign right', meaning the supremacy of the papacy in succession from Peter. Blackmore, however, confronts us with a conundrum in the last two lines, which encapsulates rather neatly the contradiction haunting each of the descriptions we have been discussing and which is inherent, in England, in the reputation of Raphael as the history painter par excellence:

> But do not ask what Raphael's notions were,
> His judgement might, his pencil cannot err.

Blackmore presents these two lines as a resolution to the implicit problem of how to manage the Catholic content of this work. The shape of the poem also serves to isolate this cartoon from the others whose meanings can more easily be understood as straightforward readings of the New Testament, if the overall Catholic significance of the programme is not acknowledged. In other words, the other cartoons can cross the boundary between Catholicism and Protestantism much more easily than this one. Blackmore's resolution is, however, no resolution and it is rather difficult to know what he might mean by it. How should we understand the suggestion that an artist's ideas may be wrong, but his execution is not? He could mean that Raphael was able, in some way, to depict the truth without intending it or that Raphael's works are available for reinterpretation without considering the authority of the

---

59   Blackmore (1718), pp. 460–61.

artist's judgement. Given what we know about the way history painting was thought about, this latter possible meaning would be most unusual. The term 'pencil' carries the weight of the ambiguity, but it may simply suggest that Raphael's practice was admirable. Just how Blackmore imagined a spectator should divide Raphael's invention from his practice must remain a matter for conjecture.

Among the group of prominent works on the Cartoons that we have considered, we have encountered a number of different strategies for dealing with their problematic elements. This diversity of responses to the problems suggests that there was no consensus on how to deal with the issue of the Catholic origins of much high art, that these problems were still actively being resolved. We have seen, moreover, that the reputation of the Cartoons as exemplary history paintings and the claims for them as religious texts (which had to follow) were ultimately irreconcilable. The Cartoons presented more of a challenge to the English spectator than those tourists saw in Italy because of their very important place in English culture. The option that tourists had to ignore a picture was not available and therefore, somehow, Raphael's Catholicism had to be managed.

A great deal of the cultural power of these paintings is held in the reputation of Raphael as artist. We noted in the previous chapter Turnbull's remarks:

> The analogy between those two ages of painting [of Apelles and of Raphael] in many circumstances is indeed surprising; but it is well vouched and not imagined.[60]

Indeed, Turnbull argues elsewhere:

> The art in both ages advanced at first very slowly; came to a certain pitch, and then made a stand for some time. But beginning afterwards in both to soar above the first small advances, it improved exceeding fast, till it came in both to a degree of perfection, the description of which in the one, from the works of Apelles, is precisely correspondent to that which is most justly given of it in the other, from the works of Raphael.[61]

The idea that Raphael embodied this modern rise of the arts is a common trope, but the conclusions drawn from it could vary considerably. Leonard Welsted (1688–1747), in his *Epistle to Mr Steele, on the King's Accession to the Crown* (1714), provides us with a good example of the broad meanings Raphael's name could carry in a quite different context. Welsted anticipates the expected benefits George I's accession will bring:

---

60 Turnbull (1971), p. xxii.
61 Ibid., p. 48 fn. 117.

His influence shall extend to farthest shores,
Unite th' Allies, and bind their weaken'd powers:
The pure Religion, the Reform'd, shall share,
Amidst oppression, his protecting care;
By him and Heaven assisted, spread at length,
Insensibly prevail, and rise in strength:
Refulgent Rome from her proud height shall stoop,
And see her long-supported honours droop:
The worship'd image shall neglected stand,
And boast in vain the work of Raphael's hand;
Mankind, to freedom wak'd, her pride shall tame,
Restrain her Pontiff, and his laws disclaim.[62]

Welsted uses Raphael both as a defining figure of modern Roman art and as a Roman Catholic artist. The shape of the argument demonstrates just how closely identified with Roman Catholicism Raphael could be. This identification had two quite different aspects to it. First, there are the negative associations of erroneous belief and superstition we have seen raised, in different ways, by Richardson, Addison and Blackmore. Welsted's argument is unusual in making a direct link between Raphael's art and Catholic idolatry. We noted towards the end of the previous chapter how Richardson, again unusually, acknowledged the idolatrous potential of the greatest art but firmly dismissed its dangers for Protestants, an argument we will explore further in the following chapters. Richardson's argument differs slightly, but significantly, from Welsted's because Richardson separated more clearly Raphael's art from 'its abuses', suggesting that it was possible to quarantine Raphael's works as art from the superstitions of Catholicism.[63] We have explored a number of different approaches to the works of Raphael adopted by English spectators, which acted to isolate the pictures from connections with the idolatrous image. By contrast, Welsted denies Raphael this special status by using the emotive and significant word 'image' to describe his work rather than the words 'painting' or 'art'.[64]

The second aspect of this close association of Raphael with Catholicism was a more ambivalent attitude towards papal patronage. We noted in the previous chapter that extensive patronage was understood as one of the keys to cultural success and that there was a consensus among concerned observers that the English elite was not fulfilling its duties in this regard. Explanations of the rise of the arts in Ancient Greece and Rome, and in Modern Rome, focused on the liberal qualities of both patrons and artists in those times. So, when Richardson described how Raphael came to be the

---

62   Welsted (1714).

63   Richardson, *The Science of a Connoisseur*, (1792 edition), p. 189.

64   We will explore this distinction further in Chapter 5.

greatest modern artist, he stressed not just the society in which he lived but the quality of his patrons:

> [He] was one of the politest, best natured gentlemen that ever was; and beloved, and assisted by the greatest wits, and the greatest men then at Rome ... [He] lived in great fame, honour, and magnificence, and died extremely lamented; and missed a cardinal's hat only by dying a few months too soon; but was particularly esteemed, and favoured by two popes, the only ones who filled the chair of St Peter in his time, and as great men as ever sat there since that apostle, if at least he ever did.[65]

The artist and miscellaneous writer George Keate (1729–97) makes a similar point in his poem *Ancient and Modern Rome* (1760):

> ... such were the happy times,
> When Plato trod the academic grove,
> And spoke of wisdom. Such, when Rome beheld
> Augustus throned; such too, in later years,
> When Leo ruled ...[66]

Keate is also clear that religion is an essential element in the success of Rome in promoting the arts:

> Yet hence, the arts, in ev'ry age, have found
> A sure protectress; by Religion called
> To raise her temples, decorate their walls,
> And with unwearied toil her sainted shrines
> Illumine ...[67]

It is important to note the context in which Keate discusses religion's vital role in the encouragement of the arts. He does so directly after repeating the story of the entrance of Petrarch's Laura into the convent. English tourists were often keen to see the kind of ceremony that Keate describes in the poem and accounts of them in the tour literature exhibit a mixture of Protestant distaste for such superstition, horror and sensual pleasure.[68] More relevant to us is the way in which the proximity of Keate's description of this 'superstitious' practice to his discussion of the important part religion has played in cultural patronage appears to manage both sides of the troubling

---

65 Richardson (1719) in Richardson (1792), pp. 250–51. For a similar comment see the well-known closing section of Reynolds's First Discourse to the newly-founded Royal Academy in which he urges that the Academy should contribute to make the 'present age vie in Arts with that of Leo the Tenth' (Reynolds (1992), p. 87).

66 Keate (1760), See Mason (2004) and Waterhouse (1981) for Keate.

67 Keate (1760).

68 See Chard (1999), p. 128 for a brief discussion of this common trope of tour writings.

coin of Catholicism. The word 'yet', which links the two episodes in Keate's poem, carries the weight of this meaning and recalls the comments of Shaftesbury and Edward Gibbon who both lamented the fact that, as Gibbon put it, 'Catholic superstition ... is often the parent of taste'.[69]

In trying to understand how this uneasy balance might have been maintained, the temptation to resolve it in some way, to try to find a single key must be resisted. During this period a very similar but slightly less uneasy balance was maintained with respect to the authority of the ancients. Turning again to the comparisons that were made between ancient and modern cultures that we discussed in Chapter 2, there are strong parallels between the management of Catholic culture and the ways in which problematic aspects of ancient culture were handled. Comparisons between ancient and modern Rome, or between pagan and Christian superstitions (such as those made by Conyers Middleton) had a wide currency. The two fields, the ancient and modern, were associated in this culture in religious history, anti-Catholic polemic and in the history of art.[70] Such comparisons may well have functioned to manage problems of superstition and idolatry at a distance from the works of ancients and moderns, in order that their authority might be maintained. I am not arguing that a kind of exclusion zone operated around the works of, for example, Homer or Raphael, but that, with rare exceptions, criticism and questioning was pursued rather lightly in close proximity to canonical works of art, as we have seen in our discussion of the Cartoons.[71]

I argued in the previous chapter that the association of modern canonical art with antiquity (through a history of art which emphasized the revival of ancient values necessary for art to flourish again) was crucial to its reputation in England and explained a good deal of the prestige an otherwise alien art carried in the culture. However the authority of the ancients was not unassailable and in a number of areas it was undergoing considerable challenge during this period, particularly in natural philosophy and medicine. In literature there was a great deal of heated argument over the relative merits of the ancients and moderns. A dispute, known as the 'Battle of the Books' that was widely satirized as too 'curious' in its close attention to minute distinctions of literary criticism, nevertheless had much broader implications for the whole question of authority in England.[72] Of central importance to the reputation of the ancients was the way in which

---

69 Gibbon (1990), p. 135.

70 This has been recognized for some time in religious history and anti-Catholic polemic as we will discuss shortly.

71 See Patey (1984), p. 84.

72 Levine (1991). See Levine (1981) for a revision of Jones's pioneering work *Ancients and Moderns,* first published in 1936.

the superstitious practices of ancient religion and the anti-realistic devices of literature (such as 'miracles' and grotesques) were interpreted.

After the Reformation, the nature of religion itself became an important focus of enquiry. Increasingly during the seventeenth century, the 'primitive' religious practices and beliefs of the ancients and of those peoples being encountered in the New World were subject to considerable and rigorous attention. Comparative studies were a key component of the study of religion and, as Manuel has pointed out, studies of contemporary societies fashioned a new understanding of ancient religion. The idea of progress was both evidenced in this comparative programme and was used to justify the superiority of modern Reformed religion over that of the ancients, and other 'primitives'.[73] Although the 'superstitious' nature of these religions identified them as irrational and corrupt, the characteristics and stories of the pagan deities were used extensively in poetry, opera and dramas as allegories of moral virtues. In representing them as allegories (an approach with a long history), eighteenth-century writers and painters depended on a universalist understanding of moral virtue, albeit one that had occasionally to manage conflicts between classical narratives and contemporary Christian morality. The test of probability, explored in relation to history painting, was used extensively here too. Indeed, the problem appears to be of exactly the same order as the one we are dealing with: how might a work of superstition be made acceptable to the English?

We observed in Chapter 2 that tourists made connections between the contemporary religious practices of Catholics and their pagan ancestors in ancient Rome. These connections were seen by some to be more than mere parallels, rather as indications of a direct inheritance from paganism of unchristian practices. In the hands of men such as the Deist-leaning Anglican clergyman, Conyers Middleton, or the Presbyterian James Owen (1654–1706), such comparisons were used to develop a very strongly anti-Catholic line, which also took into its ambit aspects of orthodox Anglicanism.[74] As Leslie Stephen recognized, Middleton's, and we might add Owen's, arguments were by no means new and were repeated extensively in formal treatises and in casual references in tour literature, for example.[75] The points of comparison ranged from the institution of ranks of priesthood in both religions to the forms of ceremonies. Of central importance, to all such arguments, was the

---

73 Manuel (1959), pp. 1–53, esp. pp. 18–19.

74 This was most famously exercised in relation to the debate over miracles. See Cragg (1964), *passim* but esp. pp. 54–7, 84–6. Probability was a test increasingly applied by Christians, Protestant and Catholic, to the Bible and the question of revelation. See Walsh (1997) and Weinsheimer (1993), esp. pp. 23–71.

75 Stephen (1902), vol. 1, p. 256. See for example Dorrington's *Observations Concerning the Present State of Religion in the Romish Church* (1699) which is in the form of a tour diary (p. 25). See Pailin (1984), pp. 121–8 and Harrison (1990), *passim*.

role of the image and the idolatrous nature of all superstitious religions. In *The History of Images, and Image-Worship* (1709), James Owen argued:

> The Romanists worship consecrated images with the same ceremonies with which the pagans worshipped theirs

a claim which he supported by descriptions of 13 different elements of their idolatrous use of images, which they shared, quoting ancient sources as evidence of pagan practices, such as:

> the pagans honoured their idols with garlands, crowns, flowers, altars, music &c. the same is done by the Papists to their images ...

> Arnobius saith, they prostrated themselves before their images; the same is done by the Romanists.

> The pagans kept fasts in honour of Ceres, and abstained from certain meats as the Papists do by the saints and their images.[76]

Elements of Owen's argument are familiar to us from the comments of Edward Wright as well as Jonathan Richardson's on the Popish use of paintings. Similar comments are to be found scattered through religious texts and writings about art. A history of idolatry was, I suspect, uniquely prominent in the English history of art during this period.[77] This meant that art history was embedded in religious and political discourses in singular ways in England and that while art played a significant role in anti-Catholic rhetoric, reciprocally political considerations were active in discussions about art so that the history of idolatry was retold in places as apparently diverse as religious tracts, grand tour journals, doctrinal texts of the Church of England and theoretical writings about art.[78]

The history of idolatry, which the comparisons of paganism and Popery use and contribute to, demonstrate how entwined the problems of superstitious antiquity and contemporary Catholicism were. However there is one substantial difference between the ways that each were thought about

---

76   Owen (1709), pp. 281–2. See Mussard (1732) (trans. du Pré) and Middleton (1729) for similar arguments.

77   For example, no histories of idolatry are to be found in de Piles (1706), Du Bos (1748), Dufresnoy (1695) or de Lairesse (1778). Hence the interventions of translators such as Fritsch in the preface to his translation of de Lairesse (1778), and of Savage, in the text of de Piles (1706), discussed in Chapter 2. De Piles does, however, acknowledge implicitly that there might be some doubt about the depiction of God the Father, mentioning the decision of the Council of Nice[a] (787) in support of his contention that it was acceptable.

78   See, for example, Breval (1738), pp. 274–8 for a typical account of the rise of idolatry; see Rickey and Stroup (eds) (1968) for a reprint of the 1623 'Homily against the Peril of Idolatry' (pp. 27–8).

that we must now consider. There were a number of historical and literary perspectives on classical myths, developed over a very long period, which allowed Greek and Roman literature to be used and savoured. Diverse historical perspectives were available such as the psychological approaches developed by Bayle (1647–1706) and Fontenelle (1657–1757), the attempts to reconcile pagan myth to Scripture of Samuel Shuckford (c.1694–1754) and the work on Homerian myth by Thomas Blackwell (1701–57) in which, following Vico, he established myth as primitive (that is, pre-rational) man's understandable way of dealing with the world.[79] These perspectives did not solve all the difficulties in encountering the superstition and 'immorality' of the ancients, but they did help successfully to mediate classical literature and make it acceptable.

Of the greatest significance to this mediation was the notion that progress had been made in human society and that the moderns had consequently huge advantages over the ancients, including great improvements in religion, morality and rationalism. By contrast, Popery was still too present a danger, I believe, for similar approaches to those deployed to manage pagan culture to have been secured, even though English Protestants, in particular, felt themselves to be superior to their French and Italian Catholic contemporaries. Whereas there were ways in which one could think of myths as useful allegories or the over-imaginative responses of primitive peoples to fear, Popery represented too immediate a religious and political threat to the nature of English Protestantism to allow complicity with that form of superstition.

Instead, as we have discovered, the reception of Raphael in England involved rather fragile processes of shuffling competing intellectual and emotional concerns. The commitment to European cultural standards was strong, but so was anti-Catholicism, and because of the multiplicity of positions regarding large questions such as religious belief and hermeneutics, it is not surprising to discover that there were a diverse number of determinations made of the appropriate balance between Catholicism and high culture.[80] We have noted, for example, how writers such as Richard Steele and Jonathan Richardson devised quite different modes of approach to the problematic Catholicism of the Cartoons: whereas Steele excluded the Catholic elements of the pictures from his view, Richardson acknowledged them but sought to accentuate those parts of the pictures which were amenable to Protestant assent. Raphael was enmeshed in an English history of art that had been modified from its European origins to serve the country's particular political and religious concerns. While the English accepted Raphael as the second

---

79 See Manuel (1959) and Levine (1999). I regret we have room only for this very brief account here.

80 See pp. 1–2 and 4–8 above for the preliminary discussion of the diverse nature of anti-Catholicism.

Apelles, in common with a European art history, he had to be constructed as an object lesson in slightly different ways. We have observed that when English Protestants turned to Raphael as the greatest modern painter, they did so in a very unstable setting in contrast to the relatively secure status the painter had in France, for example.[81] Where Blackmore suggested that Raphael was wrong, or Addison suggested that Raphael depicted a Catholic version of St Paul, for example, we see an urgent transformation process under way by which Raphael's works, and the critical concepts of history painting and artist to which his reputation was tied, were reformed and made available for the use of English Protestants.

In the next chapter we will consider how paintings of Popish doctrines fitted into Protestant picture collections. It is no coincidence that portraiture was the most popular genre of art made and collected in England during this period, and that it was the way that even the most prominent artists earned their living.[82] Portraiture was comparatively safe and that safety was built into the histories of idolatry that were told in England.[83] The origins of sculpture and painting were frequently traced, using the authority of classical texts, to the innocent human need to record the faces of loved ones, before the subsequent decline into idolatry.[84] Religious painting, by contrast, was enmeshed in a web of hermeneutic difficulties for the English, as we have begun to discover.

In this chapter we have questioned the supremacy Raphael appears to have had in the English reception of art. We have ranged widely in an effort to understand how Raphael's apparently unassailable reputation was upheld in England despite being attended by apparently conflicting and troubling issues relating to his religion and the subject matter of his works. In exploring a number of different approaches adopted by English writers in relation to Raphael, we have developed further understanding of the spectatorship of canonical art that we began to discuss in Chapter 2. The fact that even Raphael was not allowed to stand free from the associations we have discussed suggests the force that Catholicism had in English reception of art. By considering the links established in religious and art history between ancient culture and modern Catholicism, and the different ways in

---

81   See Blunt (1958) and Rosenberg (1995), esp. pp. 1–117. This is not to underestimate divisions over colour and design, but debate about Raphael tended to range over theory in France and did not involve such broad issues as the ones we have been considering in relation to England.

82   A matter of considerable and sometimes bitter disappointment to artists in England, frequently expressed in grudging comparisons to the better conditions pertaining in France and Italy, where artists were more frequently commissioned to paint history paintings. See Chapter 1.

83   See Aston (1995).

84   See, for example, Aglionby (1972), Preface, and Breval (1738), p. 274.

which they were handled, we have revealed how a considerable effort had to be made to secure art for the English nation.

Chapter 4

Collecting Catholic Pictures

It was not just in the spaces of a royal palace, or a journey to Italy, or in the literature on art, that English Protestants engaged with Catholic art. Many Catholic paintings were displayed with pride as ornaments in English homes. Although the Injunctions, which directed the iconoclasm and proscription of religious imagery of the previous two centuries, did include 'public' and 'private' spaces in their orbit, religious pictures in 'domestic' or 'wholly secular settings' were tolerated.[1] In her work on the period 1550–1660, Margaret Aston has shown that it was acceptable that private spaces might contain religious art, but what the basis was of such distinctions between public/private or religious/secular and its implications remain unclear.[2] Aston suggests that it might have been possible to divorce religion from art, but I am not sure that is right.[3] In this chapter, I will demonstrate that in the period 1660–1760 religious pictures were not insignificant, nor neutral, in specifically religious terms, when hung in homes and that arguments were developed to manage the meanings of such works in the contexts of ornament and display.

I will concentrate on elite collections for two separate reasons. Firstly, the evidence for middle-class collecting has only recently begun to receive scholarly attention, and while there is some reason to expect that many of the same ideas were at work in middle-class and elite homes, I am not in a position to be certain of it.[4] Secondly, the milieu in which two key texts I wish to explore was an elite one and it seems important to attend to the context in which they were produced. Nevertheless, this does not mean that

---

1   Aston (1996), p. 103. The word 'private' was used in the Injunctions. However, it is worth remembering that the possession of such pictures could be used as evidence of Catholicism. See Collinson (1988), esp. p. 118.

2   Aston (1996), pp. 94–5, 103, pp. 119–21. Margaret Aston has done a considerable amount to illuminate the use of the portrait in this earlier period, a form, she argues, found favour because it '[filled] the gap created by Protestant fidelity to the second commandment'. See also Aston (1995).

3   Aston suggests that when Henry Peacham argued for the memorial use of religious images (that we will discuss in the next chapter), he was 'capable of distinguishing religion from art' (Aston (1996), p. 104). As this book aims to show such a distinction was not operating in the period 1660–1760. See pp. 136–9 below

4   Gibson-Wood (2002) and Galinou (ed.) (2004).

the ideas expressed in these texts were entirely exclusive to an elite context, and I will demonstrate, where I can, that some of them were not.

Colin Haydon's work on anti-Catholicism demonstrated that elite anti-Catholicism gradually declined as an active force in politics.[5] This did not mean that Catholicism became less of a cultural problem. There was a more fundamental reason than an essentially political prejudice that people, even with exceptionally tolerant views of Catholicism, would have had difficulties with pictures showing Catholic doctrine. These pictures showed ideas that they did not believe in. This was problematic in terms of an understanding of art, as we discussed in relation to Raphael, and in relation to an individual's religious beliefs. Protestantism in England was, as we will discuss in the next chapter, tied to Catholicism in a mutually excluding binary that guided people's understanding of what the Church of England (or indeed any other denomination) was – it was in many respects simply that which Popery was not. Even for sceptics such as Shaftesbury and Gibbon discussed in the Introduction, the alien qualities of subject matter were problematic. Thus, whether or not one expressed active distaste or suspicion of Catholic neighbours, pictures showing Roman doctrines could not be absorbed seamlessly into the fabric of a picture collection, elite or otherwise.

Such display was not a new phenomenon in our period, although among the middle classes it probably was. The substantial market for art that existed in eighteenth-century England was a late seventeenth-century development, with the first picture auction recorded as taking place in London in 1674.[6] Published evidence of middle-class ownership of works of art is still scarce, and it is to elite collections that we must turn to gain understanding of how people looked at these alien works of art. We have elite inventories with named pictures listed that we can match to extant works, and we have texts of various kinds that we know from library inventories were owned by the elite. The similarities between these texts and the discussions of art in journals such as *The Spectator,* and later the *Monthly Review*, suggest that we can use these texts as indicative of shared attitudes among the art-buying public. However, while it is likely that pictures of Popish subject matter did decorate some middle-class homes, we are not in a position to be certain about this, as auction lists and inventories of middle-class homes tend to be fairly unspecific. I am emphasizing this problem here because this chapter will demonstrate how, through the concept of judgement, there was a specific political relation operating between social rank and the visibility of religious art in the period.

Collections were not closed spaces in this period: they were permeable; people, meanings and knowledge flowed in and out. So we cannot deploy

---

5   Haydon (1993), esp. Chapter 5.

6   Pears (1988), Gibson-Wood (2002), Lippincott (1995) and North and Ormrod (eds) (1998).

the words 'public' and 'private' with safety here. Collections were not private, but they were qualified spaces, entry to which could be gained only by those bearing the outward markers of judgement – whether in dress, manners, language or social connections. Furthermore, the reputation of a collection was an essential element of it, providing some of the impetus for its formation. Collecting was one of the cultural practices which were directed towards a body called the 'public', the precise identity of which was debated and which concepts such as politeness and taste were designed to manage.[7] The collection's actual accessibility or visibility did not count for as much as its reputation in the 'public sphere' of the polite that we discussed in Chapter 2. While later in the eighteenth century there was a growing trend of country house visiting, collections circulated to an ever broader public throughout the eighteenth century in the form of catalogues and engravings made of particular paintings.[8]

Literature in the history of science on collecting, and other work on the collecting of objects labelled, in rather complex ways, as curiosities has demonstrated to us that collections are fruitful sources for historical enquiry, allowing us to see how culture, social relations and politics worked together.[9] It is clear that these collections operated as a focus for a variety of social relations, as a means of organizing knowledge and as a space for the deployment of judgement and taste. Art collections have seldom been used in such ways, but Iain Pears's groundbreaking study *The Discovery of Painting* and work as diverse as David Solkin's *Painting for Money* and Dukelskaya and Moore's *A Capital Collection* suggest that a 'thick description' of art collecting in eighteenth-century Britain might be possible and helpful.[10]

---

7   The key text here is Habermas (1989) for the most influential delineation of the 'public sphere'. Tony Claydon has some useful and critical comments of the 'public sphere' in his article on the sermon as an element of the public sphere (2000). See also Brewer (1997), pp. 87–114 for a discussion of taste, politeness and notions of the public. David Solkin's book *Painting for Money* (1992a) is very useful in its discussions of the relations between British painters and the public. Further to this is Solkin (ed.) (2001).

8   See Clayton (1997) for engravings of pictures in collections and Tinniswood (1989) for country-house visiting. As far as I can tell, no general work has been done on the collection catalogue of this period. However see Simpson (1951) for discussion of the sources, all published, for Martyn's *The English Connoisseur* (1766) which listed the contents of some 20 or so 'private' collections, a number of Oxford colleges, the British Museum and so on.

9   See Findlen (1994), Swann (2001) and Sloan (ed.), (2004).

10   The term 'thick description' was developed by the anthropologist Clifford Geertz to describe the multilayered social explanation that he aimed to develop by studying a single social phenomenon, such as, most famously, a Balinese cockfight: Geertz (1973). It has been taken up by cultural historians in particular as a useful term to describe their ambitions and to signal an indebtedness to Geertz's pioneering work.

Very little attention has been addressed to hanging strategies and subject matter, for example.[11] As I hope to show, there is evidence available to demonstrate that pictures were objects of active interest, which were looked at repeatedly and about which people read, thought, talked and, to some extent, argued. Collections are usually invoked by historians as tools of asserting status, in the context of the country house, but they were more than this; they were complex endeavours with multiple social and cultural resonances. It is undoubtedly true that we do not have an extensive body of primary writing about works of art in private collections, nor is it generically coherent, but, this need not imply a discursive space of little contemporary interest or engagement; rather it can indicate that assumptions were so widely shared they need not be articulated. This apart, there are in fact a number of sources which have not been used to explore questions of meaning in collections and they will be deployed here. However, research that collated and analysed the disparate accounts of collections available in inventories, catalogues, sermons, diaries, correspondence and journals could prove fruitful. This chapter, which is directed towards a particular aspect of collecting, will demonstrate that collections can play a role in generating understanding of the social and political roles of art during this period.

Having discussed these historiographical issues, we can now move to consider some specific collections. Historians have suggested that collectors were 'cautious' about religious topics, or even that a political position might have motivated collectors to concentrate on [collecting] 'works which bore no "Popish" traces'.[12] As a starting definition of what might constitute such 'Popishness', we can say that paintings which showed Catholic doctrines, such as the invocation of saints, the figure of God the Father or the Virgin Mary in ways not described in the New Testament, would be considered as Popish.[13] As we proceed we will discover other aspects of Catholic painting that were recognized as objectionable. However, there is very little evidence to suggest that the 'Popishness' of subject matter was a bar to a work's attractiveness to a collector.

---

11 The exception to this is Marcia Pointon's *Hanging the Head* (1993).

12 Pears (1988), p. 43 and Monod (1993a), p. 374.

13 This definition is carried implicitly in Pears's argument (1988, p. 43). We will be in a position to define this more closely by the end of the chapter. It will prove impossible to provide a 'Popish' test, as it were. For example, Domenichino's *Madonna della Rosa* has been described as an example of 'potentially dangerous papist subject matter' (Llewellyn (1999), p. 77). More precise historical analysis is needed before we can be sure that this subject could be read as Popish. From Graves (1907, 1969), we know that the subject of the Madonna and Child was frequently exhibited at the Society of Artists and the Royal Academy exhibitions and it is one that could easily be seen as exemplary of a mode of motherhood, which gained currency during the eighteenth century. See Jordanova (1999), pp. 203–27, esp. pp. 219–27.

Evidence for the range of works that were in English collections can be gained from the brief descriptions to be found in the sale catalogues, inventories and guide book of the period. The diaries and correspondence of men such as John Loveday (1711–89) and Horace Walpole (1717–97) are also very useful because both men were inveterate listers of the pictures they had seen on their travels round the country.[14] Loveday visited Althorp, for example, on 19 August 1742, and saw three tapestries made from the Raphael Cartoons and a painting he called 'The Elevation of the Host in a Nunnery Church'.[15] When Horace Walpole visited Althorp in August 1760, he noted different pictures, including a painting of the 'Virgin giving Child to St Christopher over a river', and a 'St Jerome reading, from Albert Durer by Stenwick'.[16]

Thomas Martyn's *The English Connoisseur* (1968) is another useful source because it brought together catalogues of a number of very prominent collections including those at Chiswick, Devonshire House and of Charles Jennens (1700–73) and Paul Methuen (1672–1757).[17] Methuen's collection at Grosvenor Street, now at Corsham Court, Wiltshire, included works such as Pitati's (1487–1553) *Madonna and Child with Saints and the Three Cardinal Virtues* [Plate 16] and Bernardo Strozzi's (1581–1644) *St Mark and St John in Consultation on their Writings*. At Stowe, Martyn records the large paintings which decorated the chapel, which included 'The Salutation of the Virgin Mary' and the 'Resurrection' by Tintoretto which was above the altar, paintings of Joan of Arc and a 'Representation of the Holy Lamb'.[18] From sources such as Martyn, Walpole and Loveday we can see that there were large numbers of religious pictures held in collections, and that a significant number of them were Popish in origin, doctrine and sensibility. In addition, a considerable number of these circulated in prints, which were made increasingly of works in such collections by entrepreneurs such as Arthur Pond, Elisha Kirkhall and John Boydell.[19]

How should we begin to think about religious pictures and their role in elite collections? As catalogues began to be developed in the 1740s and 1750s, pictures were usually described only by a very short title and the name of the artist. The hanging of several pictures of the same subject matter such as the Holy Family, together with pictures of a quite different kind, for

---

14   Markham (1984) and Toynbee (ed.) (1928).

15   Markham (1984), p. 344. See note for information about a reinterpretation of the painting. See Garlick (1976) for a modern account of Althorp's collection.

16   Toynbee (ed.) (1928), p. 31.

17   For the sources for Martyn's book see Simpson (1951). Most of Martyn's work was drawn from R.J. Dodsley (1761).

18   Martyn (1968), vol. 2, pp. 66–8.

19   See Clayton (1997), Griffiths (ed.) (1996), Lambert (1987), and for Arthur Pond, Lippincott (1983). See Plates 17–19 for Boydell engravings after pictures in the Walpole collection.

example, with portraits or scenes from antiquity, suggests that the hanging strategies were often driven by pragmatism: the size of pictures was of much importance. The common practice of architectural and decorative schemes designed to accommodate particular works of art in balanced, formal arrangements is also suggestive of pragmatism.[20] Another important factor was the degree of prominence of the artist, so that large pictures by the most renowned artists were more likely to be hung in the most formal rooms of a house, rather than smaller works by less significant figures. This attention to the artist and the size of the picture suggests that coherence of genre or narrative content was not a strong consideration.

However, the idea that some types of pictures were more suitable for certain spaces than others was current during this period. Richard Blome (d.1705), for example, presented such a formula in *The Gentleman's Recreation* (1686), which was a very substantial representation of the text of William Salmon's (1644–1713) *Polygraphice*, a hugely successful seventeenth-century drawing treatise:

> Let the porch or entrance into the house be adorned with rustick figures, and things rural. In the hall shepherds, peasants, cattle, sheep and the like.
> The stair-case ought to be set out with pieces of buildings, landskips, history, &c. The like in the dining, and withdrawing rooms, but with those of better painting.
> For the galleries, let there be good histories. In banquetting and summer houses, put those pieces that seem cheerful and merry; with good landskips.
> In your bedchambers, place your own, with your wives, children and relations.[21]

In practice, while in a number of country houses a similar scheme was used with, for example, pictures of horses and dogs in the entrance hall, other social and political considerations affected display practices.[22] The most obvious example of this is the important role of portraiture in these collections. Portraits usually made up a substantial part of any collection and were displayed a great deal more prominently than Blome suggested. Portrait galleries were a fairly common feature of substantial collections, in which portraits of ancestors, relatives and friends were collected, commissioned and displayed with a number of aims and effects.[23] Again, in the secondary

---

20 See Saumarez Smith (1993) which includes a number of these plans. The size of a work of art also had connotations of its importance; large works were likely to be filled by more figures implying a greater deployment of skill in their depiction.

21 Blome (1686), p. 229. See also Clayton (1997), pp. 3–23, esp. p. 23 for similar ideas for hanging prints.

22 See Deuchar (1988), pp. 86–91 for the display of sporting art in country houses. Deuchar makes some well-considered points here about the collecting of art, in general.

23 For example, at Blickling before 1745, the Long Gallery was decorated with family portraits and others of his friends commissioned from William Aikman (1682–

literature, the portrait collection is largely viewed as a statement of social status, but as we can see from Stella Tillyard's engaging description of the gallery at Holland House, organized by Caroline Fox (1723–74), wife of the first Baron Holland (1705–74), it could be much more than that:

> [The gallery was] designed to show to the world the image of a happy and successful marriage, family and career. Caroline invested time, money and herself in it. It constituted a kind of self-portrait. Displayed on the gallery walls were those people, those lives, that made up her own life and personality. Everyone who really mattered to her was there.[24]

This is fascinating and work on portraiture is proving an increasingly fertile ground for study; our interest here is in a different kind of art.[25] Unfortunately, we have very little evidence of a similarly intense psychological use of, or engagement with, history painting (the genre in which most religious art was located). We do know that the discourses surrounding history painting were focused rather differently from those of portraiture, which tended to concentrate on likeness, character and associations (through the use of accessories, views and so on), rather than on formal qualities of the painter's craft which dominated discussion of history painting in England. There are, however, a number of links between portraiture and religious painting, particularly in the English context. The perceived English supremacy in portraiture was constructed as an outcome of the anti-religious art strand in English Protestantism.[26] Portraiture was, thus, *the* English form. By contrast, religious painting definitely was not an English genre (as Richard Steele's comments about the geography of art in *The Spectator* that we discussed in Chapter 1 demonstrate).

There are two specific social and political associations that a fine collection of paintings generated in this period that are worth emphasizing. First, such a collection was undoubtedly only available to those with both commitment and money. It did assert status, both financial and moral (through the discourses of taste that we have considered), and thus collections were

---

1731) by Lord Hobart (1693–1756). These included major national figures as well as local minor gentry. In smaller houses, portraits were often used in drawing rooms and halls in similar ways. See Saumarez Smith (1993) for many illustrations of this practice.

24   Tillyard (1995), p. 149.

25   See Pointon (1993), Woodall (ed.) (1997) and Jordanova (2000a) for different historical approaches to portraiture. Haskell (1993) has some useful comments on the history of historians using portraits.

26   In addition, in Chapter 5 we will discuss the view that was held by some of the impossibility of portraying people from Scriptures of whom no likenesses were taken in life.

engaged politically, in a broad sense.[27] As Pears argues, collecting on a substantial scale was frequently conceived of as a social good, not as a sign of luxury; the owner was seen as a custodian and the collection as a repository. Indeed, a large collection could be thought of as a national asset, as the outcry at the sale of the Houghton Collection to Catherine the Great in 1779 suggested.[28] The fundamental idea was the ancient one that the arts were symptomatic of the health of the nation, that the greatness of a country, and therefore its leaders, could be assessed and recognized by the degree to which the arts flourished.[29] Collections were key sites where this anxiety about the state of the arts in England, for anxiety it was, got worked out. This vision of the collection was utilized in relation to all kinds of collecting. Owners of cultural resources (that is, paintings or other objects which could be construed to have a public importance or national fame) laid great stress on the notion of public responsibility, a responsibility which did not necessarily imply the granting of public access, however.[30]

This linkage of collection and national reputation was supported by the rhetoric of art treatises, which emphasized the moral implications of taste, and was reinforced by their writers, who often prefaced their works with dedicatory epistles praising, in extravagant terms, both the taste and virtue of their patrons. A good example of this is Banbrigg Buckridge's dedication to Robert Child (d.1721) of Savage's translation of Roger de Piles's *The Art of Painting* (1706):

> In speaking of painting to you, sir, I speak to one of the best judges of that noble art, which is not to be understood without penetration, delicacy, good sense, a refined taste, and a portion of that genius which inspired the painter in his performance ...

> 'Tis the happiness, sir, of men of your fortune, that they can read and see what they think fit for their pleasure or instruction; but this benefit rather exposes than improves many, who have not a true relish of the things about which they are curious ... numerous collections of pictures injudiciously made are the sport and contempt of the spectator and a reflection on the owner ... By the nicety of your

---

27　Pears quotes the case of the Wentworth family who, apparently feuding over who should 'rule' Yorkshire, invoked the quality of their picture collections in support of their case. Pears (1988), p. 161. In addition see Klein (1989).

28　Pears (1988), pp. 171–80. For the concept of luxury see Sekora (1977) and Berry (1994). For other connections between property and the responsibilities of public life see Langford (1991). For the Houghton sale see Moore (ed.) (1996), esp. pp. 56–64.

29　It is held in the concept of a civil, or in more modern terms, a civilized society. See Shaftesbury's *Letter on Design* in *Second Characters* (1969) and Barrell (1995), pp. 7–8. Sekora (1977) and Berry (1994) deal with these issues in relation to the concept of luxury.

30　For other kinds of collections see Haynes (2001), Jenkins and Sloan (eds) (1996) and MacGregor (ed.) (1994).

choice the world admires that of your *Goût*, and are surprized to see so many rare
things together in a country where painting, and the politer arts, are not so much
encouraged as in those places, where, perhaps, the nobility and gentry are not so
well qualified to judge of merit, nor so well able to reward it as in England. Yet
there are even here, some few illustrious persons, and men of worth and honour,
who are solicitous for the prosperity of the arts, and contribute, by their studies
and bounty, towards making them flourish and prevail among us.[31]

Robert Child is promoted here by Buckridge as a 'public' man; he asserts
Child's rightful place at the top of the social hierarchy, affirming the right
of those with land and money to claim authority, a claim that was made
through such symbols as high art.[32] At the top of the artistic hierarchy was
history painting and it was this genre that men like Child were most able
and desirous to claim as their own.[33] History painting, as the genre that was
meant to deal with morally elevating subject matter drawn from the Bible or
classical myth and literature, was thought by some to be only available to those
at the top of the social hierarchy, who might have the necessary education
and disinterestedness to absorb its lessons.[34] (It was also the most expensive
kind of art, usually painted on large canvases with many figures; history
paintings represented a considerable investment on the part of the artist in
one piece of work.) Given the discordant nature of some of the meanings of
these pictures, their absorption into statements of social leadership had to
be managed carefully. As we discussed in Chapter 3, the English could not
sign up to the cosmopolitan model of art without accepting all the works
of an artist, not just the secular ones. For an artist to be great, for art to be a
worthy pursuit, all of a master's work had to be of value. The tension that
existed in the English context between head and hand, the errors of the ideas
represented and the mastery of the pencil that we uncovered in relation to
Raphael is also present in the setting of a collection. However, as we shall
discover, the English could indeed absorb these works of art into collections,
setting aside problematic content through, in particular, the apparatus of
formal analysis and factual history.

The second political resonance of collections that I want to pick out here
relates precisely to the presence of Popish, or indeed any religious pictures
in the collection and the notion that idolatry was committed in the eye of the
spectator. In the context of a collection, the presence of these pictures can
perhaps be seen, paradoxically, as a positive claim for the judgement of the
collector. To possess and display proudly such pictures was not an assertion

31 Buckridge (1969 edition), Dedication (unpaginated).

32 See Barrell (1995), pp. 1–68 and Solkin (1992b), esp. pp. 1–105.

33 For Child's membership of the Virtuosi of St Luke see Bignamini (1988).

34 This idea was subject to modification through our period, as writers suggested
that other ranks might, if properly guided, learn the 'civil' lessons history painting
offered. See Pears (1988), pp. 36–51.

of Popish leanings, but of the distance of the remove from base ideas the spectator had reached. There is scope here, but this has to remain speculative, for Catholic pictures to be seen as always presenting a challenge to the English spectator. This challenge was described explicitly by Richardson:

> I plead for the art, not its abuses ... If when I see a Madonna though painted by Rafaelle I be enticed and drawn away to idolatry; or if the subject of a picture, though painted by Annibale Caracci pollutes my mind with impure images, and transforms me into a brute ... may my tongue cleave to the roof of my mouth, and my right hand forget its cunning if I am its advocate as it is instrumental to such detested purposes ... I know I speak with zeal, and an ardent passion for the art, but I am serious, and speak from conviction, and experience.[35]

Here idolatry and 'obscenity' are marked out as the dangers of religious and secular art. Religious art, even of a fairly safe subject as the Virgin, was seen by Richardson as always associated with the potential of idolatry. The challenge to the spectator is clear, for he argues that paintings can 'entice' or 'pollute' but that education, virtue and right religion – the three necessary qualities that inform good judgement – can prevent such a reaction and that 'to consider a picture aright ... [is to] have at once an intellectual, and a sensual pleasure'.[36] He argues:

> Pictures are not merely ornamental, they are also instructive; and thus our houses are not only unlike the caves of wild beasts, or the huts of savages, but distinguished from those of Mahometans, which are adorned indeed, but with what affords no instruction to the mind: our walls like the trees of Dodona's grove speak to us, and teach us history, morality, divinity; excite in us joy, love, pity, devotion, &c. If pictures have not this good effect, it is our own fault in not chusing well, or not applying ourselves to make right use of them.[37]

Richardson suggests that the collecting and looking at pictures was highly fertile ground for the exercise of judgement, on which the spectator could demonstrate to himself and others his virtue. So how might we imagine the engagements that took place with pictures like those at Paul Methuen's house, at Althorp or at Stowe? By its very nature, evidence is very hard to come by, but there are two remarkable sources which have received too little attention, each of them written as a response to the specific problem of looking at religious art in the context of a private collection. The texts – Horace Walpole's *Sermon on Painting* (1742) and Charles Lamotte's *An Essay upon Poetry and Painting, with Relation to the Sacred and Profane History* (1730) – are of quite different kinds, but each is concerned with English Protestant

---

35 Ibid., p. 189.

36 Ibid., p. 189. This can be conceptualized more broadly as a test of disinterestedness: see Stolnitz (1961–62).

37 Richardson (1792 edition), p. 189.

engagement with Roman Catholic religious art. Charles Lamotte DD FRS is a little-known figure. He was chaplain to John, Second Duke of Montagu (?1688–1749) and acted as the Duke's agent at his estate at Boughton.[38] The *Essay*, which went through five editions by 1745, begins with a flattering reference to the Duke, his collection and his taste. The essay was written, the author says, at the request of the Duke. The request was apparently made during a conversation the two men had in the Duke's picture gallery about the licences which poets and painters take when representing histories.

Horace Walpole is, by contrast, a well-known figure in the literary landscape of the eighteenth century. However, the *Sermon* is a text that has largely been ignored. The *Aedes Walpolianae*, of which the *Sermon* forms one part, was published by Walpole to eulogize his father, Sir Robert Walpole (1676–1745), through a celebration (and advertisement) of the taste he had deployed in gathering his very distinguished collection.[39] We know that Walpole wrote the *Sermon* in 1742 to be read by his father's chaplain in the Picture Gallery at Houghton, but unfortunately we have no further information about the presentation of the *Sermon*. The proximity of the chapel to the picture gallery in the house does raise the question of whether it was read during the course of a service or as a separate event.[40] It has been suggested that the text is a rather minor work, even a pastiche, but the arguments presented in the text are, I think, sufficiently well thought through to warrant serious consideration, entirely in tune with texts in favour of religious art, which we will consider in the chapter about art in churches (and with Jonathan Richardson's comments on the spectatorship of religious pictures that we have just looked at).[41]

Walpole was trying, I believe, to develop a specifically and theoretically cogent, Protestant approach to art in the *Sermon*. The *Sermon* also contributes to the overall purpose of the *Aedes* of celebrating Sir Robert in a number of ways, most obviously in a rather elaborate comparison of Sir Robert to Moses in a brief discussion of Poussin's painting of *Moses Striking the Rock* at the end of the *Sermon*: 'see the Great *Moses* himself! The Lawgiver, the Defender, the Preserver of Israel.' We are led by the encouragement in a footnote to read this as an 'allusion to Lord Orford's Life'. The *Sermon* was probably written to mark a key event in the life of the collection, the gathering of Robert Walpole's pictures, for the first time, at Houghton in 1742, after his resignation as Prime Minister. It was at that moment the collection that Horace celebrates in the *Aedes* can be said to have been born. The ways in which a collection articulated claims about political and social status in this

---

38   See Murdoch (ed.) (1992).

39   It has appeared in a modern edition edited by Andrew Moore in Dukelskaya and Moore (eds) (2002).

40   See Yaxley (1995) for a discussion of the picture gallery at Houghton.

41   See, for example, Mowl (1996), pp. 91–2.

1   Domenico Veneziano ('Domenichino'), *The Last Communion of St Jerome*, 1614. By Kind Permission of the Direzione dei Musei Vaticani.

2　William Hogarth, *The Battle of the Pictures*, 1745. Copyright The British Museum cc.1.137.12.

3 Francesco Bartoli, *Interior of the Church of the Gesù, Rome*. Early 18th Century. By kind Permission of the Earl of Leicester and Trustees of the Holkham Estate.

4 Giovanni Paolo Panini, *Capriccio*, 1741, Walker Art Gallery, National Museums Liverpool.

5   Giovanni Battista Piranesi, *Veduta dell'Anfiteatro Flavio detto il Colosseo*, 1751. Copyright The British Museum 1886-11-24-104.

6   William Pars, *Interior of the Colosseum*, c.1775. © Tate, London 2003.

7   Giovanni Battista Piranesi, *Veduta interna del Panteon volagamente detto la Rotonda*, 1751. Copyright The British Museum 1914-2-16-145.

8　Raffaelo Sanzio ('Raphael'), *The Disputation of the Sacrament*, 1509–10. By Kind Permission of the Direzione dei Musei Vaticani.

9   *The Seven Cartons of Raphael Urbin* [sic], c.1729. Copyright The British Museum 1996-7-13-1.

The Seven Famous Cartons of Raphael Urbin, Drawn
at the Command of Pope Leo the 10 as Patterns for Tapestry:
They were bought by K. Charles the first (at the Persuasion of
S.r P.P. Rubens) and brought from Flanders into England:
afterwards K.William fix'd them in his Palace of Hampton :
Court in the Gallery here Represented.
In 1707 they were drawn and Engraven by Sim: Gribelin
and by him most humbly Dedicated to Her Late Majesty —

SEMPER EADEM
ANNA REGINA·

Septem Tabulas Chartaceæ (Jussu Leonis X Pontificis
Romani) a Raphaele Urbinate in Aulæorum Texturam
pictæ quas Rex Carolus I (Suasu P.P. Rubens Equitis)
ex Flandria in Angliam advehi jussit. et quas postea
Rex Gulielmus Palatio suo Hampton-Court dicto. in
Pinacotheca hic repræsentata collocavit.
Anno 1707 eas delineavit, Ærique incidit Sim: Gribelin
et Seren. Annæ Reginæ humilissime Dedicavit.
S.G. inv. a sculp.t & excudit. 1720

10   Samuel Gribelin, *Hampton Court Gallery*, 1720. Copyright The British Museum 180b.26.

11   *Interior of the Cartoon Gallery*, Knole, Kent. © Crown copyright. NMR.

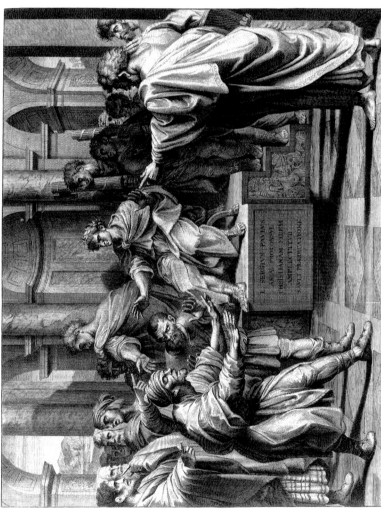

12 Nicholas Dorigny after Raphael, *Elymas the Sorceror*, 1719. Copyright The British Museum 346462.

13   Raffaelo Sanzio ('Raphael'), *St Paul Preaching*, c.1515, V&A Images/Kind permission of HRH Elizabeth II.

14   Raffaelo Sanzio ('Raphael'), *Christ's Charge to St Peter*, c.1515, V&A Images/Kind permission of HRH Elizabeth II.

15 Raffaelo Sanzio ('Raphael'), *The Miraculous Draft of Fishes*, c.1515, V&A Images/Kind permission of HRH Elizabeth II.

16 Bonifazio de Pitati, *Madonna and Child with Saints and the Three Cardinal Virtues*, Corsham Court, Wiltshire.

17   William Sharp after Guido Reni, *The Doctors of the Church*, 1775. Copyright The British Museum U.3.22.

18 After Girolamo Francesco Mazzola ('Parmigiano'), *Christ Laid in the Sepulchre*, 1775. Copyright The British Museum 1980.U.1547.

19 After Thomas Gousse (?), once attributed to Eustache Lesueur, *The Stoning of St Stephen*, 1775. Copyright The British Museum X-8-66.

20   The Chapel, Chatsworth, Derbyshire. Reproduced by permission of English Heritage. NMR.

21   The Painted Hall, Chatsworth, Derbyshire. Reproduced by permission of English Heritage. NMR.

22   The Chapel, Holkham Hall, Norfolk. Reproduced by permission of English Heritage. NMR.

23   The Marble Hall, Holkham Hall, Norfolk. Reproduced by permission of English Heritage. NMR.

24   The Chapel, Witley Court, Worcestershire. © Crown Copyright. NMR.

25 Sir James Thornhill, The East Wall of the Chapel, Wimpole Hall, Cambridgeshire, 1724. © Crown
    Copyright. NMR.

26　Interior, St Mary Magdalene, Croome d'Abitot, Worcestershire. © Crown Copyright. NMR.

27   Interior, St Swithun's, Worcester. Reproduced by permission of English Heritage. NMR.

28   *Altarpiece*, c.1680, St Martin Ludgate, City of London. Reproduced by permission of English Heritage. NMR.

29 Sir James Thornhill, *The Last Supper*, St Mary's, Melcombe Regis, Dorset, 1721. © Crown Copyright. NMR.

A View of the ALTAR PIECE lately Erected in the Church of St. James Clarkenwell.

A LETTER to the Bishop of LONDON, complaining of the New Altar-Piece in Clerkenwell Church, with REMARKS: To which is added, the late Bishop Fleetwood's Account of the Rise and Progress of placing Pictures and Images in Churches, discovering how readily such Practices lead to Superstition and Idolatry; as the Whole was published in the *Old Whig* of *October* 30, 1735.

To the OLD WHIG.

SIR,

THE underwritten Letter was sent about two Months past to the Bishop of *London*; but as I find that no Regard is paid to it, so I send it you as proper to have a Place in your Paper; the Matter of Complaint is what I think must give Offence to all *Consistent Protestants*, and be the Cause of great Triumph to their Adversaries.

My Lord, *August* 6, 1735.

AS you have shew'd great Zeal in the Discharge of the Duties of your Pastoral Office, so I hope you'll think, what I have to offer is not unworthy of your Notice. Being lately at the Church of St. *James Clerkenwell*, I observed an Altar-piece newly erected, which gave me great Offence, as I find it does many besides: The Virgin *Mary* is painted with Christ in her Arms, in the Front, with *Moses* and *Aaron* on each Side, as her proper Guard. I wish your Lordship would take a View of this new Work, which, in my Judgment, is the Reproach of Protestantism, and very near ally'd to Images, which we so justly condemn in the Church of *Rome*. And as such Fopperies are now growing upon us (and such as the common People were in all Ages, as well as the present, too fond of) so I doubt not but you'll order its Removal, and not suffer any of the like Kind, either there, or in any other Church, within your Jurisdiction. My Lord, if People will have Ornaments in that Place, I think the Commandments, with the Creed, and the Lord's Prayer, are only what they should be indulg'd in. Pictures (however dignify'd or distinguished) naturally tend to great Superstition, and to take People's Minds from what should be the Subject of their Thoughts during the Time of divine Service; and were therefore no less than Images condemned and rejected at the Reformation; all which your Lordship is too sensible of, to want any Information. I shall therefore give you no farther Trouble, but depend, that you will put a stop to this growing Evil; which will effectually convince the World, that you are in earnest for the *Protestant* Cause; but if no Care is taken to prevent such Nuisances in Religion, People, that think on such Matters, will have too much Reason for concluding, that the Reformed Religion is almost at as low an Ebb at Home, as it has been for some Years Abroad. I am,

SIR,

Your Lordship's most humble Servant,

THOMAS WATSON.

I CANNOT take upon me to say, what has been the Reason, why the Right Reverend *Prelate*, to whom this Letter was addressed, has not hitherto thought fit to comply with Mr. *W*——'s Request. Perhaps the Church of St. *James Clerkenwell* is exempt from his Lordship's Jurisdiction: Or some Circumstance or other may make it irregular for his Lordship at present to interpose in this Affair, in the Manner here desired. I offer these Conjectures, because I cannot easily be persuaded, that his Lordship does approve of these Kinds of Decorations, or that he desires to countenance or encourage the putting, or the keeping, them up in any of the Churches, that are under his Inspection and Care.

THIS Humour of placing *Pictures* in Places of publick Worship, as *Helps to Devotion*, is little suited to the plain and manly Spirit of *Christianity*. The primitive *Christians* and their *Churches* were quite unacquainted with all Ornaments of this Nature. The first *Protesters* against the Church of *Rome* expressed a great Indignation against them, and reckon'd them among her most gross Corruptions.

A LATE excellent *Prelate* of our Church, never to be mentioned or thought of without the highest Regard, has, in a very free and most agreeable Manner, let the World know his Sentiments on this Head. The late Right Reverend Dr. *William Fleetwood*, Bishop first of St. *Asaph*, and afterwards of *Ely*, was never accounted an Enemy to any *Decency* and *Order*, that was consistent with a becoming Concern for the *Protestant Religion*, and a zealous Attachment to the *Protestant Succession* in his present Majesty's most August House. To these he was a uniform, unsuspected, and declared Friend: He was so at all Times, but never more remarkably so, than at a Season, when Professions of Zeal, either for the *Protestant Succession*, or the *Protestant Religion*, were not thought the nearest, or surest, Way to Preferment. In a little Pamphlet, well known to have been wrote by him, tho' published without his Name, the Reader may see * that this truly great Man thought the Practice which Mr. *W*. complains of, to be of a very unjustifiable Nature, of a very dangerous Tendency, and likely to be attended with very mischievous Consequences; and that he judged, that any private Christian, who endeavoured to prevent, or put a stop to Innovations of this Kind, deserved Assistance, Countenance, and Commendation.

THERE he expresses himself on this Subject in the following Manner. †

"SOME Hundreds of Years had past, before any *Picture*, *Image* or *Statue* of a Saint, was placed in any Christian Church, throughout the World; tho' it is not unlikely that there were both in other Places for Ornament and Honour. It came at length into a *Painter's* Head, to represent, in as lively a Manner as he could, the Sufferings of a *Martyr'd Saint*, to which the Church was dedicated, *i. e.* by whose Name it was called; and to hang this Piece in some conspicuous Place within it. Wise Men were offended with the Novelty; not at the Picture, but at the setting it up in the *Church*; but the Common People were mightily pleased with it, and said, that Pictures were *the only Books which they could read*; and found themselves much edified by seeing how the Saints had glorified God, and confirm'd the Faith by their Constancy in suffering, and enduring Torments for the sake of Christ: And could such good Thoughts, and noble Resolutions be better raised in them than *at Church*, where they met so often to worship God? And therefore such good Pictures were most properly plac'd in Churches. There lived hard by a very devout *Statuary*, who excelled in carving Images both of Stone and Wood, who seeing the People so mightily taken with the *Picture*, asked them, one Day, whether an *Image*, of their Patron-Saint, carved out of fine Marble, and plac'd in a convenient Niche within the Church, would not excite the same good Thoughts, and good Remembrances in their Minds, that the Picture did; the Colours of which would, in Time, fade much, and wear away; and hearing nothing to the contrary, he set it up, and was commended for his Zeal and Benefaction by them: And *great gazing* there was at it; none of them making any Exception to an *Image*, which they could not make to a *Picture*; both seem'd alike Innocent; alike Useful; and alike proper, to excite good Thoughts, and devout Affections in the Minds of such as look'd on them.

"IT was not long after, that a Man of Quality and great Wealth, ordered the Statuary to make the finest Image he could of *Christ* our Lord, and fix it on *a Cross*, with all the Marks of Sorrow, and most painful Agonies that could be possibly expressed in such a Work, and place it in the *Eastern Light*, towards which he saw the People generally turn in their Acts of Worship. This was accordingly done, and the People were very fond of this *new Help to their Devotion*. Here was *the King of Saints* himself, they said, here they were hourly put in Mind of their Sins, which cost their Saviour all the bitter Pains he underwent upon the Cross, for their Redemption, which were so lively expressed in this *good Image*, that they could never view it well, without Compunction of Heart within, and knocking of their Breasts without, and other Tokens of Repentance. The Gentleman's *Wife*, and eldest Son, besought him, *out of pure Devotion*, that our Lord might not be worse attended in the *Church*, than he was upon *Mount Calvary*; and hereupon there was another Image made to represent his most afflicted *Mother*, and placed on his right Side; and another on his Left, namely his most beloved Disciple *John*, for so it was found to be in the Gospel; and thus the Church was furnished *with Books* for the Laity to read and meditate upon; and it was not long before they bowed their Heads; Incensed them; and Kneeled and said their Prayers before them. Under the Statue of the Patron-Saint, was *his Tomb* of Black Marble, in which the *precious Reliques* of this holy Martyr were deposited, *i. e.* the Bones that were not Burnt to Ashes, together with some Ashes of his Body that had been consumed by Fire: At this Tomb the People chose to say their Prayers rather than in any other Part of the Church, because they had heard that the Saint himself had Kneeled in the Place where his Tomb stood, when he offered up his Life to God. This Tomb the People prayed at constantly for whatever they wanted at God's Hands. One prayed for a sick Child, and another for a dying Husband, and another for the Cure of a Disease, under which she had long laboured: And it so pleased God that their Prayers were heard, and granted in their several Kinds; and then it came into their Heads, that their Prayers were the *rather* heard for their being put up at the Tomb of this good Saint; and that more People had been heard in what they asked at this Tomb, than in any other Place or Part of the Church; and when they reasoned among themselves how, or why this should be? *They were told*, that God might intend thereby to glorify his Saints, and to shew how precious their Death was in his Sight: And there were some, who doubted not to affirm, that the Saint himself did certainly intercede with God, in their Behalf; for who (said they) can think that the Saints in Heaven should sit and do nothing? And can they do any Thing better and more befitting them, than pray for those who live on Earth, and want all Manner of Comfort and Assistance? And can any Prayers be more Acceptable to God, than such as the Church Triumphant puts up for their Fellow-Members of the Church Militant? And can any Prayers be sooner heard, than what his Favourite Saints who died for the Truth, put up? And when it was *made so clear, by these Deductions*, that the Saints did undoubtedly intercede with God, for their Fellow-Christians on the Earth, it was very easy for the People then to ask of God, that he would grant them their Requests, *at* and *for* the Intercession, more especially of these Saints, his faithful Servants, whose Merits might prevail for what their own Unworthiness had made them neither dare to ask, nor fit to receive. And when these People had, at any Time received at God's Hands, what they had asked through the Intercession of the Saints, it was very Natural, for Ignorant unthinking Heads, to conclude, that God had truly granted what they had asked, for the Sake of that Saint's Intercession; which yet is no Consequence at all, since God *might grant* it, for his own Mercies Sake, and through the Intercession of his ever Blessed Son: But this the People did not mind; the Saints Intercession was the Means they used last, and having found as they thought, the Effects of it, they looked no farther. But Things did not long stand here; the People were not content to pray to God, to grant them what they wanted, for the Merits Sake, and at the Intercession of the Saints, but they pray'd to those very Saints themselves, that they would intercede with God to grant them what they wanted. This was *a wide Step* indeed, and a great Change. The Passage from the one Practice to the other, was not easy, natural, or consequential; but *Superstition* got over it quickly, and fancied there was but *a little Difference*, betwixt Peoples praying to God to hear the Saints praying for them, and the praying to the Saints that they would pray to God for them; whereas there is the widest Difference in the World betwixt those two Prayers; the one is directed to *God*, the sole proper Object, Omnipresent and Omnipotent; the other to *Creatures* only present in one Place, and of themselves able to do nothing. But these were Scruples that never troubled those good People; they had a Faith *that swallowed every Thing*, and seemed not to Value Consequences at all. To the Tomb they came, and pray'd the Saint to pray to God for whatever good Things they wanted; and when this Practice came to be contested a little, it was justified, as done out of *pure Humility*, because they were unworthy to Approach to God by Prayer, themselves in Person, and therefore did it by the Mediation of Saints their Intercessors. Well, in some reasonable Time, instead of praying the Saint to pray to God to give them this or that, they came to praying the Saint directly and downright to bestow this or that Blessing on them *Himself*: They thought it was too much round about, to say, *O Apollonia, pray to God to Cure me of the Tooth-ach*, and they said directly, *O Apollonia, Cure me, I beseech thee, of the Tooth-ach*. But being hard put to it to defend this Practice, they said they meant no more but to intreat her to pray to God for them; and all the good Writers of that corrupt Church of *Rome*, who have any Sense or Virtue left, desire to have all the Prayers that are put up to the Saints, to be understood to mean no more than a bare *Ora pro nobis*, or, —*Pray for us*. But my Design was not to Dispute about any Thing, but to shew how one Practice draws on another, not near so Innocent as the first, till at Length they come to Things Ridiculous, Absurd, and never to be justified.—And whosoever reads with any Observation, will find it was at first, the single Opinion or single Practice of some Private Man (and perhaps a very good Man too) that laid the Foundation of all the Superstitious Practices that prevail amongst the corrupt Part of Christians, now in the World. They were at first *Innocent* enough, and for a while they continued *Tolerable*; but by Degrees, and adding one Thing to another, they came at last to the Pass we now see them in; and who can tell at what Time the Impositions of private Fancies are to be withstood, if not at first? And can any one tell where they will Stop, *if private Men may not withstand them?*

* *A Letter to an Inhabitant of the Parish of St.* Andrews Holborn, *about New Ceremonies in the Church. Printed for* James Knapton, 1717.

† *P.* 17.

30 Anon., *A View of an altarpiece Lately Erected in the Church of St James Clerkenwell*, Broadside, 1735. Guidhall Library, Corporation of London.

31   William Snow (?), Ceiling of St Mary Abchurch, City of London, c.1708. © Crown Copyright. NMR.

32   Sir James Thornhill, Dome of St Paul's Cathedral, City of London, 1714–17. Reproduced by permission of English Heritage. NMR.

33   Interior of All Hallows', Barking by the Tower, City of London before 1940. © Crown Copyright. NMR.

34   Font Cover, attr. Grinling Gibbons, All Hallows, Barking, 1682. © Crown Copyright. NMR.

A Reprefentation *of the* ALTAR-PIECE *lately*
Set up in WHITE-CHAPPEL CHURCH.

Ja. Fellowes pinxit.

Falleris, hàc qui te pingi sub Imagine credis;
Non similis Judas est tibi; pænituit.

Sold by John Morphew near Stationers Hall, W^m gardiner a Linnen Draper in Whitechappel
High Street, and the Print-Sellers of London and Westminster   Price One Shilling.

35   *A representation of the Altar-Piece lately Set up in Whitechappel Church*, 1714. Guildhall Library, Corporation of London.

36 Robert Streeter, *Moses and Aaron*, St Michael Cornhill, City of London, after 1672. © Crown Copyright. NMR.

37   Anon., Altarpiece, St Mary's, Shotley, Suffolk, mid 18th century. Reproduced by permission of English Heritage. NMR.

38   Anon., Altarpiece, St Peter's, Ashburnham, Sussex, 1676. Reproduced by permission of English Heritage. NMR.

39 Anon., *Moses & Aaron*, St Michael Paternoster Royal, City of London, Late 17ᵗʰ Century. Photograph taken after the church was bombed in 1944. Reproduced by permission of English Heritage. NMR.

40 William Hogarth after William Kent, *Satire on Kent's Altarpiece*, 1725. Copyright The British Museum cc.1.62.11.

41 William Kent, *Last Supper*, St George's Hanover Square, London, 1725. © Crown Copyright. NMR.

period are rarely so vividly displayed than in this work, the irony being, of course, that it was Walpole's departure from the highest office that was its impetus. Horace suggests rather explicitly and elaborately in the *Aedes* what I suspect was usually tacit – that one was invited to judge the man through the quality of his collection.

Having dealt a little with the context of the *Sermon's* publication in the *Aedes*, I want to turn to the text itself. We cannot be certain why Horace chose to write a sermon for Sir Robert's chaplain to read at Houghton on the occasion of the collection being rehung at the house. We might want to think of it as an apt, formal means of marking the new life of Sir Robert, the house and the collection, a kind of dedication. The piece is notably anti-Catholic, as is Charles Lamotte's text that we will consider shortly. Walpole is concerned to mark out very clearly the idolatry of the Roman Catholic Church from the spectatorship of its art by Protestants and he offers suggestions for how art might be made use of for specifically religious purposes that we will discuss in the next chapter. The argument that Walpole develops is a conventional one, and one dependent on Richardson's writings, and the *Book of Homilies* of the Church of England among others.[42] However, it is worth following closely because Walpole discusses specific pictures with which he was very familiar.

He took as his text verse 5 from Psalm 115 in which David describes the idols of the pagans:

> They have mouths, but they speak not; eyes have they, but they see not: neither is there any breath in their nostrils.[43]

which he applies to Roman Catholic art, declaring:

> I must remark to you, that the words in the text, tho' spoken of images, which were more particularly the gods of the ancients, are equally referable to the pictures of the Romish church, and to them I shall chiefly confine this discourse.[44]

This formulation leads Walpole on to an entirely orthodox disquisition of the problems of idolatry, which he couples to the possible right uses of art in the spiritual edification of the faithful, echoing Richardson (and Luther):

> Painting, in itself, is innocent. No art, no science can be criminal; 'tis the misapplication that must constitute the sin. 'Tis when with impious eyes we look on the human performance as divine; when we call our own trifling imitations of the deity, inimitable gods: 'Tis then we sin ... Would we with other eyes regard these efforts of art; how conducive to religion.[45]

---

42 See Chapter 5 for further discussion of the *Homilies*.
43 Walpole (1752), p. 99.
44 Ibid., p. 100.
45 Ibid., p. 101.

The move Walpole makes next is noteworthy – to celebrate the greatness of artists such as Raphael in terms of the idolatrous response of spectators to their pictures. This appears, at first sight, an odd rhetorical shift to make, particularly because the *Sermon* uses examples of pictures drawn from his father's collection. In preparation, Walpole discusses the height to which God has permitted man to reach in representing the world he has created, using the fairly common comparison of God's creation and man's ability only to represent it, 'to call forth little worlds from the blank canvas'.[46] He then argues:

> Indeed so great is the perfection to which He hath permitted us to arrive, that one is less amazed at the poor vulgar, who adore what seems to surpass the genius of human nature; and almost excuse the credulity of the populace, who see miracles made obvious to their senses by the hand of a Raphael or a Guido. Can we wonder at a poor illiterate creature's giving faith to any legend in the life of the Romish Virgin, who sees even the Doctors of the Church disputing with such energy on the marvellous circumstances ascribed to her by the Catholicks? He must be endowed with a courage, a strength of reasoning above the common standard, who can reject fables, when the sword enforces, and the pencil almost authenticates the belief of them.[47]

Walpole is referring to Guido Reni's *The Doctors of the Church* [Plate 17], which hung in the Gallery at Houghton (a fact mentioned in the margin). The importance of painting as 'innocent' is crucial. This painting, considered the jewel of Walpole's collection, is the first mentioned in the *Sermon* and was described elsewhere in the *Aedes Walpolianae* as 'that capital picture ... the first in this collection'.[48] The argument which Walpole presents here allows him to stress its greatness as a work of art, to acknowledge indirectly its dubious content, and to allay fears about its unsuitability by the claim that only those are susceptible to idolatry who are 'vulgar' or 'illiterate' and who live where 'the sword enforces'. The implication is that in the enlightened liberty of an English picture gallery (in which the vulgar and illiterate are presumed never to trespass), the spectator is able, through his education and good judgement, to discern the 'fable' that the picture depicts, while he derives pleasure from the artist's performance.

Notice the enigmatic phrase 'the pencil almost authenticates the belief of them', a phrase which Walpole reinforces by mentioning the tale of Apelles being deceived exclaiming: 'no wonder then the ignorant should adore, when even the master himself could be cheated by a resemblance'.[49] This phrase skates over the responsibility of the painter because, for Walpole,

---

46 Ibid., p. 101.
47 Ibid., pp. 102–3.
48 Ibid., pp. 76–7.
49 Ibid., p. 103.

responsibility lies with the Popish clergy who are the 'real criminal[s]'. This is an unsurprising sentiment given the importance that was placed on the fame of canonical painters in the valuing of works. Walpole argues that paintings could, and should, be used to 'lead the poor unpractised soul through the paths of religion ... Then were painting united with devotion, and ransom'd from idolatry; and the blended labours of the preacher and the painter might tend to the glory of God'.[50] However, the prominence of the preacher in mediating such art is a rather different operation from the gentlemanly spectatorship of art in a collection. In support of this Walpole describes the effects paintings could have on the properly equipped spectator, using examples of some of the less problematic imagery held in the collection. Here, Walpole discusses Parmigiano's *Christ Laid in the Sepulchre* [Plate 18]:

> Then let him turn his eyes to sadder scenes! to affliction! to death! Let him behold what his God endured for his sake! Behold the pale, the wounded body of his Saviour; wasted with fasting! livid from the cross! See the suffering parent swooning! and all the passions expressed, which she must have felt at that melancholy instant! Each touch of the pencil is a lesson of contrition; each figure an apostle to call you to repentance![51]

Walpole provides a further justification for the presence of religious images in a private collection:

> When we can draw such advantages from the productions of this art, and can collect such subjects for mediation from the furniture of palaces, need we fly to deserts for contemplation, or to forests to avoid sin? Here are stronger lectures of piety, more admonitions to repentance ... Sights like these, must move, where the preacher fails; for each picture is but scripture realized ... The painter but executes pictures, which the Saviour himself designed.[52]

So Walpole asserts in a conventional way the value of pictures of subjects taken from the Scriptures, implicitly rejecting, in the context of religious edification, those pictures that depict 'fables', such as the subject of Reni's *Doctors of the Church*.[53] Thus, Walpole recognizes two categories of religious painting: one that depicts subjects guaranteed by the Word and another representing scenes from the lives of the saints or other aspects of Roman Catholic doctrine. This latter category is obviously unsuitable for religious

---

50 Ibid., p. 104. We will discuss the use of pictures in tandem with preaching in Chapter 5.

51 Ibid., p. 105.

52 Ibid., pp. 108–9.

53 It is particularly hard to know how to read the first sentence, which seems rather complacent. It may be seen in terms of the traditional argument about luxury, that it is the rich who are more susceptible to sin than the poor because of the number of temptations their wealth brings them into contact with. See Berry (1994).

edification, but such works of art can be valued in the gentlemanly collection for their qualities of execution. This depends heavily on the notion Walpole, Richardson and Lamotte each articulate, that painting is innocent. In any case, Walpole's distinction is rather an unclear one in the sense that it is difficult to see how firm lines might be drawn. For example, as Jonathan Richardson pointed out, there is no mention in the New Testament of the Virgin 'swooning' at the sight of Christ on the Cross, as she is frequently presented.[54] Obviously such judgements have as much to do with a sense of decorum, as with religious belief.[55] While the art of painting might be innocent, the choice of subject matter does indeed offer a challenge to the spectator. But tellingly, Walpole does not tackle this problem any further and Reni's *The Doctors of the Church* is the only such painting mentioned in the *Sermon*, even though there were others in the collection which were problematic in just these terms.[56] This allows unequivocally positive statements about pictures to dominate the *Sermon* and an uncomplicated sense of the greatness of the collection to emerge.

Walpole returns to the subject of Catholic spectatorship, in an attempt to make clear the distinct nature of the Protestant 'gaze', by treating the question of the invocation of the saints as intercessors and, indeed, the nature of sainthood. He asks why:

> Instead of throwing themselves into the arms of eternal mercy or infinite goodness, they barter for pardon with impotent images, or perished mortals, who died with the repute of a few less sins than the rest of mankind! But could these suppostitious deities attend to their prayers – why should canvas or stone, why men who when living were subject to all the obduracy, ill nature, and passions of humanity, why be supposed more capable of pity, more sensible of our sorrows, than that fountain of tenderness and compassion, who sacrificed His best-beloved for the sake of mankind? Or why prefer the purchase of pardon from interested mercenary saints, to the free forgiveness of him, who delighteth not in burnt offerings?[57]

The saints, for Walpole, were mere men and women whose lives may perhaps have been exemplary. Walpole uses a rather crude caricature of Roman Catholic understanding of sainthood, but given this view of it was widely shared, it raises the question of how straightforward it was for the English Protestant spectator to look at even a simple 'portrait' of a saint. Walpole does not illustrate this part of his argument by considering any of the pictures of saints that Sir Robert owned (for example, *St John the Evangelist* by Maratti

---

54 Richardson, *An Essay on the Theory of Painting* (1715) in Richardson (1792), p. 22.

55 See 'Decorum' in Murray and Murray (1996).

56 For example, two paintings by Carlo Maratti: *The Marriage of St Catherine* and *Two Saints Worshipping the Virgin in the Clouds*.

57 Walpole (1752), p. 111.

and *St Christopher* by Elsheimer), and so does not show us how he looked, or expected others to look, on such pictures. In the *Description*, the other important element in *Aedes Walpolianae*, he does describe Le Sueur's (1616–55) *Stoning of St Stephen*, which hung in the Saloon at Houghton [Plate 19]:

> A capital picture of Le Soeur [*sic*]. It contains nineteen figures and is remarkable for expressing a most masterly variety of grief. The saint, by a considerable anachronism, but a very common one among the Roman Catholics, is dressed in the right habit of a modern priest at high mass.[58]

This is, perhaps, indicative of the kind of manoeuvres the English spectator made in front of such pictures. There are two registers of appreciation: the affective and the connoisseurial, but it is still hard to gauge to what extent the affective response was, or was supposed to be, engaged in looking at scenes drawn from the lives of saints, not the New Testament. In connection to the question of reading the sensibility of Roman Catholicism, we might want to consider Walpole's description of Van Dyck's *Rest on the Flight into Egypt*:

> A most celebrated picture ... the chief part of it, is a dance of boy angels, which are painted in the highest manner. The Virgin seems to have been a portrait, and is not handsome, it is too much crowded with fruits and flowers and birds. In the air are two partridges finely painted.[59]

It is difficult to grasp the significance of this; we should see the notion of a 'portrait' as a criticism that Van Dyck did not use an idealized vision of the Virgin, that the portrayal smacks a little too much of naturalism, as does the Snyders-like attention to the natural surroundings.[60] This criticism can easily be seen to work within the standard tropes of art writings in which the figures of histories should be portrayed ideally, to promote emulation. I suspect that the earthbound quality of this painting, combined with the presence of the *putti*, might have been recognized as anachronistic, as Catholic unreason, but the presence here of such meanings is impossible to be sure of, without more evidence.[61]

These two are the only pictures to receive extended attention in Walpole's *Description* and we can see that the challenges offered by ownership and display of such pictures is not explicitly acknowledged. What is clear is that responses to these pictures included recognition of Catholic elements. There is little hope of finding evidence to produce a deeper 'psychological' understanding of this process, as yet, but perhaps we are a little further

---

58 Ibid., p. 54.

59 Ibid., p. 54.

60 For a reproduction of this painting and discussion of it see Dukelskaya & Moore (eds) (2002), pp. 208–10.

61 John Bossy discusses cognate issues briefly (Bossy (1985), pp. 95–6).

forward.[62] Charles Lamotte's work, to which we now turn, deals rather more extensively with the grounds on which objections to Catholic paintings could be raised.

Lamotte's lengthy *Essay* is different in kind from Walpole's. While it is based on the classical/Horatian trope of a comparison between the arts of poetry and painting, Lamotte's primary interest is in a scholarly elaboration of the problem of artistic and poetic licence. Lamotte argues that poets and painters depart from the 'truth' in three ways: obscenity; historical anachronism (placing people together in an image, or a poem, who did not live in the same era or rendering a person in a costume of another time or place from that in which they lived); and fabrication (introducing elements which are not licensed by the history which is represented).[63] His attention is devoted largely to the errors of painters, and while he does discuss erroneous depictions of classical subjects, he reserves his greatest attention and criticism for religious paintings. He divides religious works into two categories using the same criteria that we noticed in Walpole's argument. The first is those that depict incidents drawn from the Bible. He describes a large number of common subjects which, with one exception, the Death of Abel, come from the New Testament, demonstrating how artists have introduced variations to the narrative of the Scriptures (or in any of the most authoritative interpretations of them). The second category, which Lamotte calls 'ecclesiastical history', describes those religious subjects which are not drawn from the Bible and which deal with the lives of saints or other aspects of Roman Catholic doctrine. This division reinforces the impression we got from Walpole's argument that a vital aspect of spectatorship of religious works was this test of biblical orthodoxy. The tensions in which the ownership and spectatorship of Italian art had to be managed are becoming clearer.

Of Lamotte's types of licence we need not deal with obscenity, in this context, although it is worth noting that these two were commonly held in tension, but we should look at anachronism and fabrication and examine more closely his definition of 'ecclesiastical history'.[64] We noted in Walpole's catalogue description of Le Sueur's *Stoning of St Stephen* the mention of the anachronism of the saint wearing modern Roman Catholic vestments and Lamotte raises a number of similar examples, such as St Jerome painted in

---

62   This given that collecting is so under-researched. Perhaps when more work has been done in the archives in relation to collections we may be able to understand spectatorship better.

63   Lamotte uses the word 'truth' with confidence. In religious matters this is, for him, an admixture of a straightforward reading of the Scriptures and rational or common-sense interpretation. We will explore this further. Lamotte's treatment of the question of 'probability' should be compared to Richardson's considered in Chapter 3.

64   Lamotte's discussion of obscenity largely concerns depictions of classical subjects. Compare to Richardson's comments on the same issue quoted above.

the 'habit of a cardinal, when I know that neither the dignity nor dress were heard of 'till some hundred years after this father', or St James the Apostle, who is depicted carrying:

[A] pilgrim's staff and set out with shells and trinkets as going on a pilgrimage, when I'm very sure there were no pilgrims in his days; and yet he is drawn in this ridiculous equipage, because, forsooth, there is daily a great resort of pilgrims to his pretended shrine.[65]

There is a strong note of anti-Catholicism in these descriptions that is characteristic of the *Essay*, which distinguishes it from similar criticisms against anachronisms made by continental art theorists.[66] His examples of temporal errors in religious works have much the same flavour:

Thus one shall often see St Jerome attending our Saviour at the institution of the Last Supper, and St Francis present at the Crucifixion, though both lived many hundred years after him ... Paolo Veronese in one of his finest pieces, the Changing Water into Wine at the Marriage of Cana, which is to be seen in the Convent of St George at Venice. In this piece, by an unpardonable licence and a ridiculous compliment, he has placed among the other guests some Benedictine monks, for whose convent he wrought that piece; an order that was not known 'till above five hundred years after the working of this miracle.[67]

Lamotte has no time for painters who paint such untruths. In contrast to Richardson (whose argument he refers to), Lamotte places the blame firmly on the artist, rather than, quoting Richardson, on the 'positive directions of those for whom the picture was made'.[68] He declares that this is not a 'lawful excuse':

A great artist and a noble genius should set himself above such mean considerations ... He should not debase or prostitute his pencil, nor sacrifice his glory and

---

65   Lamotte (1730), p. 12.

66   See Blunt (1958), p. 11 for du Chambray. See also Du Bos (1748), vol. 1, p. 218. These criticisms were made on the basis of reason, as were Lamotte's, but were not harnessed to Protestant anti-Catholic rhetoric.

67   Lamotte (1730), pp. 8–9.

68   Richardson argues that 'when we see in pictures of the Madonna those of St Frances [*sic*], St Katherine, or others not contemporary ... this is not so blameable as people commonly think. We are not to suppose these were intended for pure historical pictures, but only to express the attachment those saints or persons had for the Blessed Virgin, or their great piety and zeal ... with this key a great many seeming absurdities of good masters will be discovered to be none.' Richardson, *An Essay on the Theory of Painting* (1715) in Richardson (1792), p. 47. The passage Lamotte quotes from is on p. 48.

reputation to the wrong taste and vanity of others. He should put on the same spirit and courage, and the same love of truth as an impartial historian.[69]

Lamotte goes on to argue that artists have a greater responsibility to adhere to the truth when representing religious subjects, but instead they have taken unwarrantable liberties.[70] Lamotte employs a variety of tools to criticize their works. His criticism of depictions of the birth of Christ, for example, is based on a common-sense reading of the story of the Virgin giving birth in the stable. Lamotte argues that often the Virgin is shown:

> Arrayed like a glorious queen, set of with royal robes, and a crown upon her head; and on the other side, the infant Jesus lying in a manger by her; than which, nothing can be more absurd and preposterous ... What has a queen to do with a common stable? What analogy is there between a manger and a crown? This is done, I suppose, to set off the glory of the Virgin Mary, or to add beauty and embellishment to the picture. However it be, it is certainly a direct fault against costume, a downright solecism in painting.[71]

Lamotte insists on a very tight reading of Scriptures, a plain reading, strongly naturalistic in its adherence to the text. This is even more obvious in his discussion of depictions of the Adoration of the Magi. Raising a number of objections, Lamotte reserves his strongest point until last:

> They are always represented as kings with crowns on their heads ... and this without the least warrant or authority from scripture and antiquity. The Holy Scripture calls them Magi, wise-men, and ancient writers tell us that they were philosophers, that applied themselves to arts and sciences, but especially to the study of astronomy which led them to the observation of the new star, which they followed as their guide but without the least hint ... of their regal dignity.

He goes on to argue that whatever the motivation of these artists, whether to beautify the picture or to 'emphasize the glory of the Infant-Saviour' by showing the kings at his feet, it is unwarranted:

> The Christian religion disclaims such false and deceitful props ... A judicious painter therefore, in matters so sacred and solemn, should be more prudent and cautious, should strictly confine himself to truth, should have recourse to the Scriptures, those divine springs, ... and not build upon such weak and sandy foundations as forged and fictitious legends.[72]

This is a Protestant manifesto for religious painting: there should only be plain readings of the Bible with very little licence, or scope for probability, using

---

69   Lamotte (1730), pp. 9–10.
70   Ibid., p. 57.
71   Ibid., p. 69.
72   Ibid., pp. 73–5.

either the painter's own invention or traditional iconography.[73] Furthermore, no painter should treat non-scriptural subjects of religious figures, which he describes as 'those sandy foundations…[of] forged and fictitious legends'. Lamotte identifies this category of images, which he categorizes as 'ecclesiastical history' as specifically Popish and argues that he need not deal with them because the subjects of these paintings are fabulous:

> If I were to pass to the ecclesiastical history … I could prove that many of the pictures that are drawn, nay that are with great devotion worshipped in Popish countries, are mere ideas, such as never existed in the world.[74]

He gives several examples, such as St Christopher, who is 'only an emblem of labour, constancy and perseverance in religion', and St Catherine, 'who is held in so much veneration in the Church of Rome'. His emphasis on the subjects of the pictures, not on the images themselves, leaves their reputation rather ambiguous. Indeed this is further compounded by his concluding comments. Having discussed the currency of St Catherine's reputation not just in Catholic countries but also in England, where young women celebrated on 25 November a festival which Lamotte calls 'Catherning', he says:

> But as most of these stories and fictions are grounded upon some old legends, which are held in veneration by a great part of the world; and as a legend may be perhaps thought a sufficient foundation for a poet or limner to build upon, I shall insist no farther upon them here; nor shall I lay this to the charge of the gentlemen of the profession.[75]

We must take this as sarcasm, given his strictures about artists quoted above, and the list of the skills and virtues an artist must possess that he includes towards the end of the *Essay*, the last of which is:

> He must also be perfectly skilled in history, both sacred and profane, which will enable him to discern truth from falsehood, to distinguish the history from the fable … he must, in his historical performances, rise above even common errors, despite vulgar and groundless traditions, and make truth and veracity the very rule and standard of his judicious pencil.[76]

---

73   One is reminded of the famous debate between Charles Le Brun and Philippe de Champaigne over Poussin's depiction of the story of Rebecca and Eliezer at the Well. Champaigne, a Jansenist, argued that Poussin had taken too much licence with the text by excluding the camels. I have found no evidence that Lamotte knew of this specific argument. However the writings of Roger de Piles and André Felibien were available to Lamotte in French.

74   Ibid., p. 124.

75   Ibid., p. 126.

76   Ibid., p. 164.

The painter must not only be learned, something that Richardson also insisted on, he must be much more than this: he must be a theologian who can rise above the local custom of his own religion. The strength of these assertions represents a rather different relationship towards religious pictures from Walpole's or Richardson's. For it is hard to say how one might, with Lamotte's arguments ringing in one's ears, as it were, approach the religious pictures in Sir Robert Walpole's or the Duke of Montagu's collection.[77] Whereas Walpole justifies these pictures in terms of both the artist's reputation and the execution of the work, Lamotte implies that such work cannot be praised because those artists are not great who depict the fables of 'ecclesiastical' history.

The implications of this argument for English admiration of Italian art are not acknowledged by Lamotte, that artists who served the Catholic church cannot be great, who describes Raphael as great even when he criticizes him. One conclusion we may be expected to draw is that only sound Protestants can be truly great artists. It is revealing perhaps that Lamotte does not discuss any specific pictures held in English collections. This perhaps allowed him to distance his arguments from the actual problems of interpreting such pictures in Protestant spaces, to focus on production rather than reception. Lamotte's *Essay* helps us to identify many problematic areas of content and execution in these foreign works, and although he does not help us to see in what positive terms they were prized, he does give ample testimony to the force which these works had in this culture: for, in the end, even he does accept that the best nine works of art, still extant, are all religious, eight of them are by Catholics and several of them contain licences of precisely the kind he has been arguing against. Lamotte argues that Domenichino's *Last Communion of St Jerome* is 'esteemed the finest next to the Transfiguration of Raphael, that is the 2d Picture in the World' and then proceeds to seven other paintings including *The Nativity of Christ* by Correggio, Daniel Volterra's *Descent from the Cross*, *The Last Judgement* by Michelangelo, Van Dyck's *Crucifixion* and Holbein's *Dead Christ*.[78] Only the last painting might possibly be described as a Protestant work, dating from Holbein's first residence in Basle in the early 1520s, although it was painted before the Protestant regime was introduced in 1527, with its iconoclastic purges of the city's churches and before Holbein's formal declaration of his faith in 1529. It may have been more significant to Lamotte that both Van Dyck and Holbein had long been co-opted into an English history of art and they had been 'Englished' in an even more thoroughgoing fashion than Raphael, and thus Lamotte's list can be said to have a patriotic aspect to it.

---

77 See Murdoch (ed.) (1992), pp. 75–89 for an account of the Montagu picture collection.

78 Lamotte (1730), p. 127.

To return to our main theme, both Lamotte's and Walpole's essays demonstrate how the subject matter, the doctrinal content, of Catholic paintings was not ignored by spectators even in the space of a collection, but that 'errors' of doctrine were recognized and sometimes commented upon. We can also see that reactions to them, and the implications drawn from them, could vary. What becomes clearer after this analysis is that the language and methodology of art criticism played a crucial part in mediating religious images, through two rhetorical mechanisms. The first is the idea that painting is, in itself, innocent, a claim that is made explicitly and implicitly by both Walpole and Lamotte and which is to be found commonly in the literature. This claim allows paintings of alien subject matter to be absorbed into collections and discussions of art for their qualities as works of art, as we saw in the case of Reni's *The Doctors of the Church*. The second is the notion that the painters whose works were so prized were the greatest of modern times (a claim which Walpole asserts but which Lamotte seems to reject, albeit, rather ambiguously). These two arguments often work in tandem. Thus, a painting of an unsympathetic subject could be hung with pride as a work by a great artist, could be appreciated through the processes of art criticism, and judgements made about how to account for the dubious subject matter. For Walpole and others who might want to talk about their *own* pictures, the territory seems to have been particularly difficult to navigate. I suspect that Walpole would not have thought of using the force of argument that Lamotte deployed because he was talking about his father's pictures and therefore a way had to be found to manage the troubling content within a positive reading of them. The light touch of Walpole's comments about the dress of St Stephen in the Le Sueur exemplifies this.

We are fortunate to have another discussion of Reni's *The Doctors of the Church* by Walpole that we can usefully draw on here. In the *Description* (the catalogue element of *Aedes Walpolianae*), Walpole describes the painting as the greatest in the collection, but this greatness is measured only in the briefest of formal terms:

> In this picture, which is by Guido in his brightest manner, and perfectly preserved, there are six old men as large as life. The expression, drawing, design and colouring, wonderfully fine. In the clouds is a beautiful virgin all in white, and before her a sweet little angel flying.[79]

However, this short appreciation appears only after an extensive description of the theological debates in the Roman Church over the immaculate nature of the Virgin. Walpole's discussion, the details of which need not detain us, begins with the statement that 'this has been a most controverted point in the Romish Church' and while the tenor is neutral, Walpole's motivation for such an extended account of an aspect of Roman Catholic doctrine might

---

79   Walpole (1752), p. 79.

appeinterestar to be elusive. It is true that another painting, Poussin's *The Continence of Scipio*, receives a fairly lengthy treatment too, although most of this is taken up with an extended quotation from Livy, on which the painting is based, and an English translation of it. However, Walpole's description of the Reni appears significantly more thoroughly researched, containing references to many more texts than any of the other entries and the only one to mention the doctrinal significance of a religious picture. While Walpole may have believed that his account would be of interest and use to his audience, it is also likely that the painting's prominence in the collection (it was 'the first picture in the Collection') demanded that the painting should receive a description of a length apt to its fame. The account given of the picture in the *Sermon* that we dealt with earlier was different; Walpole used it to demonstrate the dangers of idolatry of such works in that memorable phrase 'the pencil almost authenticates the belief of them'. Both the descriptions in the *Aedes Walpolianae* exemplify how the Popish identity of such pictures was, indeed, visible and that it was a hurdle that had to be overcome. It is precisely because commentary on pictures had to negotiate with the troubling content of pictures that English art criticism appears so reticent about the experience of spectatorship.

We can usefully think further about the roles of religious art, and turn particularly to the significant aspect of rank that it entailed, by considering the presence of religious art in country house chapels.[80] Large country houses built during this period often included a chapel in their plans and it is remarkable how exuberant some of the chapel decorative schemes were.[81] The decoration was frequently conceived as part of the scheme for the whole house and the schemes suggest that the chapel was seen as a room whose importance was on a par with the state rooms. For example, at Chatsworth the vigorous ornamentation of the chapel is completely in tune with that of the Painted Hall and the suite of state rooms, with large-scale narrative paintings and marble wall furniture. At Holkham the use of marble in the chapel is strongly reminiscent of the famous Marble Hall [Plates 20–23]. This suggests that there were few obstacles, during this period, to decorating a private religious space in ways impossible for a parish church.

W M Jacob suggests that 'the practice of Anglican Christianity seems to have been central to the self-understanding of aristocratic and gentry society', a comment of considerable interest and Jacob uses the decoration of chapels to support his point, arguing that 'given the expense of employing the most

---

80   There is very little secondary literature on country house chapels. Girouard (1978), for example, pays little attention to them in his, still influential, text. See the brief survey of 'Lordly Chapels' in Robinson (1995a). The posthumous publication of Annabel Ricketts's work on private chapels of the sixteenth and seeventeenth centuries is eagerly anticipated.

81   For a representative sample see Campbell's *Vitruvius Britannicus* (1715–25).

distinguished architects and artists of their generation, Christian worship must have been seen as playing a significant part in the life of these great country houses. The best of design and craftsmanship was lavished as much on the chapel as on the saloon'.[82] There is much in this argument, but I am not sure that one can map so directly the elaborateness of decoration onto the significance of worship. For example, many of these houses stood largely empty for the majority of the year, as families lived in London for the sitting of parliament or resided at other houses. The grandeur of these chapels, in which the formal hierarchy of family and servants was so carefully maintained, but in which everyone was present (rather than in the saloon, the library or the kitchen) suggests that we might look for other possible readings of the decorative schemes of chapels. In addition, much of the valuable picture collections owned by these families were to be found in London during this period, not at the great houses, and so further investigations are needed to locate the decorative schemes of such houses more securely in relation to the understanding of the role of art in the country house.[83]

Some historians have sought to establish the style of building and decoration of elite country houses as party political statements, so that taste for the rococo or Palladianism is an indication of Tory or Whig allegiances.[84] However, such claims cannot be sustained for very long. Chapels were built by Tories and Whigs, and it is mistaken to look to styles or even subject matter for party messages in these spaces; I suggest that decorative schemes are better seen within a tradition of cosmopolitan aristocratic culture. Responding to this, English patrons used both émigré and English artists to make schemes similar to those to be seen in the courts of Europe, although a considerable level of negotiation (whether tacit or explicit we cannot be sure) was necessary to ensure that Catholic elements were removed. A suggestive example is the work of Sebastiano Ricci (1659–1734) at Bulstrode Park (1713–14), for which, unfortunately, only *modelli* survive (an idea of the finished quality of Ricci's work can be gained from the apse ceiling painting which survives at the Royal Hospital, Chelsea). The New Testament scenes painted by Ricci at Bulstrode appear to have been designed with Protestant sensitivies in mind for they are quite different iconographically from his work for the churches and chapels of Venice.[85]

---

82 Jacob (1996), pp. 98–9.

83 For example, how important was the portability of pictures? Wall painting may also have been, *contra* Jacob, cheaper than either more elaborate architectural treatments or substantial canvases, which are, in any case, rare.

84 See Hook (1976) and Whinney and Millar (1957) for claims about the use of Baroque and Palladianism. See Colley (1984) for the care one must exercise over these kinds of judgements which she discusses in the context of the rococo in England. Following from Colley is Crown (1990) who develops the arguments further.

85 See Martineau and Robison (eds) (1994) and de Grazia et al. (eds) (1996) for discussions of Ricci's work in the Venetian context.

At Canons, James Brydges, First Duke of Chandos, built a chapel (before 1720) which can be compared to Chatsworth and Bulstrode Park for the vivid multiplicity of its decoration. The Duke employed Antonio Bellucci (1654–1726) to paint the ceiling panels. Francesco Sleter (1685–1775) designed the windows, Giovanni Bagutti (b.1681) was in charge of the extraordinary plasterwork and Joshua Price (1672–1722) made the stained-glass windows, and together the four created a space which must have seemed extraordinary in the countryside of Middlesex. Chandos had a full orchestra on his staff, Pepusch was his master of music and Handel was also employed by the Duke, for whom he composed the Chandos Anthems. The house was broken up in 1747, but, fortunately, the chapel interiors (paintings and stained glass) were bought for his own recently completed chapel by Lord Foley of Witley, who had Bagutti's ceiling plasterwork reproduced [Plate 24].[86] The resulting reconstruction is an extraordinarily light, joyous scheme, which is in some ways, with its creamy white and gilt colourings, more reminiscent of pared-down German or Austrian church decoration of the period, than of anything else to be found in England at this time. Bellucci had decorated much of the rest of Canons. Unfortunately we have little idea of what those interiors looked like, although a surviving Inventory suggests they were very rich with many painted ceilings.[87]

The work at Canons, it has been suggested, was a spur to Edward Harley, Second Earl of Oxford, who employed James Gibbs (1682–1754) to add two wings to the house at Wimpole. One wing housed the famous library at the west end of the house and the other, the chapel in the south-east corner.[88] Both of these rooms had anterooms connected with them: the book-room and the ante-chapel. Our interest lies with the decorative scheme of the ante-chapel and the chapel itself. The calm order of Gibbs's exteriors do not prepare one for the abundant complexity of Thornhill's decoration of the chapel (1724) [Plate 25].[89] Giving structure to Thornhill's plan is the *trompe l'oeil* architecture deployed on each of the walls and the elaborate coffering of the ceiling. The east end, decorated with Thornhill's masterful portrayal of the *Adoration of the Magi*, is conceived as a continuation of the architectural scheme with its Venetian-window-shaped portico, with *putti* pulling back a curtain as a dramatic gesture above. Below, a reredos, also by Thornhill, of Christ and Nicodemus, which seems to have been lost, completed the east end.[90] On the North wall, the four Doctors of the Church are shown as statues in niches

---

86 Watson (1954), p. 300. Handel's organ at Canons was also installed at Great Witley.

87 Collins Baker and Baker (1949), pp. 162–72.

88 See Lees-Milne (2001) and Harris (1985) for a discussion of Harley and the group of artists and writers to whom he acted as patron.

89 For brief discussions of Thornhill's work at Wimpole see Osmun (1950), Allen (1985) and Souden (1991).

90 Milles MS (1735), p. 44.

and between them are *putti*. The work on this wall is strongly reminiscent of that of Louis Laguerre (1663–1721) for the Duke of Chandos at St Lawrence's Church, Whitchurch, Middlesex (after 1715), near to Canons, and it also recalls Thornhill's own decoration of the spaces between the windows of the west wall chapel at All Souls, Oxford (before 1719).[91] The scheme at Wimpole was completed by the west wall of the gallery (the family pew), on which Thornhill painted three vases with reliefs of the Baptism of Christ, the Last Supper and the Resurrection.

Unlike the other houses we have looked at, this room was singular, in the context of the house, in its painted decoration, suggesting that the chapel was a statement of special significance for Harley. What makes this plausible is the decoration of the ante-chapel located between the hall and the chapel, which gave access to the family pew in the gallery of the chapel. The hall was decorated with a substantial number of hunting scenes by John Wootton (?1668–1765), but the ante-chapel was, in abrupt contrast, clearly a religious space.[92] Here were two other paintings by Thornhill: *St John Preaching in the Wilderness*, which hung over the mantelpiece, and a *Salutation*, on the right of the door into the chapel.[93] These were accompanied by a number of portraits by Michael Dahl (?1656–?1743) of whose work Harley owned many examples. In 1735, Jeremiah Milles (1675–1746), on a tour round the area, noticed portraits of Archbishop Laud and Bishops Sprat (1635–1713), Smalridge (1663–1719) and Gastrell (1662–1725) as well as of Dr Stratford (Harley's tutor at Christ Church, Oxford), in the ante-chapel.[94] The display of a portrait of Laud may be interpreted as a High Church gesture, but perhaps the fact that Sir Robert Walpole had one hanging in his drawing room at Houghton may cut across this. Walpole's portrait of Laud was significantly claimed as a Van Dyck and was just one amongst eight portraits by the artist (which included one of Charles I) which hung in that room.[95] However, the choice of situation for Harley's portrait of Laud, at Wimpole, may be more significant. Each of the other portraits represented a family friend who was tied in to the networks of Tory (and Jacobite) allegiance that Harley had been introduced into by his father, Robert Harley, First Earl of Oxford (1661–1724). I do not want to give the impression that I think Harley intended a polemical function for the scheme – there is no evidence of such intent – but it is difficult

---

91   I hope that in further research I will be able to look at university and other institutional chapels.

92   See Meyer (1985) for information on Harley's extensive patronage of Wootton. The religious works were sold, along with most of the pictures, in 1742 after Harley's death. These were not repurchased for the house subsequently, but many of the pictures by Wootton were. See Cock (1742) for details of the sale.

93   See Allen (1985).

94   Milles MS (1735), p. 44. See Ingamells (1981) for discussion of these portraits in the context of episcopal portraiture.

95   See Moore (ed.) (1996), pp. 105–7.

not to view the ante-chapel as a statement of Harley's High Church Toryism through which we might be encouraged to view, literally, the chapel. This is in contrast to the other schemes we have looked at, which seem less clearly partisan in their use of imagery.

In any case what is most striking about these schemes is the deployment of rich ornament and narrative images. Within the decoration of the rest of the house, such vivid imagery in a place of worship is a statement of confidence in the judgement of the household and all those who would enter into it. It is significant that on estates where there was no chapel in the house itself, but a separate estate church, decoration appears to have been a great deal more restrained in its use of narrative decoration and painterly effects. One striking exception to this is the Duke of Chandos's scheme at St Lawrence, Whitchurch. That example apart, the decoration of an estate church tended to be less dependent on figure painting, although it could still be vivid, thus declaring the patronage of the commissioner as at Croome d'Abitot in Worcestershire, the interior of which may have been designed by Robert Adam [Plate 26].

However, there were no guarantees that everyone would consent to country-house chapel schemes representing a safe Protestantism. In 1764 Lady Beauchamp-Proctor visited Holkham from her home at Langley Park, Norfolk and, as she recorded in her journal, found the pictures which hung on the walls of the chapel [see Plate 22] to look 'so like the Roman Catholic superstition', but she added that it was 'very elegantly fitted up' and praised the marble of the communion table and the cedar from which the altar rails, reading desk and gallery were made.[96]

In this chapter and the previous one, we can see that anxieties expressed about visual images in the Church of England can now be seen to be operating on a kind of scale. In the country house, imagery could be tolerated for two reasons: first, it was the home of a gentleman who, in the terms of the operating discourses, by his very nature, could not have looked at these images in any other way than rightly, and second, the household would be expected to be properly guided and educated by his leadership to use them wisely. So in this setting, with access both limited and properly controlled, religious imagery was acceptable, whereas in the parish church, where the unlettered and the uncontrolled might be drawn into idolatry, it could be less safely tolerated. This demonstrates once again how the removal of imagery from public spaces must be seen as an act of political significance, as well as of theological prescription. It also reveals another aspect of the intimate relation between religious imagery and political authority, which we have explored in a number of different ways and which we will pursue in the next chapter.

---

96   Quoted in Ketton-Cremer (1957), p. 191.

It is clear that 'Popish' art was accepted more easily in the spaces of the art collection than the private chapel and, as we shall see, the parish church. Although access to pictures in art collections was controlled, much of the work collections were engaged to do was 'public', as we have seen. The degree to which an orthodox reading of problematic pictures could be guaranteed seems to have been the principal test of religious imagery, both Protestant and Catholic. In our discussion of collections we established that there were two categories of religious imagery, one describing subjects drawn from the Scriptures and the other from what Lamotte called 'ecclesiastical history'. Neither category was completely unproblematic (the manner of depiction could still cause the spectator concern, as we saw in relation to the concept of anachronism), but the latter group of subjects was the most difficult for the English spectator. We have explored how the discourses of art were used to manage the complex relations operating between the content of these pictures, the idea of the great artist and the public reputation of their owners. Nevertheless, orthodox religious art could still carry 'Popish' connotations in the privacy of the country house.

Chapter 5

Ornamenting Anglicanism: Images and Idols

The attitudes to art that we have been exploring in this book were informed by two key ideas held in tandem: a vision of Catholicism as superstitious and idolatrous and an uncomfortable sense that Catholicism had been, as Gibbon put it, 'the parent of taste'. I suggested earlier that a considerable part of the uncertainty towards art was probably due to the rather unstable position of the Church of England towards religious imagery. This chapter aims to show how ambiguous the role of the image was in the Church of England. This is essential in order to understand more fully the central concern of this book, which is to show how art was, as a category, associated with Catholicism in England. The role of images in the Church of England is such an underexplored area of eighteenth-century studies that I hope that this chapter will also serve to suggest ways in which further work on the production and reception of art for churches in England might contribute to our understanding of the religious history of the period.[1]

Among the paintings made for churches and chapels that are still extant, there are a few works by well-known artists such as Copley, Hayman, Hogarth, Kent, Streeter, Thornhill, and West. A host of foreign artists found work in this field including Andrea Casali, Giovanni Battista Cipriani, James Parmentier and Sebastiano Ricci.[2] In addition, many now little-known or completely unknown artists fulfilled commissions for their local parish church. Most of this work is unrecognized for its own sake, nor is it recognized as a significant part of eighteenth-century English art production. It has not been ignored completely: for example, Addleshaw and Etchells's *The Architectural Setting of Anglican Worship* (1948), Clarke's *The Building of the Eighteenth-Century Church* (1963), Croft-Murray's *Decorative Painting in England, 1537–1837* (1962–70) and Friedman's *The Georgian Parish Church* (2004) each discussed it to a limited extent, describing a wide range of church decoration. More recently, the historians Jeremy Gregory and Jonathan Barry have both used some of the evidence of church decoration to argue a broader point about the use of all forms of culture in the competitive

---

1   I plan to make a more substantial contribution to this field in a book provisionally entitled *Idol or Ornament?: Art in the Church of England*.

2   See Croft-Murray (1962–70).

experience of parishes in urban communities.[3] However, the idea that the Church of England found roles for religious art has yet to have an impact in art history, and much more work is needed to reveal its wider religious and socio-political significance. In the context of this present study, it must be sufficient to survey some of the art that was to be found in churches in the period and consider some of the debates about religious art that took place within the Church of England. This will enable us to understand more clearly the challenges that the English Protestant spectator encountered in looking at religious art, and those that the English artist faced in making art of a kind that was so intimately associated with Catholicism.

There are perhaps two hundred ecclesiastical paintings left to us from this period, using a conservative estimate, but the number of undisturbed church interiors is considerably less, perhaps needing only two hands to count.[4] We cannot be sure of how many churches were decorated with paintings or sculpture: surviving parish records are unreliable in this regard. Even when we know that an altarpiece did exist in a church, mention may not be made of it in the vestry minutes or churchwardens' accounts. Indeed, by law, a parish should have requested the grant of a faculty from the diocese for any addition or change to the church fabric, but they were rarely applied for. This means that it would not be sensible to hazard a quantitative estimate of altarpieces or other decorative schemes to be found in the Church of England in the period as a whole. There are other resources that we can use to try to establish a sense of how art was used in churches: paintings, prints and drawings of church interiors and copies of individual works, textual descriptions in guidebooks and journals, newspaper accounts and court cases, as well as poetry and works of Church of England apologetics. This evidence suggests that the works that survive are probably an unreliable guide to the variety and extent of church decoration of the period. However, the evidence does suggest that art was used much more widely than has so far been realized, and that, simultaneously, it was a live issue of debate throughout the period.

Before we discuss these works of art, it will be worthwhile to point out that church interiors were not all of the plainness commonly associated with Puritanism [Plate 27]. In line with Elizabethan injunctions, the coat of arms of the monarch, highly coloured and frequently gilded, was a prominent feature of most church interiors. These could be flatly painted or sculpted, and range

---

3   Gregory (1991) and (1997) and Barry (1988) and (1993). This is borne out by the high incidence of altarpieces in the City of London churches rebuilt after the fire. The City of London churches are valuable examples for us because, despite the destruction during the Second World War, many of them retain more of their seventeenth- and eighteenth-century fittings than is the case elsewhere. These fittings are not different in kind from those deployed outside the city, as we will see.

4   Chatfield (1989).

in size from two or three feet across to ones which spanned the whole width of the nave.[5] The display of the texts of the Commandments, Lord's Prayer and Creed was also required, and these were often painted surrounded by ornamented borders.[6] Frequently, hatchments of the local elite family were also to be found in churches. These black-bounded, usually diamond-shaped wooden panels bore the arms of a deceased family member, and were often displayed in groups in the church, after they had hung outside the house immediately after death.[7]

In addition to these objects, there was some stained glass, woodwork and other objects remaining from the pre-Reformation period.[8] Pulpits, fonts and covers were sometimes quite plain, but could be highly decorated, and often of a size to present a striking visual effect. Altar rails, sometimes of iron, often of wood, were usually fairly plain, but again could be more elaborate, as were the sword rests and special pews for the local civic elite. In many churches altar frontals, linen and lace, as well as cushions, frequently made of red velvet, for the Bible and the *Book of Common Prayer* to rest on, were to be found. Altar screens, organs and ornate memorials to individuals were often made to make strong visual statements, and there were frequently objects of local significance and commemoration too, such as votive ships, only a very few of which survive.[9] This complex visual setting is the one in which people worshipped, and the one in which we must consider the painted figural representations that are our focus.

As the altar was moved back to the east end of all churches in the years after the Restoration, some form of elaboration of the east end was widely adopted.[10] This usually took the form of the prescribed texts painted on boards to form a reredos, which might be highly ornamented with symbols [Plate 28]. Moreover, the text panels were frequently accompanied by 'portraits' of Moses and Aaron, or sometimes by paintings of the Last Supper or the Nativity [Plates 29–30]. New coloured glass might be installed in the east window and fictive curtains were apparently also a common feature, painted on the wall dividing the chancel from the nave, or on the east wall itself, serving to focus attention on the altar.[11] Ceilings could be painted blue with stars or clouds; sometimes they even presented a vision of heaven, as at St Mary Abchurch in the City of London [Plate 31].

---

5   Hasler (1980) and Munro Cautley (1974).
6   Ibid.
7   Summers (ed.) (1976).
8   Woodforde (1954), Robinson (1995b).
9   Cox (1915), Cox (1933), Randall (1980), Vallance (1936), Harley (1994).
10   Fincham (2003), Addleshaw and Etchells (1948) and Yates (2000).
11   See Hatton (1708) and Malcolm (1803–07). Walpole mentioned that the artist Robert Brown was known for his 'skill in painting crimson curtains'. Walpole (ed.) (1862), p. 667.

The most famous ecclesiastical painting of the eighteenth century is probably Sir James Thornhill's work in the dome of St Paul's [Plate 32]. In grisaille, the paintings of the life of St Paul drew heavily on the Raphael Cartoons (which Sir James copied three times). The commission was only awarded to him after some protracted negotiations among the officials in charge of the scheme: Sir Christopher Wren's preferred medium of mosaic was not thought to be suitable, nor was the work of foreign painters who competed for the job.[12] Both medium and artists were objected to on the grounds of Popery. However, by the time Sir James began work in St Paul's, many of the newly restored and rebuilt churches around the cathedral in the City of London, and others across the country, were already decorated with paintings (and a few sculptures), and many more would be by the 1760s when this present survey ends.

There is not a simple historical trajectory to be traced of an increasing acceptability of religious imagery in the Church of England after the Restoration of Charles II in 1660, although it is probably true that images did become more acceptable as time went on. Rather, we will trace continuities in the acceptability and rejection of images that go back to the beginning of the Reformation and which lasted through our period and beyond. As we discussed in Chapter 1, when Richard Terrick rejected the proposal to erect paintings in St Paul's in 1773 on the grounds that it would encourage Popery, he was not behind the times. It is worth remembering the anti-Catholic Gordon Riots in 1780 would be the worst riots London had ever known. Popery was still a live issue in the 1820s as the debates over Catholic emancipation amply testify. We can cast this in another way: the Oxford Movement and its subsequent influence on church decoration in the nineteenth and twentieth centuries was not inevitable.

What we will see is that to use images in the service of God entailed calculations about a number of factors, not least of which was the trust that could be placed in the judgement of those who would look at them. Images were put up *and* taken down in the Church of England throughout the eighteenth century and the same image could be derided as an idol and valued as a suitable means of encouraging religious devotion. The history of images in the Church of England reaches to the heart of the Reformation: to the debate about the proper way to worship God, the primacy of the Word over the image and the question of an individual's power to judge properly. Thus it has much to tell us about the Church itself.

It is important to recognize that religious images were frequently identified not just as against God's law as laid out in the Second Commandment, but as specifically Popish. Idolatry was a Popish sin. As we will discuss, images were seen by those antagonistic to them as a Roman corruption of the 'true church'. This was the church founded by the apostles and in which

---

12 See Tindal Hart (1957).

the teachings of the Church Fathers were established. Edmund Sherman, a City of London merchant and churchwarden of whom we will hear more later, described images, in 1681, as 'inseparable badges of [the Papists]', for religious images could indeed be symbols of Popery in English society.[13] However, if it were as simple as Sherman suggested, there would have been no images in the Church, because maintaining a clear distinction from Popery was essential to everyone's idea of the Church of England's religious identity. However, as we discussed in the previous chapter in relation to Horace Walpole's *Sermon on Painting*, there were some who believed that a properly Protestant engagement with art was possible and necessary for the education of the 'common people' and to encourage devotion. This tension remained unresolved, as we shall see, and figured in religious writings and in writings about art throughout the eighteenth century.

The great move from visualization as the primary method of religious engagement to the contemplation of the Word that the Reformation entailed was not sustained simply on the basis of anti-Catholicism. There were three rather different theological positions, which were employed in the substitution of the Word for the image. Some believed that all representational images were corrupt because man's handiwork was always bound to be inferior to God's. As John Phillips points out, 'artifice was perilous not only because it might be merely extraneous to furthering the work of God – but because it might also be the work of the Devil ... [who] was periodically awaited in a form not perfect – but *nearly* perfect.' Thus good works were preferred over works of art and this was the cause of what Phillips calls the 'revulsion against man-made objects of beauty'.[14] This extreme view of representation was not widely shared, but the associated idea, that God was a matter of inward faith and knowledge and that these visual practices were merely man-made symbols, inessential and suspect in intention, was.[15] From this viewpoint, the Roman Catholic Church, with its elaborate liturgy, and heavy dependence on visualization, represented a form of luxurious decay from the principles of simple dignity widely believed to characterize the early or 'primitive' church, which was the ideal to which Reformers were reaching.[16]

The third position, the notion that images were traps for the unwary, which might lead the spectator into sensuous contemplation, superstition and idolatry at worst, was probably the most widely held. Most attention

---

13   Sherman (1681b), p. 13.

14   Phillips (1973), pp. xi–xii. See also Aston (1988), p. 155.

15   The distinction of necessary and unnecessary ritual practices is hugely significant in Reformation theology but cannot detain us here. See Phillips (1973), *passim* and Aston (1988), p. 40 for Luther and the principle of *adiaphora* which we will discuss further.

16   See Aston (1988), p. 58. It is perhaps worth reiterating that I am dealing with broad Protestant perceptions of Roman Catholicism, not with the realities of Roman Catholic doctrine or belief.

was directed at the role of religious images in promoting idolatry.[17] Protestants saw idolatry not just as a sin committed by an individual, but as institutionalized in, for example, the Catholic doctrine of transubstantiation, the practice of lighting candles at shrines or in front of pictures, suggesting a superstitious mode of engagement, and the intercessionary role given to the saints. The implicit recognition in this position that idolatry was a failure of judgement or understanding, and that images were not (except in the case of representations of God) of themselves sinful, had been made right from the start of the Reformation process.[18] It was the use to which images were put that was crucial, but because idolatry was invisible – a sin of the mind – the outward sign, the image itself, had to be regulated. Whichever of these three lines of argument was deployed, the effect was the same: they justified attempts to remove all images and other external signs of belief, such as gestural routines, ornament and so on, from religious practices.[19]

While these negative views of images were invoked periodically by iconoclasts and more or less constantly in anti-Catholic polemics, other perspectives were possible during the period before the Restoration. The innovations of Archbishop Laud (1573–1645) were adopted quite widely (although they were largely destroyed or removed by the iconoclastic purges of the 1640s) and there were always people within the Church who were attached to a religion of 'mind *and* eye' or 'mind *and* body as Julia Merritt's work on the pre-Laudian period demonstrates.[20] Religious pictures or sculptures were erected during the 100 years before the Restoration, and the necessity for repeated programmes of destruction suggests immediately that there were differing standards of what constituted a Reformed church.[21] Religion in England was thus not all of the plainness of Puritanism, the fervour and political dominance of which tends to overshadow our understanding of this period.[22]

---

17 For a useful summary of the arguments see Freedberg (1975). Phillips (1973) offers a more sustained account focused on England.

18 Phillips (1973), *passim*.

19 It should be mentioned that discussions of images usually carried the implication of 'priestcraft', which was an important criticism of the Roman Church. The Church's use of images was widely seen as open to abuse as well as another manifestation of the improper Roman intervention in the direct relation of God and the believer.

20 Merritt (1998). See also Addleshaw (1941), esp. pp. 20–69 and Aston (1988), pp. 80, 147–52, 451, 461–2.

21 Aston (1988), Phillips (1973). See Freedberg (1982) for Netherlandish iconoclasm in the sixteenth century. See Freedberg (1975) as well as the other papers in Bryer and Herrin (eds) (1975) and Gutmann (ed.) (1977) for comparative approaches to iconoclasm.

22 See Tyacke (ed.) (1998) which discusses the different ways in which we can view the Reformation in England *c*.1500–1800 and Walsh and Taylor (1993).

It is also worth remembering that the iconoclasm of the sixteenth and seventeenth centuries was never completely about religion, as Margaret Aston and John Phillips have shown. The Reformation, or, perhaps more correctly, the Reformation movements, involved a social and political as well as a religious revolution for, by turning from the doctrines of the Roman Catholic Church to emphasize the authority of the Word and a more direct relationship with God in prayer, the institutions of church and state were necessarily challenged as well. Each time iconoclastic activity took place, it was the result of particular political, social and economic factors as well as theological ones. For example, during the Henrician Reformation, images were destroyed because they also represented the foreign, antagonistic institutions and power of the Roman Catholic Church and later, Parliamentarians used iconoclasm to compel adherence to the republican project in which images stood for the corruption of royalty as well as Popery.[23]

Iconoclasm was thus driven by political as well as religious imperatives and was a tool of social control in which the legislative, judicial and military apparatus of the state was involved. This meant that images could carry quite specific local identities: for example, during the Commonwealth, commissioners sent by Parliament might be defeated in their aim of destroying religious images by local people dismantling and hiding them.[24] It is rather difficult to weigh the various impulses that drove this, but certainly political resistance and local allegiances, as well as different religious views, played their part.[25] I am placing particular emphasis on the socio-political dimension of iconoclasm here because these factors remained crucial in arguments about religious imagery throughout the long eighteenth century. As we shall see, political circumstances often influenced people's trust in the orthodoxy of images.

As we discussed in Chapter 1, the identity of the Church of England was a matter of intense concern and vigorous, even violent, debate both in and out of the Church.[26] The Church's claim to be the true church of God in England, which was the safe path to salvation, was energetically defended. There was one standard for this, the degree to which the Church adhered to the arrangements and doctrines of the early or 'primitive' church. However, as seventeenth- and eighteenth-century scholars were only too well aware, what the practices and doctrines of the early church were, were not a matter

---

23 See Phillips (1973), which offers a chronological account of the changing roles of iconoclasm during the period 1535–1660.

24 Spraggon (2003) and Cooper (ed.) (2001).

25 See Aston (1988), p. 84 for suggestive comments in this regard.

26 See Duffy (1977), which concentrates on High Church use of histories of primitive Christianity, Marshall (1985) on Latitudinarian ecclesiology and Young (1998a) on the variations in ecclesiology within the Church, which has some suggestive comments on the use of the Church Fathers. See Holmes (1976) on the Sacheverell Riots in 1710.

simply of fact, but of interpretation and judgement. Take for example St Paul's injunction that in the worship of God 'let all things be done decently and in order'.[27] The question is, what did this mean? For some it meant that current and local ideas of dignified worship were necessary; for others it meant that nothing that was not of St Paul's understanding of worship could be permissible.[28] Was the wearing of a surplice showing a proper veneration or a Popish adherence? Where should the altar stand and what was it – a table or an altar of sacrificial remembrance? What roles might art and music have in the worship of God, or had they been completely corrupted by their use by Catholicism? Each of these apparently minor questions of liturgical practice mobilized fundamental questions about the kind of Reformation that the Church stood for.

Within the Church, this problem was often approached using the concept of the *via media*, a path it chose to tread between the perceived idolatry of the Church of Rome and the broad spectrum of schismatical Dissent. The *via media* was crucial to the Church's identity and should not be confused with Latitudinarianism, a term which was used to describe (often pejoratively) those who had a looser attachment to certain aspects of Church doctrine (often because of a strong, principled toleration of different religious beliefs).[29] The *via media* was an outlook informed by the concern of the Church, as a reformed religious body, to mark itself out from the equally dangerous alternatives of 'Popery' and 'Protestant schism', in order to better assert its rights as the 'true church'. This was reinforced, indeed was inseparable from, the political exigencies that demanded a similar contradistinction. The *via media* was essentially a negative concept involving not the careful definition of a unique and authoritative theology, but rather the policing of the boundaries of Dissenting and 'Popish' identities.[30] The scholarship deployed in the Church of England to identify and defend its position as the 'true church' was formidable and often informed by a deep spirituality,

27 1 Corinthians 14:40.

28 See Sommerville (2004) regarding the debate about things 'indifferent'. Many of the other essays in Braun and Vallance (eds) 2004 discuss the role of the conscience in the understanding of ecclesiology and liturgy.

29 The identity of Latitudinarianism is still very problematic. John Spurr's important article (Spurr (1988)) questioned the existence of a group that can be identified as Latitudinarians and its identification with the new science, an association Margaret Jacob emphasised in *The Newtonians and the English Revolution* (1976). Such a link is still being depended on (see, for example, Mayhew (2000)). Spurr argued 'no specifically "latitudinarian" party or outlook can be distinguished among the Restoration churchmen'. See Walsh and Taylor (1993), pp. 35–43 for a review of the various trends in scholarship on Latitudinarianism, but note their modifying emphasis of something they call 'liberal Anglicanism'. See Sykes (1962), pp. 338–43, Marshall (1985) and Greene (1971) for other useful contributions.

30 See Walsh and Taylor (1993), pp. 55–7.

but in the absence of a single, authoritative account of the primitive church, consensus was impossible. An important element was dependent on an individual's judgement, in which the tone of one's spiritual aesthetic was likely to be influential in the formation of a doctrinal position.

Thus, we can see that at every turn the quotidian practice of Anglicanism was endowed with intense significance, that the conformity of the liturgical practice of a parish church could carry implications, for some, for the integrity of the nation state. Conformity was a sign of the security of the nation, as we shall see when we turn to consider the case of All Hallows Church in the City of London where there was a heated dispute over an image. There was plenty of room for debate as to what constituted a fit form of Anglican worship and even where firm rules did exist, these were ignored in parishes where different beliefs were espoused. Thus a diversity of ritual was a feature of the Church, but practice was keenly observed and sometimes just as keenly policed. Liturgical innovations instigated by the clergy were often examined by the parish (or its officers) in terms of the identity of the middle path between superstition and schism and each parish was periodically surveyed, at diocesan level, for its conformity at the time of the bishop's visitations.[31]

Against this background, the re-emergence of religious art is striking. As 'badges of popery', religious images would appear to be so compromized that their use within the Church of England might be thought untenable. In the course of this chapter we will identify a number of reasons why images were brought back into use. It is reasonably certain that images were most easily admissible, after the Restoration, by those of a Laudian outlook, but there is evidence to suggest that it was only a fairly short time before a broader spectrum of the Church placed value on religious imagery. Such a position cannot be described as 'High Church', a label which was coined as a negative term in the seventeenth century, and which carries a raft of 'political, ecclesiological, liturgical, spiritual and sacramental' associations.[32] Such a label can hardly be imagined as capable of accurate application to individuals, or indeed communities, in regard to a single issue. As Mather, Nockles, Gregory and Walsh and Taylor have shown, an attachment to ritual might be shared, albeit in different sets of associations, by those with rather different political and ecclesiological views.[33]

---

31   See Addleshaw and Etchells (1948), p. 162 and Spurr (1991), pp. 331–75. Also see Spurr's comments on the lack of power of the ecclesiastical courts which were, consequently, not very effective in maintaining uniformity (ibid., pp. 188–90). See below for discussion of the danger of 'innovations'.

32   Nockles (1993), p. 335.

33   See Mather's important article on the varieties of Anglican worship which coexisted in the Church of England 1714–1830 (1985). Gregory (2000) discusses the common phenomenon in the Canterbury diocese of High Church Whigs. See Walsh and Taylor (1993) for a general discussion of church parties in the period and Nockles

Importantly, images do not map directly onto the concerns most commonly associated with either 'High' or 'Low' Church parties, as the questions of episcopacy or the role of the Church in the state, can be seen to. By contrast, the associations of imagery with 'Popery' were a concern, as we shall see, for all. Indeed, it was possible that one could view images as 'superstitious' in one setting, while finding them useful in one's own milieu.[34] For those who believed in the dignified enrichment of the liturgy, the ornamentation of the east end served to underline its identity as the most important and sacred part of the church. This was manifested not just in the placing of pictures or stained glass, but also in the installation of altar rails, use of altar frontals, carpets and cushions and in the use of gestures, such as bowing, and in liturgical procedures, such as the position from which certain parts of the service were said. This can be considered to be, to some extent, within the Laudian tradition. This was a vision of a Church that could bring the whole nation together in a collective, uniform and highly visible act of worship in which the authority of the Church and the king were to be reinforced by ritual and aesthetic pleasure. As Graham Parry puts it, in his discussion of the Laudian reforms:

> Beauty was a form of church discipline, a sign of conformity to regulations imposed by a central authority, obedience to a uniform mode of worship. Laud's policy of restoring dilapidated churches and tidying up the interiors, his insistence on placing the communion table as an altar at the east end ... railed off as a holy place, on the use of the Prayer Book, on the wearing of ceremonial vestments and on the proper consecration of churches, all was intended to bring order, dignity and holiness to a Church that should be uniform in its practices and beliefs.[35]

This vision of the Church of England was still anathema, 50 years later, for some, but it is worth remembering that by the 1720s the altar was nearly always to be found orientated north–south at the east end of the church and it is becoming clear that parishes with no obvious High Church agenda put in train schemes of ornament before and after Laudianism took its brief hold. The existence of imagery in a church cannot be ascribed simply to one mode of belief or another, as we will discover, for images were enmeshed in complex relations. For example, the Church of St Lawrence Jewry in the City of London, which has been identified as a centre, during the post-Restoration period, for those holding Latitudinarian ideas, had paintings of

---

(1993) who demonstrates the changing political associations of the term 'high church' in the 'pre-Tractarian' period.

34   See Aston (1988) pp. 23–34, 147–54.

35   Parry (1981), p. 250. For seventeenth- and eighteenth-century High Church attitudes to the aesthetics of liturgy see Addleshaw (1941) and for its impact on the decoration of the church see Addleshaw and Etchells (1948) esp. pp. 148–202. See also Mather (1985).

the martyrdom and apotheosis of St Lawrence by Isaac Fuller II (*fl.*1678–1709) on the overmantel and ceiling of the vestry (1679).[36]

Given the wide variety of religious and political beliefs which members brought into the Church's body, and the difficulty of fixing an ecclesiology, it is not surprising that there was passionate debate over almost all aspects of the liturgical practice of the Church and the theology on which it was based. This is best appreciated through specific, local examples. For example, in 1681 the Parish of All Hallows Barking (by-the-Tower), London witnessed the collision of these forces in a dispute over an image which had been moved, six years before, from above a clock at the west end to the east end where it was placed over the Ten Commandments.[37] All Hallows was not, by any means, unique – there are a number of incidents throughout the eighteenth century in which the law (civil or ecclesiastical) was needed to settle disputes, and others where debate was enjoined in the press, which forced action to be taken over images. To consider this issue through such disputes is useful because such conflicts forced their participants to articulate clearly what otherwise might have remained unsaid. We will look at a number of these cases quite briefly, but I want to begin by considering the case of All Hallows in some detail because the bile which the dispute stirred up in the participants makes it particularly vivid and the arguments engaged by each side were deployed by others throughout our period.

The figure in question had hung above a clock between two other figures, one of Time and the other of Death, since 1659/60. Alterations to the building, which included the installation of an organ, apparently necessitated the removal of the central figure and it was placed above the altar in 1675. In 1681, an indictment was presented to a session of the Grand Jury at the Old Bailey by a Mr Whitaker, who accused the Vicar, Lecturer and Churchwardens of suffering 'the graven image of St Michael to remain undestroyed ... to the great danger of introducing idolatry and superstitious worship among the King's liege-subjects'.[38] The indictment was answered in two proceedings: at the first, Edmund Sherman, the leading Churchwarden and writer of two pamphlets defending his actions, pleaded guilty to the offence (with another of the Churchwardens); at the second Dr George Hickes (1642–1715), the Vicar, pleaded innocent to the charge and it was dropped, ostensibly for technical reasons.[39] Jonathan Sanders, the Lecturer, appears to have authored

---

36   See Marshall (1985), p. 408 for the Latitudinarianism of a number of the clergy at St Lawrence Jewry, Croft-Murray (1962–70), vol. 1, p. 221 for Fuller's paintings. See Hatton (1708), vol. 1, p. 306 for the altarpiece which consisted of the texts painted in red on black with 'gilden cherubim'.

37   I have discussed this case at length elsewhere (Haynes (2006) in McElligott (ed.)) and I am grateful to Dr McElligott for allowing me to reproduce some parts of that text here.

38   [Sanders] (1681a), p. 2.

39   See [Sanders] (1681c) for an account of Dr Hickes's hearing.

each of the three pamphlets which appeared in defence of the image, but whether he went to court to answer the charges does not appear to have been recorded.[40] The results of the two hearings were therefore somewhat contradictory and it is clear that the legal status of images was uncertain.[41]

The tone of the pamphlet war between Sherman and Sanders was vituperative, and it appears that the parish was divided and that this dispute was representative, even the working out, of a wider battle between two different visions of the proper ecclesiological identity of the Church. A sermon given by the Vicar, Dr Hickes, against Dissent may have been the immediate trigger for the troubles, but it is clear that there were wider concerns in the parish.[42] Hickes, who had been appointed Vicar in 1680, became Chaplain to Charles II in 1681 and would, in 1690, refuse the oath of allegiance to William and Mary. He was defended in this case by a 'Mr Genner' who, it might be worth speculating, was the barrister Thomas Jenner (1638–1707). Jenner was sent to the Tower in 1688 for attempting to escape to France with James II. The Lecturer, Jonathan Sanders, was also indicted and attacked by Sherman in his pamphlets for his liturgical practice (Hickes was not mentioned directly by Sherman). In his life of George Hickes, Hilkiah Bedford (1663–1724) (who would be a fellow Nonjuring Bishop of Hickes's) records that there was a concerted campaign to attack Hickes for his anti-Dissenting activities and that Sherman, together with another Churchwarden and the republican Sheriff Slingsby Bethel (1617–97), got up the plot using the image as a pretext.[43]

The two main opponents Sherman and Sanders were men of opposing views on liturgical matters. While Sherman makes strong claims for the superiority of the 'established religion of the Church of England', his loyalty cannot be questioned; he inveighs against any sign of elaboration of the liturgy, including, significantly, the increasingly common practice at this time of the placing of the 'table' at the east end which looks 'so like an altar ... standing close to the Commandments, with ends North and South'.[44]

---

40   A Lecturer was a minister appointed by a parish to deliver regular preaching.

41   It would appear that this remained the case until the 1870s. Certainly during our period the verdicts of two cases heard by the Court of Arches (Moulton in 1684 and Clifton in 1731) were contradictory. See Phillimore (1895), pp. 733–4.

42   Hickes (1680).

43   I am very grateful to Dr Mark Knights for allowing me access to his unpublished notes from the papers of George Hickes kept at the Bodleian (Bod. Ms Eng Misc. e.4).

44   Sherman (1681b), p. 6. The question of the placing of the altar was a very significant one. For further discussion of this question see Addleshaw and Etchells (1948), pp. 148–202. However, as we have already noted this would change by the 1720s. I regret that I do not have the opportunity to develop this more fully here. We will, however, deal with associated ideas about the ornamentation of the chancel

Sanders, by Sherman's account at least, was a man convinced of the pursuit of the 'beauty of holiness'. Both men were aware of the public attention the quarrel was generating, and each saw the wider significance of it for the Church and the nation. The heated way in which it was carried out was, I want to suggest, not just the result of a clash of perspectives in the sometimes fraught life of a parish church, but because in 1681 the Popish Plot and the exclusion crisis had created a great deal of anxiety about Popery.[45] Thus surveillance and speculation were particularly intense at this period and this perhaps explains why it was only then that the image at All Hallows was challenged, having stood over the altar for six years apparently without causing alarm.

Sherman had the image taken down from above the altar and carried to court and afterwards he proceeded to dismantle and burn sections of it in the vestry. His opponent's account of this ably sets the tone for our discussion:

> And whereas he then burnt a wing of the angel, affirming, that neither the Pope nor St Peter should have any piece of it; so after sermon, before all the gentlemen of the vestry then present, he pull'd some part of the feet of it out of his pocket, telling them, that as it could not fly, so neither should it walk to Rome.[46]

Such theatricality can be taken with a pinch of salt if we choose; what is obvious from the accounts is that the issues were, for both sides, but for Sherman in particular, serious and pressing. Sherman described the statue he had burned in this way:

> This *image* was a *great, carved, gilded image*, and about a yard and half long with great, broad, spreading wings, each wing about three quarters of a yard long; the right arm and hand was in its full proportion, just coming out of its shoulder, holding up the end of a label of lead, the other end of the label hung down to his right foot. On the label was wrote to this effect, *Arise you dead, and come to judgement*; his face, hands and feet painted, all the rest of it was gilded. It had not dragon under it, yet in weight about 18 or 20 stone.[47]

Sherman's emphasis of the image's physicality, underlined by the carefully detailed description suggests, I think, not that the precise appearance of the image is, in itself, very important (the description appears at the end of the first pamphlet in the postscript), but rather that every detail of description

---

area in more detail. Although I have expressed concern over the use of such labels, the conclusions Sherman draws of the political and ecclesiological implications of Sanders's liturgical practice are broadly in line with the range of concerns evoked by the term Low Church.

45   For the Popish Plot and the Exclusion Crisis see Kenyon (1972), Knights (1994), De Krey (1990) and Scott (1990).

46   [Sanders] (1681b), p. 2.

47   Sherman (1681a), p. 14.

is another point of justification for his actions, another proof of the image's superstitious identity.

In one passage in the text he describes how he came to the decision to plead guilty to the charge, saying that he had been advised by Dr Hickes that one of the possible defences he might offer was that 'it is indicted in the name of S. Michael, and everyone ... knows that S. Michael is always pictured with a dragon under him, and this hath no dragon; therefore let them prove it to be S. Michael and that it was ever called S. Michael before'. Sherman rejected such nice distinctions and did not offer a defence because, he argued, 'seeing that it is a *great, gilded, carved image*, it will look as if we had a mind to defend images'. The size and elaborate nature of the figure are called upon by Sherman to condemn it – it is '*a great silly image*'.[48] Sherman parades the figure's physicality because it is its very materiality, not its subject matter, that is the crux of the issue.

He defends his destruction of Church property thus in his first pamphlet:

> Single me out, any man of you, or doctor and all of you together, that can convince me or any man living (but a *Tory* or *Papist*) that such a great carved image is any ornament at all to a Christian church, where God will be worshipped in spirit and truth, and adds the least force to the Commandments of God.[49]

and in the second:

> And who ever blames me in print or pulpit for burning this abominable badge of superstition, they cannot distinguish themselves from being pleaders for images; and they that plead for images in churches, are as near akin to superstition, as superstition itself is of kin to Popery; and whoever bows to an image, or fathers such texts ... can never quit themselves from a suspicious leaning towards superstition.[50]

Both of Sherman's texts are shot through with similar innuendoes and accusations that the Lecturer, Jonathan Sanders, was a Papist in disguise, intent on leading the parish towards Popery.[51] Sherman collects a huge amount of evidence in support of this damning assertion. He highlights the installation of the organ, the placing of the image above the altar and the gift of a 'rich crimson carpet ... [by] Mr Whitebread (a kinsman of that Father

---

48 Ibid., p. 4.

49 Ibid., p. 11.

50 Sherman (1681b), p. 13.

51 This was a common accusation levelled by one party against the other, 'high' against 'low', 'low' against 'high', that somehow the other's opposition to their position was either a Popish plot or would give hope to the hated Jesuits who were everywhere seeking to reintroduce Popery at a moment's notice. See Haydon (1993), pp. 252–3.

Whitebread, that was hang'd for the damnable Popish Plot)' as examples of Sanders's Popish innovations.[52] In addition he describes at length the ways in which Sanders has changed his liturgical practice (and how it diverges from that of the rest of the Church) since the image and carpet were installed in the chancel. He argues that Sanders introduced 'ceremonies' which are not 'positively' commanded by the Act of Uniformity, unlike the 'services' which are 'therein injoyned':

> else if it be indifferent, why did you press it, especially at such a juncture of time as 78 when the Popish Plot was discovering; O the time, the time, the critical minute.[53]

Sherman dates the moving of the statue to 1678, but in fact the parish records show that it was moved three years before in 1675. The association of image and Popery is thus strengthened. His use of the word 'indifferent' (a distinction also made in his implicit opposition of ceremonies and services) is highly significant within the complex associations of liturgy at this period. As mentioned earlier, things 'unnecessary', 'indifferent' or inessential could be highly charged, viewed as potentially dangerous, as suspect accretions to the doctrines of the primitive church as witnessed in Scripture and the writings of the Church Fathers. As we have discussed, conformity and uniformity were widely seen to be the bastion against schism and Popery and Sherman makes this point very clearly towards the end of the second pamphlet:

> God Almighty, who equally hates superstition and sedition, blast the designs of all those on either hand that tend to seek the destruction of this true *Protestant* Church of England (as it is now established by law) *especially those of her own household*, for I am an enemy to all that go beyond (as well as to those that come short of the Church of England). For every step beyond, if it be a superstitious step, it may soonest of all be a *Popish* step, the rather because at this day, *Rome's* agents are so ready to take men by the hand and dance them into *Rome's* fopperies, with the pleasant song of welcome *John Sanderson* [sic], welcome, welcome.[54]

Sherman's accusations of Sanders's Popery may have been partly intended to provoke a reaction from him. He demands that Sanders answers a number of points of fact and of doctrine, but, as far as I can tell, Sanders never did respond directly to Sherman's accusations and questions in print, other than to dispute the facts of the case. The three anonymous pamphlets which Sanders wrote contain only one direct, but general, refutation of his opponent's account of the affair, which takes the form of an advertisement

---

52   Thomas Whitbread (*c*.1618–1679) was one of the five Jesuits who were executed on the evidence of Titus Oates in 1679.

53   Sherman (1681b), p. 8.

54   Ibid., p. 15.

placed at the end of the third of the Lecturer's pamphlets, *A Sham Indictment Quash'd*. The advertisement states that at a meeting of the Vestry (at which Dr Hickes was present) it was registered:

That his [Mr Sherman's] narrative was a rude, scurrilous, and insolent paper, and asserted that it had very many falsities, and prevarications in it, and that it highly tended to the dishonour of the established Protestant Religion, and was a libel upon the whole parish ... .[55]

Needless to say, Sanders's accounts of the affair are quite different from Sherman's and he argues that the Churchwarden has 'gratified the enemies, and much offended, and scandalized the friends of the Government, and the Church' suggesting that Sherman's actions were politically motivated.[56] While I have devoted a considerable amount of space to Sherman's part, Sanders's defence of the image is as revealing, if more concise. The first of the three very short pamphlets is called *A Narrative of a Strange and Sudden Apparition of an Arch-Angel at the Old-Bayly* [sic] and it is dedicated 'to all the ministers and churchwardens of the whole nation'.[57] Sanders argues that defending the indictment was necessary because:

Otherwise they should render his Majesty's chapels-royal, the cathedrals, and collegiate churches and chapels, and most of the parish churches of this city and kingdom obnoxious to the lash of every factious and disaffected person, upon the account of the church ornaments.[58]

Sanders appeals, as Sherman had done, to the national interest and argues that it is he that is the conformist, not Sherman.

Sanders's use of the word 'ornament' is of importance because I believe it suggests an attempt to carve out a Protestant category of religious imagery, safe from charges of idolatry.[59] Sanders probably meant to indicate reference to a Rubric, which formed part of the *Order for Morning and Evening Prayer* in the *Book of Common Prayer*:

The Morning and Evening Prayer shall be used in the accustomed Place of the Church, Chapel, or Chancel...And the Chancels shall remain as they have done in times Past.

---

55 [Sanders] (1681c), p. 3. This is a transcription of the vestry minutes of the meeting held on 24 April 1681 (All Hallows: AH/RR/C1/2).

56 [Sanders] (1681a), p. 1.

57 Both of Sherman's pamphlets run to 16 pages of very closely set print whereas the longest two of Sanders's are each four pages long, the shorter just two.

58 Ibid., p. 1.

59 We will explore this further in the case of St Margaret's Westminster.

> And here is to be noted, that such Ornaments of the Church, and of the Ministers thereof at all times of the Ministration, shall be retained, and be in use, as were in this Church of *England* by the Authority of Parliament, in the Second Year of the Reign of King *Edward* the Sixth.[60]

This insubstantial and rather unspecific text was the piece of legislation, which was all the Church of England had to manage the liturgical conformity of its churches and ministers. The reference to the second year of King Edward VI's reign was probably intended to signify the situation that pertained before the Edwardian reforms got under way, and thus a period when there was a little more latitude and elaboration in worship.[61] However, the wording of the Rubric meant that it had little force in dictating practice. In each of the cases that I have researched, there is no specific mention of the Rubric, but when the word 'ornament' was used, it probably carried a certain authority of orthodoxy because of it.

This connotation of orthodoxy was mobilized by Sanders, supporting his argument that the statue had been accepted for a long time without a suggestion being made of Popery:

> This image (as they call it) was not a thing erected of late ... it is strange that no body could discover either the thing itself, or the mischief of it, till 1680.[62]

Sanders disputes the term 'image' suggesting that the word itself is tainted with idolatrous significance, a point on which both he and Sherman agree (remember Sherman's phrase: 'images are such inseparable badges of [the Papists]'). He claims that the 'image' was invisible until the time of the indictment:

> This figure was so far from having any respect or veneration paid to it, that few or none of the inhabitants took any notice of it; and had the Doctor, or Lecturer, been asked two or three weeks before this bustle, where it stood, I dare confidently pronounce they had ... to seek for an answer.[63]

The Lecturer insists that the figure did not claim that attention which an idolatrous image must. We may read this as slightly disingenuous if we look at the interior of the church [Plate 33]. Although some of the details have changed, the broad uninterrupted view down the nave would have meant that the 5 ft gilded statue would have been a prominent feature of the east end. In any case, Sanders goes on to declare, ironically, that the Churchwarden made the 'happy discovery ... to know ... when a thing is done *pravae mentis*,

---

60   1662 Version (in Everyman Edition, 1999), p. 68.
61   Micklethwaite (1897).
62   [Sanders] (1681b), p. 2.
63   Ibid., p. 3.

and when a man bows to an idol under the colour of adoring his God'.[64] In other words, Sanders is suggesting that Sherman was able to discern the act of idolatry even though it takes place in the mind.

While Sanders refutes the idolatrous nature of the figure on a number of grounds, he provides no justification for the statue, other than by characterizing it as an 'ornament', thereby choosing to downplay its status. This strategy is reinforced by Sanders's assertion that the statue did not represent St Michael: 'That it had not the shape of St. Michael, nor was ever known or reputed to be the image of that, or any other saint.' Crucially, he does not say what it does represent, other than it:

> Had no relation, but to the two figures of *Death* and *Time*, betwixt which it might handsomely enough stand with its trumpet and motto, to mind men of the last judgement.[65]

Sanders's avoidance of the issue of what it was, exactly, that the figure represented can be seen, I believe, as another strategy to underplay the representative and symbolic potential of the figure. This enables him to claim, much as Sherman had done, that Popery lay hidden behind the indictment:

> There is not a more serious and regularly-devout Parish in the City of London than this of All Hallows Barking is: and when they shall be exposed to the censure of the world as Popishly-affected, 'tis not only an ill thing, but it is an ill sign; 'tis a token that some among us are either ignorantly, or cunningly, running into that Popery which they pretend to hate and fear.
> This is the mighty engine that carries on the business of the Jesuits, and other Papists at this time; for if men can at pleasure take away the reputation and honour of the Church of England, then the Romish faction have gained the field, and have no more to do but to sit down and divide the spoil. Yet so it is, we are fallen among a generation of things (whom I was going to call men) which call every man Papist, and everything Popish, which doth not just jump with their little self-conceited models.[66]

There is much to interest the historian of anti-Catholicism here, but what is most significant for us is that 'images' were indeed for both sides in this debate 'inseparable badges of Popery'. Rev. Sanders claims the conformity of the Parish by denying the figure the status of *image*; by denying that anyone even looked at it; and that, therefore, the figure had no idolatrous potency. This is a line of argument we will come across again.

It is worth noting that very soon after this event one of the parishioners gave a magnificent font cover to All Hallows [Plate 34]. This suggests

---

64 Ibid., p. 3.

65 Ibid., p. 3.

66 Ibid., p. 3. This argument had already been advanced in Hickes's polemical pamphlet *The Spirit of Popery Speaking out of the Mouths of Fanatical Protestants* (1680).

that the parish wanted to reassert a commitment to the visual celebration of the sacramental life of the church.[67] The cover, said to be by Grinling Gibbons (1648–1720), is an astonishing piece of work, gloriously energetic in execution, with three *putti* surrounded by garlands of fruit and wheatears. Five years later in 1686, a new altarpiece was erected in the church. It is no longer extant, but a description of it is given in Edward Hatton's *A New View of London* (1708):

> The altarpiece is mostly carved and neatly adorned with four columns and their entablement of the corinthian order. The intercolumns are the commandments done in gold, on black bet[wee]n Moses and Aaron, finely painted, and without the columns, are the creed and Lord's Prayer done in black, on gold each under a pediment with a dove descending. Over the 2 inner columns, are acroters; and betn [*sic*] them an open pediment, under which is a glory painted on the expansed [*sic*] figure of a holy lamb skin, (alluding to Leviticus 7 and 8 compared with Heb 9. 25, 26) done in basso relievo, between two gilded cherubims; over each of the outer columns is a lamp; and the whole has curious enrichments of cartouches, leaves, fruit, palm-branches &c.[68]

The depiction of the lamb's skin is not as unusual as we might suspect. In a subsequent description of a very similar altarpiece of St Bartholomew's Exchange, Hatton explains the symbolism of the lamb's skin:

> By the Levitical Law the priest was to have the skin of the lamb offered; so that is here placed, to demonstrate, that our high priest Christ Jesus, the Lamb of God, hath offered himself a sacrifice for us, of which that under the Law was only a type.[69]

The lamb's skin emphasizes the sacrificial aspect of the Last Supper, but no simple conclusion can be drawn from it about the parish's liturgical or political leanings. Views on the degree to which communion was mysterious, and what kind of representation of Christ's sacrifice was being enacted, were various during this period. As Spurr suggests, they were also rarely articulated precisely because the risk of dispute was considered too high.[70] This underlines the argument advanced earlier that we should not associate imagery too readily with any particular Church party. We will discuss the inclusion in the altarpiece of Moses and Aaron later on for, as we will discover, they were the most commonly depicted figures in altarpieces of this period.

This extended discussion of the All Hallows case has allowed us to witness not only the complexity of the arguments advanced on either side of the

---

67　Cox and Norman (eds) (1929), p. 50.
68　Hatton (1708), vol. 1, p. 98.
69　Ibid., p. 139.
70　See Spurr (1991), pp. 279, 294–5 and esp. 344–6.

image debate, but the heat that the issue could generate. We have identified very clearly the Popish associations of imagery and a number of strategies, which were developed for deflecting the charge of encouraging idolatry from religious imagery, such as the idea of invisibility and the refusal to identify the subject of an image. The use of the word 'ornament' appears to signal an attempt to distinguish a safely Protestant category of imagery and we will develop our understanding of the significance of this term in the Church of England context shortly. Before we do that, I want to explore another case, more briefly, because it will allow us to explore the Church's doctrinal position on images.

While the dispute at All Hallows was dealt with locally, another parish quarrel, which took place in 1685, was taken to the Court of Arches, the highest ecclesiastical court of the Archdiocese of Canterbury.[71] It centred on a dispute between the parish of Moulton in Leicestershire and the Bishop of Lincoln, Thomas Barlow (1607–91), over the erection of pictures of the Apostles in the church. As I mentioned, a parish was legally bound to seek the permission of the archdeacon or chancellor or their diocese to make any alteration to a church or churchyard.[72] This permission, called a faculty, was necessary because, in legal terms, the parish church was the property of the bishop. It appears that faculties were not routinely sought for the erection of an altarpiece or other ornaments in churches, but the lack of one could be used as grounds for challenging them.[73] Such was the case at Moulton, when 37 parishioners petitioned the Bishop protesting against the setting up of images in the church. The parish did obtain permission in the midst of erecting the pictures from the deputy chancellor of the diocese, but when the Bishop's permission was sought after they had all been erected, Barlow turned their application down and the members of the parish who had been responsible for the scheme appealed to the Court of Arches.[74] Bishop Barlow, a noted anti-Catholic polemicist, wrote a pamphlet before the case was settled by the court (in favour of the parishioners) – *A Breviate of the Case Concerning Setting up Images in the Parish Church of Moulton* – which provides such a

---

71 I have discussed this case in an article in *Historical Research* (2005), which explores judgement, rank and art. I am grateful to Dr Jane Winters for her agreement that I might use some of that material again here.

72 See Prideaux (1701), pp. 9–27, *passim* for the guidance offered to churchwardens by Humphrey Prideaux, who was then Archdeacon of Suffolk, in his influential, and much-reprinted, *Directions to Churchwardens for the Faithful Discharge of their Duties*.

73 This claim is based on an informal survey of the records of the dioceses of London, Norwich and Canterbury.

74 There are no extant vestry or diocesan court records for this period. A copy of one of the petitions requesting permission to erect the paintings is extant (Lincolnshire Archives, Add. Register 3 ('The Red Book'), f306v).

lucid and authoritative justification of his decision that it was reprinted in 1714, at the time of another parish dispute.[75]

Barlow's basic argument in the pamphlet is straightforward: the Church's law on images is, for Barlow, very clear and neither he, nor the Deputy Chancellor, have the right to approve something which is against that law. The temper of the pamphlet is more even than those issued in the All Hallows affair, but the intention is just as resolute. Whereas neither side in that dispute argued with any precision about the law, Barlow builds his case on the basis of the relevant ecclesiastical and civil laws, quoting passages from a substantial number of statutes and Church writings with legal status (especially the *Second Book of Homilies*), which are carefully referenced. Barlow makes a number of manoeuvres in his argument, that are useful to us in trying to understand some of the subtler distinctions that could be made in thinking about religious imagery.

To begin with, Barlow establishes that he is not altogether against images, distancing himself from the more extreme positions outlined at the beginning of the chapter. He says that is a 'malicious calumny' that:

> formers have been so zealous and indiscreetly fierce against images, that they have condemn'd the ingenious art of painting, and even the civil use of images.[76]

His defence of this accusation is twofold. Firstly, he demonstrates that the law explicitly excludes the civil use of images from its scope and secondly, he argues that images are only unlawful:

> In some places and some circumstances when they may (especially to poor ignorant people) be dangerous occasions of superstition and idolatry.[77]

However, he does add an important caveat to this statement in his classification of religious subject matter:

> The Church of England absolutely condemns all images of the Trinity, or any person in it, (Father, Son, or Holy Ghost) as absolutely unlawful, and expressly condemned in Scripture. Such images are not to be tolerated neither *in nor out* of Churches [my emphasis].
>
> No images of our Blessed Saviour, of any Saints and Martyrs, (which with stupid superstition and idolatry have been, and still are worshipped in the Popish Church) are, in the judgement of our Church, to be tolerated in our temples, or any place of God's public worship. For if they be, it will be to the great and unavoidable danger of idolatry.[78]

---

75 This took place at St Mary's, Whitechapel in London and is discussed below.
76 Barlow (1714), pp. 15–16.
77 Ibid., p. 16.
78 Ibid., pp. 18–19.

The distinctions Barlow makes between spaces, and his emphasis of the danger of idolatry for the 'poor ignorant people', are fundamental assumptions for those antipathetic to church imagery. They also demonstrate the contingency of the category of 'image'. Iconoclasm had been directed almost entirely towards images in public spaces, and religious works continued to be prized by some in collections of art as we discussed in the previous chapter. This distinction is based on rank. It distinguishes the 'private' spaces in which pictures are viewed (that is, the gentlemanly collection), from the 'public' ones of church and square, in which all ranks mix.[79] It also marks out those thought fit to make fine judgements, from those who were considered susceptible to error and sensuousness.[80] Superstition was the province of the multitude, understanding of a broadly composed elite.[81]

Barlow's position is not, however, as straightforward as it might appear at first glance. Earlier in his pamphlet, Barlow had disposed of the Gregorian argument that images are useful as 'laymen's books' for the poor, or as the good Protestant Barlow describes them, 'idiots' who cannot read the Scripture.[82] He argues, quoting Habakuk, that 'images are teachers of lies', in contrast to the sentences of Scripture painted up in their place in churches, 'whence (without fear of error) the people might learn divine and infallible truths.'[83] But if images are 'teachers of lies' then how are we to understand the spectatorship of 'images' in any setting?

Perhaps the problem lies in the word image itself. Until now, I have used the words picture, painting and image interchangeably. However the weight of significance the word image seemed to carry for Edmund Sherman and Rev. Sanders at All Hallows suggests that they should not be used interchangeably and we are now in a position to explore this a little more. One of the texts Bishop Barlow relies upon is 'The Sermon against the peril of Idolatry, and superfluous Decking of Churches' which appeared in the

---

79   We might wonder if such a distinction may have been operating between the spaces of the altar and the vestry of St Lawrence Jewry, London that I mentioned earlier.

80   Margaret Aston mentions the distinction of public and private spaces in regard to iconoclasm suggesting that after 1560 'it still seemed reasonable to suppose and defensible to argue that in secular places and out of harm's way a religious image would not automatically be idolised' (Aston (1996), p. 95). I think this probably begs more questions than it answers. When somebody was suspected of being a Roman Catholic, for example, their private possession of religious images was used as a test of Popery. It is clear that there was some hidden system of regulation at work here. The most important regulatory idea would appear, however, to be that of rank: during this period, the overwhelming majority of Roman Catholics were poor.

81   This is discussed further in Haynes (2005).

82   For the question of education and the force of the Word see Gregory (1998).

83   Habakuk 2:18, Barlow (1714), p. 9.

Second Book of Homilies, first published in 1563.[84] The two Books formed a body of doctrinal guidance with the authority of law and its continued currency was essential to the maintenance of the stability of the establishment.[85] The *Sermon ... on Idolatry,* which is the longest of all, is in three parts and it is both a scholarly defence of the Church's position on images and a strong admonition against those who permit images to remain in churches or argue that they are 'indifferent'. The significance of the word image is made explicit in the first part of the Sermon in which it is argued:

> Although in common speech we use to call the likeness of similitudes of men or other things images, and not idols; yet the Scriptures use the said two words ... indifferently for one thing always. They be words of diverse tongues and sounds, but one in sense and signification in the Scriptures.[86]

This strategy is aimed at answering the argument, presented by those sympathetic to the use of images in Christian worship, that an idol is 'a thing set up amongst the heathen in their temples' and therefore not the same kind of thing as a Christian image.[87] The argument is further rebutted by the historical assertion that:

> Our images also have been, and be, and if they be publickly suffered in churches and temples, ever will be also worshipped, and so idolatry committed to them ... . Wherefore our images in temples and churches, be indeed none other than idols, as unto the which idolatry hath been, is, and ever will be committed.[88]

This idea that an image, when placed in a church, is bound to 'breed' idolatry is built upon in the Homily, so that the Church's position, appears to be unequivocal: 'images placed publicly in temples, cannot possibly be without danger of worshipping and idolatry'.[89] An elaborate history is engaged to support this point, the basic outline of which is this. When the Christian faith was in its primitive state it was 'most pure' and it had no use for images. Image-making began when a man wanted to commemorate the likeness of his dead son and slowly other things began to be represented. Gradually 'they who privately had them [that is, images], did err of a certain zeal, and

---

84   Rickey and Stroup (eds) (1968), p. viii. The two Books were reprinted unofficially and in authorised versions 22 times before 1687.

85   The 33 homilies are strongly anti-Catholic in tone and message, as one would expect, but many were directed to reinforcing the moral, social and political stability of the nation more generally (for example, 'Against Whoredom and Adultery' (Book I) and 'Against Disobedience and Wilful Rebellion'(Book II)).

86   Rickey and Stroup (eds) (1968), p. 12.

87   Walpole relied on the same elision in his *Sermon on Painting* discussed in Chapter 4.

88   Rickey and Stroup (eds) (1968), p. 13.

89   Ibid., p. 44.

not by malice: but afterwards they crept out of private houses into churches, and so bred first superstition, and last of all idolatry among Christians.'[90] Images first influence the 'simple and unwise (unto whom images, as the Scriptures teach, be specially a snare) but the Bishops and learned men also, fall to idolatry by occasion of images' and it is argued that idolatry is so pernicious that within a space of 100 years, between the time of Gregory the First and the Second Nicean Council, the worship of images was made a part of the Church's doctrine.[91]

Bishop Barlow's position did not necessitate making nice distinctions between different genres of religious imagery. He ends his description of the events at Moulton in this way:

> This is the sum of what the painter and parishioners have done, (in setting up so many and such images, as (I believe) no church in England has seen since our Reformation, and (I hope) never will permit).[92]

Nonetheless, 'so many and such images' is a phrase that does suggest that Barlow might have recognized that there were different kinds of images. Indeed, that recognition is in the Homily:

> Men are not so ready to worship a picture on a wall, or in a window, as an imbossed and gilt image, set with pearl and stone. And a process of a story, painted with the gestures and actions of many persons, and commonly the sum of the story written withall, hath another use in it, than one dumb idol or image standing by itself.

Thus paintings, stained glass and sculpture were perceived as different kinds of image, and each form could be judged as being more or less likely to encourage idolatry. Of all kinds of representation, narrative painting is granted an orthodox role of religious instruction, but it is, as a form, still implicated in the rise of idolatry as 'from learning by painted stories, it came by little and little to idolatry'.[93] Thus the term image was not a straightforward one. As the Homily demonstrates, it could be used both to describe representations neutrally and to communicate negative associations.

Barlow's pamphlet, which, as I mentioned, was reprinted in 1714, provides us with an authoritative summary of the arguments advanced by those who

---

90 Ibid., p. 61 and p. 27.

91 Ibid., p. 33. See Aston (1988), p. 58 for the use made of the chronology of the primitive church in this regard.

92 Barlow (1714), p. 5.

93 Rickey and Stroup (eds) (1968), pp. 27–8. This discrimination between flat and three-dimensional religious imagery probably accounts for the extreme rarity of religious sculpture during the late seventeenth and eighteenth centuries. See below for a brief discussion of the statues of Moses and Aaron from All Hallows the Great, London, now at St Michael Paternoster Royal, London.

were against images. For those in favour of religious painting within the Church of England, justification was elaborated on a number of grounds. With different degrees of strength, most advocate a commemorative aspect to religious imagery, suggesting that it is to be used to call to mind the figures and actions of Christ and the saints. This aspect of remembrance is advocated as unproblematic for having been the primitive purpose for which the art of painting was instituted, before it was tarnished by the rise of idolatry. This commemorative role had, however, to be managed within a quite narrow compass. The influential Bishop Henry Ferne (1602–62) provided a succinct account of this in an essay *Of Images* in his *Appeal to Scripture and Antiquity ... against the Romanists* which was published, after his death, in 1665:

> We allow not only the historical use of images, but in some sort the affective also; yet that only as to meditation and preparation; not for or in the exercise of prayer or worship: much less to be the medium or instrument of conveying the worship, hereby images in the Church of Rome become great stumbling blocks to the people that are not capable of the nice distinctions and limitations which their learned ones are fain to use in defence of this image worship.[94]

This affective role was emphasized by Richard Welton (?1671–1726), Vicar of Whitechapel, who was at the centre of the scandal in 1714 caused by the erection of a picture of the Last Supper, which was said to contain the portrait of White Kennett (1660–1728) depicted as Judas [Plate 35].[95] Just as at All Hallows, the attack on the image seems to have been motivated by broader political concerns. Kennett was a Whig, who figured prominently on the Latitudinarian side in the vigorous debates that were enjoined on a variety of doctrinal issues in the 1710s and 1720s, which threatened to split the Church.[96] Welton, by contrast, was a friend of the High Churchman Dr Henry Sacheverell (c.1674–1724), who was impeached by the Whig government in 1709 over a sermon he had preached on 5 November 1709 in St Paul's, which advocated high Tory principles and inveighed against toleration being extended to nonconformists. The sermon probably sold 100,000 copies, a vast number, and Sacheverell became a cause célèbre. Welton, who supported Sacheverell with a sermon of his own on similar lines, would later become a Nonjuror.[97] After the picture had been taken down by order of the Bishop of London, Welton preached a sermon, which was later published as *Church Ornament without Idolatry Vindicated*. Welton's argument ranges widely, but at its heart is a substantial claim for the use of images in churches:

---

94 Ferne (1665), p. 80.

95 The painting is no longer extant. The only record we have of it is this engraving, which may not be an accurate record of the original painting.

96 For Kennett, see Bennett (1957).

97 See Broxap (1924), p. 88 for Welton.

And here, far be it from us to make use of any argument that may favour of a Romish principle, so as to give the least encouragement to idolatry or superstition; which we detest and abhor, as truly impious and abominable to God, and every good Christian. But so far as these things are ornamental and becoming the house of God, so far as they may be supposed to take the mind off from inferior objects, so long as we carry flesh and blood about us, and the soul may be supposed to receive impression thro' the senses; it cannot be irrational, but far from impious, to deck and adorn our Churches with such innocent resemblances as these are.[98]

This passionate argument, which calls on the language of the Homily, was not the preserve of men of suspect allegiances. Welton was, after all, using the language and arguments of the Homily. The view that such ornament was both fitting and of use in public worship received its most extensive treatment in the treatise *The Ornament of Churches Considered*, which was published in 1761, to defend the installation of a stained-glass window in St Margaret's, Westminster.[99] There was a tremendous row at St Margaret's, not least because the money for the renovations of the church had been provided by a House of Commons committee.[100] Much of the book is taken up with rehearsing the arguments we have already discussed, but the work is useful to us here because the question of genre is raised in an interesting way that takes up the argument advanced, 200 years before, in the Homily, which I quoted from above:

As ornament and instruction are all we contend for, I should prefer large historical paintings to single figures; and this the more willingly, because adoration has at no time, nor in any place, been paid to them. Indeed it is scarcely possible to conceive, when a number of objects are before the eye in one picture, that a particular one can be selected for this purpose. And yet it must be done, unless we can suppose men ridiculous enough to adore the thieves that were crucified with our Saviour, or the guards that attended.[101]

Thus history paintings are preferred to portraits for public spaces, not because they are superior in moral force – the usual reason for ranking them higher as an artistic genre – but because they do not allow the eye to settle on one figure. This is, at first glance, a reasonably convincing argument, but it does ignore the fact that most religious narratives have at their centre the actions of an individual. Exceptions might be depictions of episodes such as

---

98 Welton (1714), pp. 16–17.

99 The main body of the text was written by William Hole, but the preface and appendix were written by Thomas Wilson (1703–84), a curate of the parish, under whose name the book appeared. See Wayment (1981), fn. 3. Wilson went on to be rector of St Stephen Walbrook, where there are a number of religious paintings from this period. See Meyer (1976).

100 See Wayment (1981), Archer (1982) and Friedman (2004), pp. 79–110.

101 Hole (1761), p. 31.

the Last Supper at which the corporate nature of the apostolic mission can be emphasized. The Last Supper was indeed a popular subject for altarpieces during this period, and a very unusual carved version by Sefferin Alken (1717–82) was installed at St Margaret's at this time. However, there were schemes where single depictions of the Apostles, Evangelists or Church Fathers were hung in groups, as at Moulton. For example, 'portraits' of the Apostles were erected at St Andrew's Undershaft in London after 1707, in Prestbury, Cheshire in 1719, and Sir James Thornhill's oil sketches for the rose window in Westminster Abbey were set up in St Andrew's Church, Chinnor probably after his death in 1734.[102] It is quite probable that this grouping of 'portraits' was seen as an efficient guard against idolatry, because I have not been able to find a single instance of the hanging of one picture of a single figure.

There is one other objection offered, in some of the literature, to the portrayal of religious figures that I want to deal with before we turn finally to look at depictions of Moses and Aaron. In a section of the Homily, the matter of portraying God, Christ and the Saints is explored. God cannot be depicted, the Homily argues, for the reasons that we have already discussed:

> For how can God, a most pure spirit, whom man never saw, be expressed by a gross, bodily, and visible similitude? How can the infinite majesty and greatness of God, incomprehensible to man's mind, much more not able to be compassed with the sense, be expressed in a small and little image?

The problem of representing Christ is slightly more complex because He had the nature of both God and Man. The Homily suggested two arguments against depicting Christ. The first was that any such image could be only a partial one, only capable of depicting Christ's humanity, not his spiritual nature. It would therefore amount to a lie. The second argument advanced against such depictions was historical:

> No true image can be made of Christ's body, for it is unknown now of what form and countenance he was. And there be in Greece and at Rome, and in other places, diverse images of Christ, and none of them like to other, and yet every of them affirmeth, that theirs is the true and lively image of Christ, which cannot possible be.[103]

Similarly, the saints should not be represented (whose souls 'the most excellent parts of them, can by no images be presented and expressed') and

---

102 See Addleshaw and Etchells (1948), p. 104; Cray (1990) and for Robert Brown's decorations at St Andrew Undershaft see Croft-Murray (1962–70), vol. I, p. 264 and vol. II, p. 322.

103 Rickey and Stroup (eds) (1968), pp. 40, 42. See MacGregor (2000) for the history of the depiction of Christ, particularly for the question of the development of a traditional 'likeness' of Christ.

this complete denial of the possible truthful role for any image is summed up thus:

> Wherefore seeing that religion ought to be grounded upon truth, images which cannot be without lies, ought not to be made, or put to any use of religion, or to be placed in churches and temples, places peculiarly appointed to true religion and service of God.[104]

These arguments were rehearsed by Gilbert Coles (1617–76) in one of the many anti-Catholic pamphlets published during this period. A pattern can be discerned in the rhetorical shape of these pamphlets (although the detailed arguments presented certainly do vary) in which the superstitious practices and beliefs of idolatry, transubstantiation, the invocation of saints and prayers said 'in an unknown tongue' are described in turn, in order to mark out the Church of England from Popery. Coles presents a discussion of the problems of depicting holy figures:

> You must show they be true resemblances and copies, of their countenances, pictures very them whom they represent; whereas now in the images of the saints there is no regard had to their likeness, but only to set up an image that shall signify, and not represent. An old man with a sword, stands for Paul; with keys for Peter ... so in our Saviour's pictures you shall observe as many forms as there are faces or fancies of men. If a painter, designing to draw Our Lady's picture, should take a beautiful courtesan for his pattern, it would serve. Now such pictures, which have no likeness to the persons represented, deserve no regard, neither are they useful for commemoration. Should anyone send you your grandfather's picture, much unlike him ... you would not honour it so much, as to hang it up in your hall or parlour.[105]

For Coles religious imagery was therefore impossible in the 'true church', for to signify religious truth by the untruthful means of iconography and artistic creativity was unthinkable.

No such concerns seem to have attended the depiction of the figures of Moses and Aaron, who were used so commonly in altarpieces during this period. Their currency cannot be disputed but has been largely ignored. The usual argument, offered by Addleshaw and Etchells, Croft-Murray and Graham most recently, is rather dismissive: that they were considered 'safe' accompaniments to the texts because they are Old Testament figures.[106] They may also be considered 'safe' because they were used to ornament the title-page of the *Book of Common Prayer*. This argument has some merit, but there is probably more to it than that. It implies that there was some urge to image-

---

104 Rickey and Stroup (eds) (1968), pp. 40–42.

105 Coles (1688), pp. 101–2.

106 Addleshaw and Etchells (1948), p. 161; Croft-Murray (1962–70), vol. I, p. 48; Graham (1987), p. 81.

making, but in fact there were many 'plain' altarpieces made at this period
without any human figures (see Plate 28). The argument is also insufficient
because it is based on the premise that Moses and Aaron had no significance
beyond their role as apt figural ornament to the Commandments. I want to
suggest here that there were some more positive and pressing reasons why
Moses and Aaron were depicted in altarpieces at this period: that they were
used not as mere 'decoration' or 'ornament' but as part of a visual rhetoric
about the Church of England.

Robert Streeter I's paintings for St Michael Cornhill [Plate 36] show us
the engaging manner in which Moses and Aaron were usually depicted.
Streeter's paintings, like so many, do not survive in their original setting and
were fitted into an elaborate neo-Gothic alabaster reredos by Gilbert Scott in
the late 1850s. This tends, as in many other cases, to diminish the effect of
the depictions of Moses and Aaron, making them appear rather plain and
understated, which perhaps explains why they have been passed over as a
subject of scholarly interest. The nineteenth-century frame serves to obscure
their polished execution, the solid magistry of the figure of Moses and the
animated pose and fine drapery of Aaron's vestments. Although few of the
original arrangements survive, the intact altarpieces at St Mary's, Shotley
in Suffolk and that at Ashburnham in Sussex [Plates 37–8] give us a good
idea of the way in which the figures were associated with the text of the
Commandments, Creed and Paternoster. As with all these paintings, the
figures are designed, in their pose and gesture, to bring the viewer's attention
to the texts.

Sometimes the figures were made like dummy boards, as were those
for St Swithin London Stone, which gave the figures a more sculptural
quality.[107] There were more elaborate treatments, such as that at All Saints',
Northampton, which had detailed painted settings for the figures. There were
also many others, which display less refinement. We can see that there was a
sophisticated visual repertoire in play here, albeit one restrained or confined
to panels to the side of texts. The manner in which Moses and Aaron were
depicted was completely consistent with pre-Reformation iconography,
although their depiction as a pair of single-figure portraits, rather than
in narratives, makes them rather unusual in the body of Christian art.[108]
Moses, bearded and wearing vaguely classical drapery holding the tables
of the Commandments, is in marked contrast to the figure of Aaron, who

---

107 See Graham (1987). I am grateful to Jonathan Fuller, who pointed out to me
that the two panels of Moses and Aaron at St Margaret Lothbury, London appear to
have once been in this form. There were also similar paintings at St Giles Cripplegate,
London during this period. The boards at St Swithin are over 7 feet high and are now
in the Victoria and Albert Museum, Furniture and Woodwork Dept. (W.8-1939 and
W.9-1939). See Graham (1987).

108 See 'Moses' and 'Aaron' in Murray (1996).

wears the fine vestments described in Exodus Chapter 28. The censer that Aaron carries, which is a traditional iconographical addition to the Biblical description (signalling Aaron as the prototype priest), is maintained in these Church of England depictions. The two figures can be seen to represent the two fundamental aspects of a church – both of which were of profound political significance throughout the period – magistry and priesthood. In a period when there was such diversity of opinion over what Establishment actually meant for the Church of England, its role in the state and the nation, the deployment of these two figures over the altar in so many parish churches is, I believe, significant.

Before we explore this further, I want to discuss the depiction of Aaron a little more because his presence is not as straightforwardly determined as this argument might seem to suggest. Firstly, in his embroidered vestments carrying a censer, the figure of Aaron as priest strikes the eye as more akin to the worship practice of the Roman Catholic Church, not at all in sympathy with the plainer ceremonial of the Church of England. It appears that the established iconographical tradition and the authority of the Old Testament meant that these vestments and symbols could be absorbed in a Church of England setting.[109] Secondly, Aaron was the idolater who made the golden calf that the Israelites worshipped and so his fitness as a subject for this most sensitive of spaces would appear, at the very least, problematic. As one writer of a pamphlet against images in churches put it, in his only criticism of specific subjects for depiction:

> A great many of our churches have only the pictures of Moses and Aaron on each side the Commandments. I have nothing to object against them, but what I have before assigned, yet have I often wondered, why Aaron, who made the molten calf, which occasioned the breaking the first two tables – why he, I say, who was the Jewish high-priest, should be placed at a Christian altar?[110]

However, as someone might perhaps have pointed out to the anonymous writer, Aaron was forgiven by God and it was Aaron who was appointed as the only one permitted to enter the Holy of Holies, just as some priests were beginning, again, to stand in the Church of England, behind the newly re-erected rails at the time of Communion.

It is clear that these images refer not just to the texts but also to the act of Communion which took place in front of them. I will give only the briefest of outline of the complex ideas that were at work here because they are not entirely germane to the central purposes of this chapter, which are

---

109 We discussed above how in the All Hallows battle over St Michael, the iconography of the saint was well known. The continuity of a visual memory of religious subjects, despite the fracture in the tradition of physical depiction, is very interesting and surely worthy of further exploration.

110 Anon. (1725), p. 21.

to demonstrate that religious imagery was widely used, and to discuss the ambiguity of image-making within the Church of England.[111] There are two principles that it will be worthwhile to sketch here. The first is that Moses was recognized as the prototype of Christ, and Aaron as that of the Christian priesthood. The figures therefore reverberate with the sacrament and the priest celebrating it in a variety of ways, reinforcing the liturgy of the Church of England with the ancient authority of the Old Testament. The spectators of these images had a variety of interpretative options available to them depending on their view of Communion. This has three dimensions, which can be usefully, if crudely, outlined as religious, political and legal. First is the notion of the identity of Communion as a 'sacrament'. For those who placed an emphasis on the sacramental, Communion was, in basic terms, a mysterious sacrifice made by a priest at an altar as a re-enactment of the sacrifice of Christ through which the forgiveness of sins and thus redemption is made possible.[112] For those who did not, put simply, it was an act of communal remembrance in which priest and people participated equally at a table. The meanings that could be ascribed to the depiction of Moses and Aaron at the east end, their political and doctrinal associations, can be seen to shift in these different perspectives. The second dimension is the notion of Communion as an act of unity of the Church and therefore, in some way, of the nation. If, as some believed, the Church was the nation and the nation the Church, the presence of Moses and Aaron, who ensured both the physical and spiritual survival of the Israelites, was particularly apt. The third association is that Communion was an act of legal status. To receive Communion at least annually was necessary to legally qualify for some public offices. Although this test was sometimes circumvented, this aspect of Communion was nevertheless an important one, especially given the infrequency at which most people received. I want to suggest that in this context Moses and Aaron appear most clearly as visual declamations of the authority and truth of the Church of England, asserting, through tradition and the associations we have observed, the rightness of its special status.

A further association of these two figures, worthy of a more extended discussion than can be attempted here, is the commonly invoked notion of the English as the 'elect nation'. War against the French, Jacobite invasion, plague, fire, drought and flood were all matched to the vicissitudes of the Israelites. Thus, we can see, in this context, these altarpieces as patriotic claims for the justness of the nation's cause and the central role of the Church of England

---

111 I will explore representations of Moses and Aaron in more detail in a forthcoming article, provisionally entitled 'Moses and Aaron, Magistry and Priesthood'.

112 Addleshaw (1941), pp. 105–7. For different ideas about Communion see Addleshaw and Etchells (1948), pp. 148–202, Spurr (1991), pp. 344–6, Mather (1985), esp. pp. 256–7.

in it as the national Church. The presence of Aaron, who challenged the Law, and Moses, who compelled obedience to it, is thus highly significant in the context of the Established status of the Church. Such altarpieces can also be seen as making a composite statement of the sure expectation of salvation. Combining the essential texts of the faith and the figures, they can be seen as promoting and affirming that the Church of England was the true path to God.

That these images did have signifying potential is evident when we consider the statues of Moses and Aaron now at St Michael Paternoster. The two statues, which were erected at All Hallows Thames Street, London towards the end of the seventeenth century, are of exceptional quality. They are very rare objects and, as such, they allow us to consider the problematic status of religious sculpture a little further [Plate 39].[113] They have been separated from the altarpiece for which they were made and were damaged during the Second World War. Aaron no longer carries the censer, which was lost – the figure was restored so that he now makes a gesture of blessing – and the stick with which Moses pointed at the texts is also missing. Given the distinctions made between painting and sculpture that we discussed above, it is not surprising to discover that these statues are very rare examples and that idolatry was linked to them. In his extensive record of the churches of London published in the early years of the nineteenth century, J.P. Malcolm recorded that the statues were nearly moved from the altar because 'some persons having been seen to bow to them on entering the church'.[114] I have not been able to ascertain the truth of this story, but in some ways it does not matter, for the fact that it was worth recording early in the nineteenth century suggests the continuing currency of the anxiety caused by religious sculpture. These figures of Moses and Aaron, then, are not mere decoration, simply appropriate accompaniments to the texts which the law of the Church of England demanded should be set up in churches. They are there because the figures of Moses and Aaron had particular resonances for the Church of England in this period.

In this chapter the evidence we have considered has been drawn mostly from before 1720, but we have observed that voices in favour of and against pictures in churches were to be found throughout the period of this study. It is possible to observe a gradual broadening of subject matter deployed in churches during the period, but to infer that the Church of England's attitude towards religious imagery in public spaces softened would be mistaken.

The range of subject matter that was considered acceptable can be illustrated with a small number of examples, although more work is needed to ascertain the full repertoire of imagery deployed in the Church.

---

113 Since 1894, when All Hallows was demolished, the statues have been at St Michael Paternoster Royal, City of London.

114 Malcolm (1803–07), vol. I, p. 43.

In addition to those subjects already mentioned, there were paintings of Christ's ascension at St Peter's Church in Lincoln by Vicenzo Damini (*c*.1727), St Mary Magdalen, City of London by Robert Brown (1720) and at St Mary Redcliffe painted by William Hogarth (1754).[115] The life of St Peter was treated in paintings by Francis Hayman, at Malpas in Cheshire, of St Peter's Denial of Christ (1763), and by Charles Catton, of St Peter's Deliverance from Prison at St Peter Mancroft, Norwich. The 'Wise Men's Offerings' was the subject of the altarpiece installed at Bath Abbey in 1726 and there were frescoes of the *Life of Christ* by Robert Brown (?1672–1753) painted in 1732 at St Andrew's Undershaft, London.[116] Each of these schemes must be seen as the outcome of local negotiations over the problem of religious art, not of any institutional shift by the Church, nor of any change in anti-Catholic discourse, which continued to focus on idolatry.

Sometimes such negotiation resulted in the pictures being taken down, as at All Hallows, Whitechapel in 1714 and St Clement Dane's in 1725, where there was an outcry over William Kent's (1685–1748) altarpiece of musician angels (which was parodied by Hogarth in an engraving [Plate 40]).[117] His enormous painting of the Last Supper for St George's, Hanover Square (1724) [Plate 41] received no such criticism, however. The St Clement Dane's painting was viewed suspiciously because it was said to contain a portrait of the contentious figure of the wife of the Pretender, Princess Clementina Sobieska, just as the one at Whitechapel was accused of bearing the face of the Rev. White Kennett as Judas Iscariot.[118] In both cases, I suspect that the portrait idea may have been cooked up so that parish leaders could be accused of using the chancel to make sordid political capital, just as it was becoming more difficult to criticize such works on the grounds of idolatry alone, since many parishes had altarpieces and other painted schemes. As at All Hallows, the status of images was so uncertain, they could be used for such political purposes.

This chapter has surveyed briefly some of the key issues involved in the use of images in the Church of England. We have seen that a concept of ornament was used to signal an orthodox religious image, but that this was by no means secure. We have also observed that what was a uniquely

---

115 Robert Brown's painting is now at St Martin Ludgate, City of London and Hogarth's painting is in the City of Bristol Museum and Art Gallery. Damini's painting is known only in the form of an oil sketch kept at Lincoln Cathedral. See Croft-Murray (1962–70).

116 For a general impression and information about specific paintings see Croft-Murray (1962–70). Pevsner's *The Buildings of England* series now published by Yale University Press makes mention of these objects too. For the altarpiece at Bath Abbey see Sloman (1991).

117 Kent's altarpiece has been lost and is only known from a rather muddy photograph.

118 See Bennett (1957), pp. 127–31 for an account of the affair.

Anglican form of altarpiece, the texts with figures of Moses and Aaron, was not simply ornamental but potentially richly significant. It is clear that there were no consistent rules, doctrines, laws or legal precedents used to distinguish the acceptable from the unacceptable image. The Church of England was so heterodox a body, that the firm articulation of rules was very difficult, and frequently undesirable, if some part of the Church was not to be alienated. Preventing further schism was an overarching concern for the national Church. Thus a wide variety of practices and ideas existed within it. Nevertheless, at times of political uncertainty, practices previously tolerated could suddenly appear Popish or schismatical.

Chapter 6

Conclusions

It is worth recalling a passage from Jonathan Richardson's *Discourse of the Science of a Connoisseur* that we discussed in Chapter 2:

> It is the glory of the Protestant church, and especially of the church of England, [which is] the best national church in the world. I say it is the glory of the Reformation that thereby men are set at liberty to judge for themselves. We are thus a body of free men; not the major part in subjection to the rest. Here we are all connoisseurs as we are Protestants; though (as it must needs happen) some are abler connoisseurs than others. And we have abundantly experienced the advantages of this, since we have thus resumed our natural rights as rational creatures ...
>
> A man that thinks boldly, freely, and thoroughly; that stands upon his own legs, and sees with his own eyes, has a firmness, and serenity of mind, which he that is dependent upon others has not, or cannot reasonably have.[1]

Richardson suggests that the Reformation ensured that individuals were able to 'judge for themselves', but also that the Church of England was the most secure route to salvation, because it was the best (that is the truest) church. The tone in which Richardson makes this claim for the Church of England is compelling, but there is also to be glimpsed in this passage a recognition that the Church of England did not have the loyalty of all. As I have discussed more fully elsewhere, it was precisely because the Reformation was not thought by everybody to be complete or safe in the Church of England that judgment in matters of art was so highly charged.[2] In a nation where the established church had such an unstable doctrinal position on images (and a wide variety of practice), the secular domain of art connoisseurship could hardly be more certain about religious images. Thus we can see, having looked at the Church of England's difficulties with regards to images, the works of Raphael and Domenichino were problematic because they raised questions that were unresolved, ambiguous and still fraught at the heart of English Protestantism.

The question of judgment has a strong class dimension to it too and while art historians have engaged with issues of the socio-political order (largely

---

1   Richardson (1792), pp. 259–60.
2   Haynes (2005).

in relation to civic humanism), the questions of rank and judgement raised by religious images have been overlooked. We have observed how central issues of rank were to both the debates within the Church about the propriety of using images and in different ways to the connoisseurship of art more generally. Religious images were thus a political matter, mostly in the broad, social sense of that word, but we have seen that they could become political in the narrower party political sense too. The question of the security of the Reformation was such a fundamental issue that religious images, or more correctly, the risk of idolatry they represented, could be used as political capital.

Art was engaged in other political debates, particularly about nationhood. We have observed in relation to the grand tour, for example, how admiration for foreign culture was tempered by an apparently unswerving belief that Britain's political settlement was the best that had been seen in modern times.[3] Richardson, Shaftesbury, Berkeley and Gibbon all wrote in various ways addressing what appeared to be a gross anomaly: it was widely accepted that British art could not be considered on a par with the best of ancient and modern art, so what of Britain's much vaunted greatness? In order for Britain to take her rightful place in the world, for her supremacy to be complete, something had to be done to allow the arts to be brought forward (as both a symptom and a demonstration of the nation's greatness). The prominence given to the problem of idolatry in texts written to encourage greater understanding and thus patronage of art is proof of what contemporaries saw as the fundamental obstacle to the rise of the arts in Britain. Thus, in his famous *Anecdotes of Painting* in 1762, Horace Walpole gave a prominent place to resolving the problem of idolatry:

> The art, that is chiefly the subject of these pages, is one of the least likely to be perverted; painting has seldom been employed to any bad purpose. Pictures are but the scenery of devotion. I question if Raphael could ever have made one convert, although he had exhausted all the expression of his eloquent pencil on a series of popish doctrines and miracles.[4]

In the light of his praise of Guido Reni's painting in the *Aedes Walpolianae* that we considered in Chapter 4 (which was couched precisely in the terms of its ability to engender an idolatrous response), this argument may seem disingenuous. In addition, it seems to diminish the art of painting that Walpole was advocating (and to be out of tune with much of the praise which Raphael received in Britain). Walpole may have had a much broader

---

3   It is impossible to speak of nationhood in terms of anything other than Britishness here, despite the emphasis that I have placed on England in the rest of the text. The claims that these writers were making were made, I believe, in terms of the whole of Great Britain – a nation that they might call England or Britain.

4   Walpole (1862), p. xii.

audience in mind for this text, than for the *Aedes*, which meant that he did not rely on his audience to respond appropriately, but in any case it is another example of the irreconcilability of the paradox that has been identified.

Walpole went on to argue:

> Pictures may serve as helps to religion; but are only an appendix to idolatry; for the people must be taught to believe in false gods and in the power of saints, before they will learn to worship their images. I do not doubt that but if some of the first reformers had been at liberty to say exactly what they thought, and no more than they thought, they would have permitted one of the most ingenious arts implanted in the heart of man by the Supreme Being to be employed towards his praise. But Calvin, by his tenure, as head of a sect, was obliged to go all lengths. The vulgar will not list but for total contradictions; they are not struck by seeing religion shaded only a little darker or a little lighter…Happily at this time there is so total an extinction of all party animosity both in religion and politics, that men are at liberty to propose whatever may be useful to their country, without its being imputed to them as a crime, and to invent what they mean should give pleasure, without danger of displeasing by the very attempt.
> At this epoch of common sense, one may reasonably expect to see the arts flourish to as proud a height as they attained at Athens, Rome, or Florence.[5]

Walpole's cavalier way with Calvinism is striking, as he works a particular vision of the past into a future in which Britain might emulate 'Athens, Rome or Florence'. Walpole suggests that images had been caught up in the politics of Reformation and Revolution, but that 'common sense' had at last prevailed. In the first few months of George III's reign, when he probably wrote this preface, perhaps all things seemed possible to him. Walpole's apparent disregard for the Calvinist principles of a sizeable minority of the population is a symptom of the same problem that he, Richardson, Shaftesbury and Gibbon each encountered when they addressed the same question: how could art be unshackled from its associations with Popery, so that it could serve Protestantism and the nation effectively, so that indeed Britain could stand next to 'Athens, Rome or Florence'? As we have seen, there was no way of working this out intellectually, but only in practice. The British did indeed advocate the truth and power of the art of Raphael, hang pictures in their churches, admire and want to own works showing Catholic doctrine, but at each step this was achieved using arguments that were fragile and partial.

The association of art with Popery was, I believe, the most significant brake on the production of art in Britain. Other than William Hogarth's efforts in that direction, there was a surprising unwillingness to reimagine art outside the Vasarian scheme in which the work of Romano-Florentine artists dominated. When writers discussed art, they did so, without fail, with reference to this highly problematic culture. This culture exerted tremendous

---

5   Richardson (1792), p. xiii.

power because it was pan-European; it dealt in matters still relevant to the English, both past and present, ancient and modern. To turn from it was impossible. However, the popularity of portraiture could well be seen as a kind of turning – from genres much less comfortably associated. The celebrity that Reynolds may have created for his sitters, and for himself, was precisely a substitute for that which painters like Reynolds and his patrons should have sought according to the discourses of art that they themselves assented to. This suggests that the practices of looking at and collecting foreign art should be woven into the history of British art much more intimately than they are at present.

I suggested at the beginning of this book that no key was to be found to unlock the paradox of British taste for Catholic art. While it is to be hoped that the paradox stands in more light than it did before, there is a great deal more that could be done to further enlighten the role of religious images. The most fundamental task is probably to enable art made for the Church of England to be recognized in the history of British art. This is very likely to be rewarding in terms of enhancing our understanding of the Church of England (as the small amount of work already done by religious historians shows). In addition, once we have a firm grasp on how much, and what kind, of art was made for the Church, our understanding of the possibilities for British art as a whole, and for individual artists, will inevitably change. While we are not in a position to say to what degree this will affect our understanding of British art, it can only be beneficial to explore an aspect of eighteenth-century visual experience that has largely been disregarded.

Bibliography

Note: Attributed authors are shown in square brackets

Manuscripts

All Hallows Barking by the Tower, City of London
    Vestry Minutes AH/RR/C1/2
    Churchwarden's Accounts AH/RR/C1/2
    George Fletcher, *A Survey of the Parish Church of All Hallows Barking, London*, 1773 AH/46

British Library
    Milles MS (1735) Add Ms 15776
    MS Lansd. 1024

Canterbury Cathedral Archives
    DCb/D/I-   Parish Inventories
    DCb/E/F-   Faculties
    DCb/V/A/1/1   *Notitia Archidiaconalis Cantuariensis* Archdeacon
                      Samuel Lisle 1724–48
    DCb/V/A/1/2   *Notitia Archidiaconalis Cantuariensis* Archdeacon
                      John Head 1759
    DCb/V/E-   Articles of Enquiry
    DCb/V/P/76–81 Churchwardens' Presentments 1724–26
    DCb-Z.3.34   Archdeacon's Visitation Book 1711–15
    U3/1–200   Parish Records

Guildhall Library
    MS9538   Episcopal Visitation 1693
    MS9450   St Mary Abchurch Inventories 1691 and 1732
    MS9538   Answers for Visitation 1693
    MS9532   Diocese of London Vicar General Records Vol. 1:
                      1685–1704

Lambeth Palace Library
    D429, D1054, E30/86   Court of Arches Records (re Moulton)

Lincolnshire Archives
>Additional Register 3   *The Red Book*, f306v (Moulton Parish petition)

Norfolk Record Office
>L'Estrange NRO: NF2
>Harvey NRO: MS20677, T140B
>Lee Warner NRO: Box 10, 441X3
>Rolfe NRO: MS21GUN3 362X5

Periodicals

>*The Gentleman's Magazine*
>*The Guardian*
>*Monthly Review*
>*The Spectator*
>*The Tatler*

Primary Sources

Addison, J. (1718), *The Resurrection. A Poem*, London: E. Curll.
Addison, J. (1753a), *Remarks on Several Parts of Italy*, First Published 1705, London: J. Tonson.
Addison, J. (1753b), *A Letter from Italy to the Rt Hon Charles Lord Halifax in the year MDCCI*, First Published 1701, London.
Aglionby, W. (1972), *Painting Illustrated in Three Diallogues*, First Published 1685, Portland, OR: Collegium Graphicum.
Anon. (1703), *A Rare Show*, London: A Baldwin.
Anon. (1704), *Dictionarium Sacrum Seu Religiosum. A Dictionary of All Religions Ancient and Modern Whether Jewish, Pagan, Christian or Mahometan*, London: J. Knapton.
Anon. (1717), *A Letter to an Inhabitant of the Parish of St Andrew's Holbourn* [sic], *about New Ceremonies in the Church*, London.
Anon. (1725), *A letter from a Parishioner of St Clement Danes to Edmund ..., Bishop of London, occasion'd by his ... causing the picture [of a certain Saint] over the Altar, to be taken down; with some observations on the use and abuse of Church paintings, etc*, London.
Anon. (1736), *A Letter on the Nature and State of Curiosity as at Present with us*, London.
Anon. (1738), 'A Description of the Choir of St Peter's Church in Leeds, Yorkshire, at Evening Prayers', *The Gentleman's Magazine*, 8, 429.

Anon. (1739a), *An Historical and Chronological Series of the Most Eminent Painters ... Chiefly collected from a manuscript of the late famous Father Resta,* London.

Anon. (1739b), *The Portraits of the Most Eminent Painters, and other famous artists ... collected from the best authors extant,* London.

Barlow, T. (1679), *Articles of Visitation and Enquiry,* London.

Barlow, T. (1714), *A Breviate of the Case Concerning setting up Images or Painting of them in Churches,* First Published 1684, London.

Barrett, W. (1789), *History and Antiquities of the City of Bristol,* Bristol: William Pine.

Barri, G. (1679), *The Painter's Voyage of Italy,* trans. W. Lodge, London.

Barry, J. (1775), *Inquiry into the Real and Imaginary Obstructions to the Acquisition of the Arts in England,* London.

Bell, H. (1728), *An Historical Essay on the Original of Painting,* London.

Berkeley, G. (1721), *Essay towards the Preventing the Ruin of Great Britain,* London: J. Roberts.

Bickham, G. (1742), *Deliciae Britannicae, or the curiosities of Hampton-Court ...,* London.

Bisset, W. (1714), *The Modern Fanatick Part III. Being a further account of the famous doctor, and his brother of like renown, the director of the New Altar-Piece ... With a postscript, demonstrating from some very fresh instances, the most pernicious effects of arbitrary power ...,* London: James Roberts.

Blackmore, S.R. (1718), *A Collection of Poems on Various Subjects,* London.

Blackmore, S.R. and Hughes, J. (1714), *The Lay Monastery,* London.

Blome, R. (1686), *The Gentleman's Recreation,* London.

Boswell, J. (1980), *Life of Johnson,* (ed.) R.W. Chapman, Oxford: Oxford University Press.

Boyer, A. (1702), *The English Theophrastus,* London.

Breval, J. (1738), *Remarks on Several Parts of Europe,* First Published 1726, 2 vols, London: H. Lintot.

Brewer, S. (ed.) (1995), *The Early Letters of Bishop Richard Hurd, 1739–1762,* vol. 3, Church of England Record Society, Woodbridge: The Boydell Press.

Britton, J. (1813), *An Historical and Archictectural Essay relating to Redcliffe Church Bristol,* London.

Bromley, W. (1705), *Remarks in the Grande Tour of France and Italy,* First Published 1692, London: J. Nutt.

Buckridge, B. (1969), *The Art of Painting to which is added an Essay towards an English school,* First Published 1706, trans. J. Savage, London: Cornmarket Press.

Burnet, G. (1687), *Some Letters Containing an Account of What Seemed Most Remarkable in Switzerland, Italy &c,* Rotterdam.

Campbell, C. (1715–25), *Vitruvius Britannicus, or the British Architect,* 3 vols, London.

Castiglione, B. (1724), *The Courtier,* trans. R. Samber, London.

Cock, C. (1742), *A Catalogue of the Collection of Right Honourable Edward Earl of Oxford Deceased*, London.

Coles, G. (1688), *Theophilus and Philodoxus, or Several Conferences between two friends*, London.

Dalton, R. (1752), *Remarks on XII Historical Designs of Raphael, and the Museum Graecum et Aegyptiacum*, London.

Dart, J. (1726), *History and Antiquities of Canterbury*, London.

Dart, J. (1742), *Westmonasterium*, 2 vols, London.

de Blainville, M. (1743), *Travels through Holland, Germany, Switzerland but especially Italy*, trans. G. Turnbull and W. Guthrie, 2 vols, Dublin.

de Lairesse, G. (1778), *The Art of Painting in all its Branches ...*, trans. J.F. Fritsch, London.

de Piles, R. (1706), *The Art of Painting, and the Lives of the Painters ... To which is added, an essay towards an English-school*, trans. J. Savage, London: J. Nutt.

de Piles, R. (1969), *Abregé de la vie des peintres*, Hildesheim: Georg Olms.

Dodsley, R.J. (1761), *London and Its Environs Described*, 6 vols, London.

Dorrington, T. (1699), *Observations Concerning the Present State of Religion in the Romish Church ...*, London: John Wyat.

Du Bos, Abbé. J.B. (1748), *Critical Reflections on Poetry, Painting and Music*, trans. T. Nugent, London: J Nourse.

Dufresnoy, C.A. (1695), *De Arte Graphica. The Art of Painting ... with remarks ... An original preface containing a parallel betwixt Painting and Poetry by Mr Dryden. As also a short account of the most eminent painters, both ancient and modern ... by another hand*, Second Edition, London.

Dyer, J. (1971), *Poems*, First Published 1761, Menston: Scolar Press.

Elsum, J. (1700), *Epigrams upon Paintings*, London.

Elsum, J. (1704), *A Description of the Celebrated Pieces of Painting of the Most Antient Masters*, London.

Ferne, H. (1665), *An Appeal to Scripture and Antiquity ... Against the Romanists*, London.

Gibbon, E. (1961), *Gibbon's Journey from Geneva to Rome: his journal from 2 April to 22 October 1764*, (ed.) G.A. Bonnard, London: Nelson.

Gibbon, E. (1990), *Memoirs of My Life*, (ed.) B. Radice, Harmondsworth: Penguin.

Gother, J. (1687), *A Discourse of the Use of Images*, London: Henry Hills.

Graham, R. (1695), *Short Account of the Most Eminent Painters*, London.

Gwynn, J. (1749), *Essay on Design*, London.

Gwynn, J. (1766), *London and Westminster Improv'd*, London.

Hatton, E. (1708), *A New View of London*, 2 vols, London.

Hickes, G. (1680), *The Spirit of Popery Speaking out of the Mouths of Fanatical Protestants*, London.

Hogarth, W. (1968), 'Hogarth's "Apology for Painters"', (ed.) M. Kitson, *Walpole Society*, 41, 46–111.

Hogarth, W. (1997), *The Analysis of Beauty*, (ed.) R. Paulson, New Haven and London: Yale University Press.

Hole, W. (1761), *The Ornaments of Churches considered, with a particular View to the late Decoration of the Parish Church of St Margaret Westminster*, Oxford.

Hughes, O. (1735), *The Veneration of Saints and Images, as taught and practised* ..., Second Edition, London: R. Ford & R. Hett.

Hume, D. (1985), *Essays Moral, Political and Literary*, (ed.) E.F. Miller, Indianapolis: Liberty Fund.

Hurd, R. (1764), *Dialogues on the Uses of Foreign Travel*, London.

Junius, F. (1694), *The painting of the Ancients in three Books: Declaring by Historicall Observations and examples, the Beginning, Progresse and Consumation of that most Noble Art, etc*, First Published 1638, London.

Keate, G. (1760), *Ancient and Modern Rome. A Poem Written at Rome in the Year 1755*, London: R. & J. Dodsley.

Kennett, W. (1714), *Images an Abomination to the Lord: or, Dr Kennet's reasons for pulling down the Altar-Piece at White chapel*, London.

Keyssler, J. (1756), *Travels through Germany, Bohemia, Hungary, Switzerland, Italy, and Lorrain*, 4 vols, London.

Lamotte, C. (1730), *An Essay upon Poetry and Painting, with relation to the Sacred and Profane history. With an Appendix concerning Obscenity in Writing and Painting*, London.

Malcolm, J.P. (1803–7), *Londinium Revidium*, 4 vols, London.

Markham, S. (1984), *John Loveday of Caversham 1711–1789. The Life and Times of an Eighteenth-Century Onlooker*, Salisbury: Michael Russel.

Martyn, T. (1968), *The English Connoisseur*, First Published 1767, Farnborough: Gregg.

Middleton, C. (1729), *Letter from Rome, Shewing an exact Conformity between Popery and Paganism: Or, The Religion of the Present Romans, derived from that of their Heathen Ancestors*, London.

Misson, M. (1695), *A New Voyage of Italy*, 4 vols, London.

Mount, H. (ed.) (1996), *Sir Joshua Reynolds: A Journey to Flanders and Holland*, Cambridge: Cambridge University Press.

Mussard, P. (1732), *Roma Antiqua and Recens or the Conformity of Ancient and Modern Ceremonies* ..., trans. J.D. Pre, London.

Nelson, R. (1704), *Festivals and Fasts of the Church of England*, London.

[Newbery, J.] (1755), *The New Testament adapted to the Capacities of Children*, London: J. Newbury.

Newton, B. (1760), *The Church of England's Apology for the Use of Music in Her Service. A Sermon ... 10 September 1760*, Gloucester.

Northcote, Sir J. (1818), *The Life of Sir Joshua Reynolds*, 2 vols, London: Collum.

Nugent, T. (1756), *The Grand Tour*, Second Edition, London.

Owen, J. (1709), *The History of Images, and of Image-Worship*, London.

Paterson, J. (1714), *Pietas Londinensis*, London.

Peacham, H. (1906), *The Compleat Gentleman*, (ed.) G.S. Gordon, Oxford: Clarendon Press.

Pelling, E. (1687a), *A Letter to a Person of Quality*, London: Benjamin Griffin.

Pelling, E. (1687b), *A Third Letter to a Person of Quality, being a Vindication*, London.

Pilkington, M. and Descamps, J.B. (1770), *The Gentleman's & Connoisseur's Dictionary of Painters*, London.

Pope, A. (1993), *Alexander Pope. A Critical Edition of the Major Works*, (ed.) P. Rogers, The Oxford Authors, (ed.) F. Kermode, Oxford: Oxford University Press.

Prideaux, H. (1701), *Directions to Churchwardens for the Faithful Discharge of their Duties*, Norwich.

Ralph, B. (1759), *The School of Raphael or, the Student's Guide to Expression in Historical Painting*, London: John Boydell.

Ralph, B. (1764), *A Description of the Cartoons of Raphael Urbin, in the Queen's Palace*, First Published 1759, London.

Reynolds, J. (1992), *Discourses*, (ed.) P. Rogers, Harmondsworth: Penguin.

Richardson, J. (1715), *An Essay on the Theory of Painting*, London: J. Churchill.

Richardson, J. (1719), *Two Discourses*, London.

Richardson, J. (1722), *An Account of Some of the Statues, Bas-Reliefs, Drawings, and Pictures in Italy, &c, with Remarks*, London.

Richardson, J. (1792), *Works*, First Published 1773, London.

Rickey, M.E. and Stroup, T.B. (eds) (1968), *Certaine Sermons or Homilies Appointed to be Read in Churches in the Time of Queen Elizabeth I. A Facsimile Reproduction of the Edition of 1623*, Gainesville, FL: Scholars' Facsimiles & Reprints.

Rouquet, J.A. (1970), *The Present State of the Arts in England*, First Published 1755, trans. J. Wills, London: Cornmarket.

Russel, J. (1750), *Letters from a Young Painter Abroad*, First Published 1746, London: W. Russel.

Salmon, W. (1672), *Polygraphice*, 2 vols, London.

Samber, R. (1722), *Roma Illustrata*, London: W. Chetwood & S. Chapman.

[Sanders, J.] (1681a), *A Narrative of a Strange and Sudden Apparition of an Archangel at the Old-Bayly*, London.

[Sanders, J.] (1681b), *A New Narrative of a Fiery Apparition seen on several days about Tower-Hill*, London.

[Sanders, J.] (1681c), *The Sham-Indictment Quash'd*, London.

Sanderson, W. (1658), *Graphice*, London.

Shaftesbury, Ashley Cooper, the Third Earl of (1964), *Characteristics of Men, Manners, Opinions, Times*, (ed.) J.M. Robertson, Indianapolis and New York: Bobbs-Merrill.

Shaftesbury, Ashley Cooper, the Third Earl of (1969), *Second Characters: or, the Language of Forms*, (ed.) B. Rand, New York: Greenwood Press.

Sherman, E. (1681a), *The Birth and Burning of the Image Called St Michael*, London: Richard Janeway.

Sherman, E. (1681b), *The Second Part of the Birth and Burning of an Image Called St Michael*, London: Richard Janeway.

Smollett, T. (1766), *Travels through France and Italy*, 2 vols, Dublin.

Spence, J. (1747), *Polymetis*, First Edition (several editions through to 1786), London.

Spence, J. (1975), *Joseph Spence: Letters from the Grand Tour*, (ed.) S. Klima, Montreal: McGill-Queen's University Press.

Stevens, S. (1756), *Miscellaneous Remarks made on the spot in a late Seven Years Tour through France, Italy, Germany and Holland*, London: S. Hooper.

Stuart, J. and Revett, N. (1762), *The Antiquities of Athens*, London.

Thompson, C. (1744), *The Travels of the late Charles Thompson*, Reading.

Toynbee, P. (ed.) (1928), 'Horace Walpole's Journals of Visits to Country Seats, &c.', *Walpole Society*, 16, 9–80.

Turnbull, G. (1971), *A Treatise on Ancient Painting*, (ed.) V.M. Bevilacqua, First Published 1740, Munich: Wilhelm Fink.

Vertue, G. (1930–55), 'Notebooks', *Walpole Society*, vols 18, 20, 22, 24, 26, 30.

Walpole, H. (1752), *Aedes Walpolinae*, First Published 1747, London.

Walpole, H. (ed.) (1862), *Anecdotes of Painting in England*, (ed.) R.N. Wornum, 3 vols, London: Henry G. Bohn.

Watson, T. (1735), *A Letter to the Bishop of London*, London.

Webb, D. (1760), *An Enquiry into the Beauties of Painting*, London.

Welsted, L. (1714), *An Epistle to Mr Steele, on the King's Accession to the Crown*, London.

Welton, R. (1714), *Church-Ornament without Idolatry Vindicated*, London: G. Strahan.

Wheler, S.G. (1689), *An Account of the Churches and Places of Assembly ... with a Seasonable Application*, London.

Whitaker, E. (1681), *The Bishop's Court Dissolved ...*, London.

Whitaker, E. (n.d.), *An Argument for Toleration ...*, London.

Whitby, D. (1687), *The Errors of the Church of Rome*, London.

Woodhead, A. (1689), *Concerning Images and Idolatry*, Oxford.

Wright, E. (1730), *Some Observations Made in Travelling through France, Italy etc.*, London: A. Millar.

Wright, E. (1764), *Some Observations Made in Travelling through France, Italy etc.*, Second Edition, London.

Secondary Sources

Abbey, C.J. and Overton, J.H. (1878), *The English Church in the Eighteenth Century*, 2 vols, London: Longmans.

Adams, J.N. (1982), *Bibliography of Eighteenth-Century Legal Literature*, Newcastle: Avero.

Addleshaw, G.W.O. (1941), *The High Church Tradition*, London: Faber.

Addleshaw, G.W.O. and Etchells, F. (1948), *The Architectural Setting of Anglican Worship*, London: Faber.

Albers, J. (1993), '"Papist traitors" and "Presbyterian rogues": Religious Identities in Eighteenth-Century Lancashire', in J. Walsh, C. Haydon and S. Taylor (eds), *The Church of England c.1689–c.1833. From Toleration to Tractarianism*, Cambridge: Cambridge University Press, pp. 317–33.

Allen, B. (1985), 'Thornhill at Wimpole', *Apollo*, 122 (283), 204–11.

Allen, B. (1987), *Francis Hayman*, New Haven and London: Yale University Press (in association with English Heritage and the Yale Center for British Art).

Allen, B. (ed.) (1995a), *Towards a Modern Art World*, New Haven and London: Yale University Press.

Allen, B. (1995b), 'Rule Britannia: History Painting in Eighteenth-Century Britain', *History Today*, 45 (6), 12–18.

Altick, R. (1978), *The Shows of London*, London and Cambridge, MA: Bleknap Press of Harvard University Press.

Anderson, B. (1991), *Imagined Communities: Reflections on the Origin and Spread of Nationalism*, First Published 1983, London: Verso.

Andrieux, M. (1968), *Daily Life in Papal Rome in the Eighteenth Century*, trans. M. Fitton, London: George Allen and Unwin.

Anon. (1990), *Holkham Hall, Norfolk. Seat of the Earls of Leicester*, Derby: English Life Publications.

Anon. (1998), *The City of London Churches. A Pictorial Rediscovery*, London: Collins and Brown.

Anon. (1999), *The Church of St Mary Magdalene, Croome D'Abitot, Worcestershire*, Series 4, no. 113, London: The Churches Conservation Trust.

Archer, M. (1982), 'The Case of Superstitious Images', in P. Moore (ed.), *Crown in Glory: Celebration of Craftsmanship-Studies in Stained Glass*, Norwich: Jarrold & Sons Ltd, pp. 48–57.

Archer, M. (1985), 'Stained Glass at Erdigg and the Work of William Price', *Apollo*, 122 (284), 252–63.

Arnold, J.H. (2000), *History. A Very Short Introduction*, Oxford: Oxford University Press.

Aston, M. (1973), 'English Ruins and English History: The Dissolution and the Sense of the Past', *Journal of the Warburg and Courtauld Institutes*, 36, 231–55.

Aston, M. (1988), *England's Iconoclasts: Laws against Images*, Oxford: Clarendon Press.

Aston, M. (1995), 'Gods, Saints, and Reformers: Portraiture and Protestant England', in L. Gent (ed.), *Albion's Classicism: The Visual Arts in Britain 1550–1660*, New Haven and London: Yale University Press, pp. 181–220.

Aston, M. (1996), 'Puritans and Iconoclasm, 1560–1660', in C. Durston and J. Eales (eds), *The Culture of English Puritanism, 1560–1700*, Basingstoke: Macmillan, pp. 92–121.

Avis, P.D.L. (1975), 'Moses and the Magistrate: a Study in the Rise of Protestant Legalism', *Journal of Ecclesiastical History*, 26 (2), 149–72.

Ayres, P. (1997), *Classical Culture and the Idea of Rome in Eighteenth-Century England*, Cambridge: Cambridge University Press.

Baker, M. (1995), 'The Portrait Sculpture', in D. McKitterick (ed.), *The Making of the Wren Library*, Cambridge: Cambridge University Press, pp. 110–37.

Barrell, J. (1984), *English Literature in History, 1730–1780: An Equal Wide Survey*, London: Hutchinson.

Barrell, J. (1990), 'Sir Joshua Reynolds and the Englishness of English Art', in H. Bhabha (ed.), *Nation and Narration*, London and New York: Routledge, pp. 154–76.

Barrell, J. (ed.) (1992), *Painting and the Politics of Culture: New Essays on British Art 1700–1850*, Oxford: Oxford University Press.

Barrell, J. (1995), *The Political Theory of Painting from Reynolds to Hazlitt: the Body of the Public*, First Published 1986, New Haven and London: Yale University Press.

Barry, J. (1988), 'The Parish in Civic Life: Bristol and its Churches, 1640–1750', in S.J. Wright (ed.), *Parish, Church and People*, London: Hutchinson, pp. 152–78.

Barry, J. (1990), 'The Politics of Religion in Restoration Bristol', in T. Harris, P. Seaward and M. Goldie (eds), *The Politics of Religion in Restoration England*, Oxford: Basil Blackwell, pp. 163–89.

Barry, J. (1991), 'The Press and the Politics of Culture in Bristol, 1660–1775', in J. Black and J. Gregory (eds), *Culture, Politics and Society in Britain, 1660–1800*, Manchester and New York: Manchester University Press, pp. 49–81.

Barry, J. (1993), 'Cultural Patronage and the Anglican Crisis: Bristol c.1689–1775', in J. Walsh, C. Haydon and S. Taylor (eds), *The Church of England c.1689–c.1833. From Toleration to Tractarianism*, Cambridge: Cambridge University Press, pp. 191–208.

Barry, J. (1998), 'Bristol as a "Reformation City" c1640–1780', in N. Tyacke (ed.), *England's Long Reformation*, London: UCL Press, pp. 261–84.

Barton, J. (ed.) (1998), *The Cambridge Companion to Biblical Interpretation*, Cambridge: Cambridge University Press.

Batten, C.L. (1978), *Pleasurable Instruction: Form and Convention in Eighteenth-Century Travel Writing*, Berkeley: University of California Press.

Baxandall, M. (1985), *Patterns of Intention. On the Historical Explanation of Pictures*, New Haven and London: Yale University Press.

Baxandall, M. (1988), *Painting and Experience in Fifteenth-Century Italy*, First Published 1972, Oxford: Oxford University Press.

Beevers, D., Marks, R. and Roles, J. (1989), *Sussex Churches and Chapels*, Brighton: The Royal Pavilion, Gallery & Museums.

Bennett, G.V. (1957), *White Kennett 1660–1728*, London: SPCK for the Church History Society.

Bennett, G.V. (1975), *The Tory Crisis in Church and State 1688–1730. The Career of Francis Atterbury, Bishop of Rochester*, Oxford: Clarendon Press.

Bermingham, A. and Brewer, J. (eds) (1995), *The Consumption of Culture 1600–1800: Image, Object, Text, Consumption and Culture in the Seventeenth and Eighteenth Centuries*, London and New York: Routledge.

Berry, C. (1994), *The Idea of Luxury: A Conceptual and Historical Investigation*, Cambridge: Cambridge University Press.

Berry, V. (1979), *The Rolfe Papers. The Chronicle of a Norfolk Family 1559–1908*, Norwich: Mrs V. Berry.

Bhabha, H. (ed.) (1990), *Nation and Narration*, London and New York: Routledge.

Bignamini, I. (1988), 'George Vertue, Art Historian, and Art Institutions in London, 1689–1768', *Walpole Society*, 54, 1–148.

Bindman, D. (1981), *Hogarth*, London: Thames and Hudson.

Bindman, D. (1997), *Hogarth and his Times*, London: British Museum Press.

Bindman, D. and Baker, M. (1995), *Roubiliac and the Eighteenth-Century Monument: Sculpture as Theatre*, Paul Mellon Centre for Studies in British Art, New Haven and London: Yale University Press.

Black, J. (1986), *Natural and Necessary Enemies: Anglo-French Relations in the Eighteenth Century*, London: Duckworth.

Black, J. (1990), 'Tourism and Cultural Challenge: the Changing Scene of the Eighteenth Century', in J. McVeagh, (ed.), *All Before Them: Attitudes to Abroad in English Literature 1660–1776*, London and New Jersey: The Ashfield Press, pp. 185–202.

Black, J. (1991), 'Ideology, History, Xenophobia and the World of Print in Eighteenth-Century England', in J. Black and J. Gregory (eds), *Culture, Politics and Society in Britain, 1660–1800*, Manchester: Manchester University Press, pp. 184–216.

Black, J. (ed.) (1997a), *Culture and Society in Britain 1660–1800*, Manchester: Manchester University Press.

Black, J. (1997b), *The British Abroad: the Grand Tour in the Eighteenth Century*, First Published 1992, Stroud: Sutton Publishing.

Black, J. (1998), 'Confessional State or Elect Nation? Religion and Identity in Eighteenth-Century England', in T. Claydon and I. MacBride (eds), *Protestantism and National Identity: Britain and Ireland, c.1650–c.1850*, Cambridge: Cambridge University Press, pp. 53–74.

Black, J. and Gregory, J. (eds) (1991), *Culture, Politics and Society in Britain, 1660–1800*, Manchester and New York: Manchester University Press.

Black, J. and Penny, N. (1987), 'Letters from Reynolds to Lord Grantham', *Burlington Magazine*, 129 (1016), 730–34.

Black, J. and Porter, R. (eds) (1996), *The Penguin Dictionary of Eighteenth-Century History*, Harmondsworth: Penguin Books.

Bligh Bond, F. and Camm, D.B. (1909), *Roodscreens and Roodlofts*, London: Sir Isaac Pitman & Sons.

Blunt, A. (1958), *The Legend of Raphael in Italy and France*, Reprinted from Italian Studies XIII, London.

Blunt, A. (1982), *Guide to Baroque Rome*, London: Granada.

Blunt, A. (1995), *Poussin*, First Published 1967, London: Pallas Athene.

Boase, T.S.R. (1955), *Christ Bearing the Cross attributed to Valdes Leal at Magdalen College, Oxford. A Study in Taste*, The Charlton Lectures on Art, London: Geoffrey Cumberlege, Oxford University Press.

Boase, T.S.R. (1963), 'Macklin and Bowyer', *Journal of the Warburg and Courtauld Institutes*, 26, 148–77.

Bohls, E.A. (1995), *Women Travel Writers and the Language of Aesthetics, 1716–1818*, Cambridge: Cambridge University Press.

Bond, F. (1916), *The Chancel of English Churches*, London: Oxford University Press.

Bonham-Carter, V. (1961), *Exploring Parish Churches*, London: Routledge & Kegan Paul.

Bosher, R.S. (1951), *The Making of the Restoration Settlement. The Influence of the Laudians, 1649 –1662*, London: Dacre Press.

Bossy, J. (1985), *Christianity in the West 1400–1700*, Oxford: Oxford University Press.

Bowersock, G.W., Clive, J. and Graubard, S. (eds) (1977), *Edward Gibbon and the Decline and Fall of the Roman Empire*, Cambridge, MA and London: Harvard University Press.

Bowron, E.P. and Rishel, J.J. (eds) (2000), *Art in Rome in the Eighteenth Century*, London and Philadelphia: Merrell in association with Philadelphia Museum of Art.

Bradley, J.E. (1989), 'The Anglican Pulpit, the Social Order, and the Resurgence of Toryism during the American Revolution', *Albion*, 21 (3), 361–88.

Bradley, S. and Pevsner, N. (1998), *London: The City Churches*, The Buildings of England ((ed.) B. Cherry), London: Penguin Books.

Bradshaw, B. and Morrill, J. (eds) (1996), *The British Problem, c.1534–1707: State Formation in the Atlantic Archipelago*, Basingstoke: Macmillan.

Bradshaw, B. and Roberts, P. (eds) (1998), *British Consciousness and Identity: the Making of Britain, 1533–1707*, Cambridge: Cambridge University Press.

Brauer, G.C. (1959), *The Education of a Gentleman: Theories of Gentlemanly Education in England, 1660–1775*, New Haven: College & University Press.

Braun, H.E. and Vallance, E. (eds) (2004), *Contexts of Conscience in Early Modern Europe, 1500–1700*, Basingstoke: Palgrave Macmillan.

Brewer, J. (1995), '"The most polite age and the most vicious": Attitudes Towards Culture as a Commodity 1660–1800', in A. Bermingham and J.

Brewer (eds), *The Consumption of Culture 1600–1800: Image, Object, Text*, London and New York: Routledge, pp. 341–61.

Brewer, J. (1997), *The Pleasures of the Imagination. English Culture in the Eighteenth Century*, London: Harper Collins.

Brewer, J. and Staves, S. (eds) (1995), *Early Modern Conceptions of Property, Consumption and Culture in the Seventeenth and Eighteenth Centuries*, London and New York: Routledge.

Briganti, G. (1966), *Gaspar van Wittell e l'origine della veduta settecentesca*, Rome: Ugo Bozzi.

Brighton, J.T. (1986–7), 'The Aaron Window at Offley Church Hertfordshire', *Journal of Stained Glass*, 18 (2), 194–200.

Brigstocke, H. and Somerville, J. (1995), *Italian Paintings from Burghley House*, Alexandria, VA: Art Services International.

Brocklebank, J. (1975), *Sir James Thornhill of Dorset 1675–1734*, Exhibition Catalogue, Dorset County Museum, Dorchester: Dorset Natural History & Archaeolgical Society.

Bromwich, D. (1988), 'Review of The Political Theory of Painting from Reynolds to Hazlitt. The Body of the Public by John Barrell (Review Article)', *Yale Review*, 77 (2), 183–92.

Brooke, J.H. (1991), *Science and Religion. Some Historical Perspectives*, Cambridge History of Science ((ed.) G. Basalla), Cambridge: Cambridge University Press.

Brown, C. and Vlieghe, H. (eds.) (1999), *Van Dyck 1599–1641*, London and Antwerp: Royal Academy Publications and Antwerpen Open.

Brown, J. (1995), *Kings and Connoisseurs: Collecting Art in Seventeenth-Century Europe*, New Haven and London: Yale University Press.

Broxap, H. (1924), *The Later Non-Jurors*, Cambridge: Cambridge University Press.

Bryer, A. and Herrin, J. (eds) (1975), *Iconoclasm. Papers given at the Ninth Symposium of Byzantine Studies*, Birmingham: Centre for Byzantine Studies, University of Birmingham.

Bunker Wright, H. and Montgomery, H.C. (1945), 'The Art Collection of a Virtuoso in Eighteenth-Century England', *Art Bulletin*, 27 (31), 195–205.

Burke, J. (1976), *English Art, 1714–1800*, Oxford: Oxford University Press.

Burns, J.H. and Goldie, M. (eds) (1994), *The Cambridge History of Political Thought*, Cambridge: Cambridge University Press.

Butlin, M. (1991), 'Introduction', in P. Cannon-Brookes (ed.), *The Painted Word*, London: Heim, pp. 7–8.

Byam Shaw, J. (1967), *Paintings by Old Masters at Christ Church Oxford*, London: Phaidon.

Campbell, T. (1996), 'School of Raphael Tapestries in the Collection of Henry VIII', *Burlington Magazine*, 138 (115), 69–79.

Cannon-Brookes, P. (ed.) (1991), *The Painted Word*, London: Heim.

Carpenter, E. (1956), *The Protestant Bishop. Being the Life of Henry Compton, 1632–1713 Bishop of London*, London: Longmans, Green and Co.

Carrier, D. (1987), 'Review of The Political Theory of Painting from Reynolds to Hazlitt. The Body of the Public by John Barrell (Review Article)', *Journal of Aesthetics and Art Criticism*, 45 (4), 420–21.

Castiglione, D. and Sharpe, L. (eds) (1995), *Shifting the Boundaries: Transformations of the Language of Public and Private in the Eighteenth Century*, Exeter: University of Exeter Press.

Castronovo, D. (1987), *The English Gentleman: Images and Ideals in Literature and Society*, New York: Ungar.

Caygill, H. (1989), *Art of Judgement*, Oxford: Oxford University Press.

Chaloner, W.H. (1949–50), 'The Egertons in Italy and the Netherlands, 1729–1734', *Bulletin of the John Rylands Library*, 32, 157–70.

Champion, J. (1992), *The Pillars of Priestcraft Shaken. The Church of England and Its Enemies 1660–1730*, Cambridge: Cambridge University Press.

Chaney, E. (1990), 'Pilgrims to Pictures', *Country Life*, 184 (40), 122–5.

Chaney, E. (1998), *The Evolution of the Grand Tour. Anglo-Italian Cultural Relations since the Renaissance*, London and Portland, OR: Frank Cass.

Chard, C. (1995), 'Nakedness and Tourism: Classical Sculpture and the Imaginative Geography of the Grand Tour', *Oxford Art Journal*, 18 (1), 14–28.

Chard, C. (1997a), 'Grand and Ghostly Tours: The Topography of Memory', *Eighteenth-Century Studies*, 31 (1), 101–8.

Chard, C. (1997b), '"Grand Tour": The Lure of Italy in the Eighteenth Century', *Eighteenth-Century Studies*, 30 (4), 449–50.

Chard, C. (1999), *Pleasure and Guilt on the Grand Tour*, Manchester and New York: Manchester University Press.

Chatfield, M. (1989), *Churches the Victorians Forgot*, Ashbourne: Moorland.

Cherry, B. (2001), 'Edward Hatton's *New View of London*', *Architectural History*, 44, 96–105.

Christie, C. (2000), *The British Country House in the Eighteenth Century*, Manchester: Manchester University Press.

Clark, J. (1989), 'The Rise of English Nationalism: A Cultural History, 1740–1830 by Gerald Newman (Review Article)', *Journal of Modern History*, 61 (3), 598–600.

Clark, J.C.D. (1987), 'On Hitting the Buffers: The Historiography of England's Ancien Regime. A Response', *Past and Present*, 117, 195–207.

Clark, J.C.D. (1998), 'Lay People and Religion in the Early Eighteenth Century by W.M. Jacob (Review Article)', *Journal of Ecclesiastical History*, 49 (2), 372–3.

Clark, J.C.D. (2000), *English Society, 1660–1832*, First Published 1985, Cambridge: Cambridge University Press.

Clark, P. (ed.) (2000), *The Cambridge Urban History of Britain. Volume II 1540–1840*, Cambridge: Cambridge University Press.

Clarke, B.F.L. (1963), *The Building of the Eighteenth-Century Church*, London: SPCK.

Clarke, W.K.L. (1944), *Eighteenth-Century Piety*, London: SPCK.

Claydon, T. (2000), 'The Sermon, the "public sphere" and the political culture of late seventeenth-century England', in L.A. Ferrell and P. McCullough (eds), *The English Sermon Revised. Religion, literature and history 1600–1750*, Manchester: Manchester University Press, pp. 208–33.

Claydon, T. and McBride, I. (eds) (1998), *Protestanism and National Identity. Britain and Ireland, c.1650–c.1850*, Cambridge: Cambridge University Press.

Claydon, T. and McBride, I. (1998), 'The Trials of the Chosen People: Recent Interpretations of Protestantism and National Identity in Britain and Ireland', in T. Claydon and I. McBride (eds), *Protestantism and National Identity. Britain and Ireland, c.1650–c.1850*, Cambridge: Cambridge University Press, pp. 3–29.

Clayton, T. (1992), 'The Print Collection of George Clarke at Worcester College, Oxford', *Print Quarterly*, 9, 123–41.

Clayton, T. (1997), *The English Print, 1688–1802*, New Haven and London: Yale University Press.

Clifford, T. (1977), 'Sebastiano Conca at Holkham: a Neapolitan painter and a Norfolk patron', *Connoisseur*, 196 (788), 92–103.

Coatu, J. (1997) 'William Chambers and Joseph Wilton', in J. Harris and M. Snodin (eds), *Sir William Chambers: Architect to George III*, New Haven and London: Yale University Press in association with The Courtauld Gallery, pp. 175–85.

Coatu, J. (2000), '"A very grand and seigneurial design": The Duke of Richmond's Academy in Whitehall', *The British Art Journal*, 1 (2), 47–54.

Cobb, G. (1989), *London City Churches*, Revised Edition by N. Redman, First Published 1977, London: B.T. Batsford.

Coffey, J. (2000), *Persecution and Toleration in Protestant England 1558–1689*, Pearson Education Studies in Modern History, London: Longman.

Cohen, M. (1996), *Fashioning Masculinity: National Identity and Language in the Eighteenth Century*, London: Routledge.

Colley, L. (1984), 'The English Rococo: Historical Background', in M. Snodin (ed.), *Rococo Art and Design in Hogarth's England*, London: The Victoria and Albert Museum in Association with Trefoil Books, pp. 10–17.

Colley, L. (1986), 'Whose Nation? Class and National Consciousness in Britain 1750–1830', *Past and Present*, 113, 97–117.

Colley, L. (1992a), *Britons: Forging the Nation, 1707–1837*, New Haven and London: Yale University Press.

Colley, L. (1992b), 'Britishness and Otherness: An Argument', *Journal of British Studies*, 31, 309–29.

Collins Baker, C.H. (1947), 'Sir James Thornhill as Bible Illustrator', *Huntington Library Quarterly*, 10 (3).

Collins Baker, C.H. and Baker, M.I. (1949), *The Life and Circumstances of James Brydges, First Duke of Chandos; patron of the Liberal Arts*, Oxford: Clarendon Press.

Collinson, P. (1986), *From Iconoclasm to Iconophobia: the Cultural Impact of the Second English Reformation*, Reading: Reading University Press.

Collinson, P. (1988), *The Birthpangs of Protestant England. Religious and Cultural Change in the Sixteenth and Seventeenth Centuries*, The Third Anstey Memorial Lectures in the University of Kent at Canterbury 12–15 May 1986, London: Macmillan.

Collinson, P. (1994), 'England', in B. Scribner, R. Porter and M. Teich (eds), *The Reformation in National Context*, Cambridge: Cambridge University Press.

Coltman, V. (1999), 'Classicism in the English Library: Reading Classical Culture in the Late Eighteenth and Early Nineteenth Centuries', *Journal of the History of Collections*, 11 (1), 35–50.

Conlin, J. (2001), 'High Art and Low Politics: a New Perspective on John Wilkes', *Huntington Library Quarterly*, 64:4, 356–81.

Colvin, H. and Newman, J. (eds) (1981), *Of Building. Roger North's Writings on Architecture*, Oxford: Clarendon Press.

Connor, T.P. (1998), 'The Fruits of the Grand Tour: Edward Wright and Lord Parker in Italy, 1720–22', *Apollo*, 148 (437), 23–30.

Cooper, T. (ed.) (2001), *The Journal of William Dowsing*, Woodbridge: Boydell and Brewer.

Copley, S. (1995), 'Commerce, Conversation and Politeness in Early Eighteenth Century Periodicals', *British Journal for Eighteenth-Century Studies*, 18 (1), 63–77.

Corfield, P.J. (1991), 'Class by Name and Number in Eighteenth-Century Britain', in P.J. Corfield (ed.), *Language, History and Class*, Oxford: Basil Blackwell, pp. 101–30.

Cornforth, J. (1977), 'Kirkleatham, Cleveland - II', *Country Life*, 161 (4151), 134–7.

Cosgrove, D.E. (1984), *Social Formation and Symbolic Landscape*, Croom Helm Historical Geography Series ((ed.) R.A. Butlin), London and Sydney: Croom Helm.

Cox, J.C. (1915), *Pulpits, Lecterns and Organs in English Churches*, London: Humphrey Milford: Oxford University Press.

Cox, J.C. (1933), *English Church Fittings, Furniture and Accessories*, First Published 1923, London: B.T. Batsford.

Cox, M.H. and Norman, P. (eds) (1929), *The Parish of All Hallows Barking,*. Vol. 12, London County Council Survey of London, 2 vols, London: B.T. Batsford.

Cragg, G.R. (1960), *The Church and the Age of Reason, 1648–1789*, Harmondsworth: Penguin.

Cragg, G.R. (1964), *Reason and Authority in the Eighteenth Century*, Cambridge: Cambridge University Press.

Craske, M. (1997), *Art in Europe 1700–1800*, Oxford: Oxford University Press.

Cray, J. (1990), 'Paintings by Thornhill at Chinnor', *Burlington Magazine*, 132 (1502), 789–93.

Croft-Murray, E. (1962–70), *Decorative Painting in England, 1537–1837*, 2 vols, London: Country Life.

Cropper, E. (1991), 'La piu bella antichita che sappiate desiderare. History and Styles in Giovan Pietro Bellori's Lives', in P. Ganz et al, (eds), *Kunst and Kunsttheorie 1400–1900*, pp. 145–73.

Cross, F.L. and Livingstone, E.A. (eds) (1997), *The Oxford Dictionary of the Christian Church*, Third Edition, Oxford: Oxford University Press.

Crow, T. (1985), *Painters and Public Life in Eighteenth-Century France*, New Haven and London: Yale University Press.

Crow, T. (1995), *Emulation. Making Artists for Revolutionary France*, New Haven and London: Yale University Press.

Crown, P. (1990), 'British Rococo as Social and Political Style', *Eighteenth-Century Studies*, 23 (3), 269–82.

Cubitt, G. (ed.) (1998), *Imagining Nations*, Manchester and New York: Manchester University Press.

Cuming, G.J. (1969), *A History of Anglican Liturgy*, London: Macmillan.

Cunningham, H. (1981), 'The Language of Patriotism 1750–1914', *History Workshop Journal*, 12, 8–33.

Dalton, R. (1787), 'Remarks on the Whole Number of the Sacred Historical Designs of Raphael D'Urbino', *Gentleman's Magazine*, 57 (2), 853–5.

Daniels, J. (ed.) (1976), *L'Opera completa di Sebastiano Ricci*, Classici dell'arte, Milan: Rizzoli.

Davie, D. (1993), *The Eighteenth-Century Hymn in England*, Cambridge Studies in Eighteenth-Century Literature and Thought ((eds) H. Erskine-Hill and J. Richetti), Cambridge: Cambridge University Press.

Davies, H. (1961), *Worship and Theology in England: from Watts and Wesley to Maurice, 1690–1850*, 5 vols, Princeton: Princeton University Press.

de Grazia, D. and Garberson, E. (1996), *Italian Paintings of the Seventeenth and Eighteenth Centuries*, The Collections of the National Gallery of Art, Washington, DC: National Gallery of Art.

De Krey, G.S. (1989), 'The London Whigs and the Exclusion Crisis Reconsidered', in A.L. Beier, D. Cannadine and J.M. Rosenheim (eds), *The First Modern Society. Essays in English History in Honour of Lawrence Stone*, Cambridge: Cambridge University Press, pp. 457–82.

De Krey, G.S. (1990), 'London Radicals and Revolutionary Politics, 1675–1683', in T. Harris, P. Seaward and M. Goldie (eds), *The Politics of Religion in Restoration England*, Oxford: Basil Blackwell, pp. 133–62.

De Krey, G.S. (1996), 'Reformation in the Restoration Crisis, 1679–1682', in D.B. Hamilton and R. Strier (eds), *Religion, Literature, and Politics in Post-Reformation England, 1540–1688,* Cambridge: Cambridge University Press, pp. 231–52.

de Waal, E. (1965), 'New Churches in East London in the Early Eighteenth Century', *Renaissance and Modern Studies,* 9, 98–114.

Deuchar, S. (1988), *Sporting Art in Eighteenth-Century England. A Social and Political History,* New Haven and London: Yale University Press.

Dickey, S. (1986), 'The Passions and Raphael's Cartoons in Eighteenth-Century British Art', *Marsyas,* XXII, 33–46.

Dickinson, H.T. (1977), *Liberty and Property: Political Ideology in Eighteenth-Century Britain,* London: Weidenfeld and Nicolson.

DiFrederico, F. (1977), *Francesco Trevisani: Eighteenth-Century Painter in Rome. A Catalogue Raisonée,* Washington, DC: Decatour House Press.

Dobson, A. (1893), *Horace Walpole. A Memoir,* London: James R. Osgood, McIlvaine & Co.

Dolan, B. (2001), *Ladies of the Grand Tour,* London: Harper Collins.

Downie, J.A. and Corns, T.N. (eds) (1993), *Telling People What to Think: Early Eighteenth-Century Periodicals from The Review to The Rambler,* London: Frank Cass.

Draper, J.W. (1931), '18th Century English Aesthetics: a Bibliography', *Anglistische Forschungen,* 71.

Drury, J. (ed.) (1989), *Critics of the Bible, 1724–1873,* Cambridge: Cambridge University Press.

Duffy, E. (1977), 'Primitive Christianity Revived: Religious Renewal in Augustan England', *Studies in Church History,* 14, 287–300.

Duffy, M. (1986), 'The Englishman and the Foreigner', in M. Duffy (ed.), *The English Satirical Print 1600–1832,* Cambridge: Chadwyck-Healey.

Dukelskaya, L. and Moore, A. (eds) (2002), *A Capital Collection: Houghton Hall and the Hermitage,* New Haven and London: Yale University Press.

Durston, C. and Eales, J. (eds) (1996), *The Culture of English Puritanism, 1560–1700,* London: Macmillan.

Eales, J. (1992), 'Iconoclasm, Iconography, and the Altar in the English Civil War', *Studies in Church History,* 28, 313–27.

Earle, P. (1989), *The Making of the English Middle Class: business, society and family life in London, 1660–1730,* London: Methuen.

Eccleshall, R. (1981), 'Richard Hooker and the Peculiarities of the English: the Reception of the *Ecclesiastical Polity* in the Seventeenth and Eighteenth Centuries', *History of Political Thought,* 2 (1), 63–117.

Ekserdjian, D. (1997), *Correggio,* New Haven and London: Yale University Press.

Eliade, M. (ed.) (1987), *The Encyclopaedia of Religion,* 16 vols, New York: Macmillan Publishing Co.

Elsner, J. (1988), 'Image and Iconoclasm in Byzantium', *Art History*, 11 (4), 471–91.

Erskine-Hill, H. (1983), *The Augustan Idea in English Literature*, London: Edward Arnold.

Eustace, K. (1998), 'The Politics of the Past: Stowe and the development of the historical portrait bust', *Apollo*, 148 (437), 31–40.

Evans, G.R. and Wright, J.R. (eds) (1991), *The Anglican Tradition: A Handbook of Sources*, London: SPCK.

Everett, N. (1994), *The Tory View of Landscape*, New Haven and London: Yale University Press.

Fehl, P. (1981), 'Franciscus Junius and the Defence of Arts', *Artibus et Historiae*, 3, 9–55.

Fermor, S. (1996), *The Raphael Tapestry Cartoons*, London: Scala Books.

Fernie, E. (1995), *Art History and its Methods. A Critical Anthology*, London: Phaidon.

Ferrell, L.A. and McCullough, P. (eds) (2000), *The English Sermon Revised. Religion, Literature and History 1600–1750*, Politics, Culture and Society in Early Modern Britain, (eds) A. Hughes, A. Milton and P. Lake, Manchester: Manchester University Press.

Finaldi, G. (ed.) (2000), *The Image of Christ. The Catalogue of the Exhibition 'Seeing Salvation'*, London: National Gallery, London.

Fincham, K. (2003), '"According to Ancient Custom": The Return of Altars in the Restoration Church of England', *Transactions of the Royal Historical Society*, 13, 29–54.

Findlen, P. (1994), *Possessing Nature. Museums, Collecting and Scientific Culture in Early Modern Italy*, Berkeley and London: University of California Press.

Finn, M. (1989), 'An Elect Nation? Nation, State, and Class in Modern British History', *Journal of British Studies*, 28 (2), 181–91.

Fleming, J. (1958), 'Cardinal Albani's Drawings at Windsor: their Purchase by James Adam for George III', *The Connoisseur*, 142, 164–9.

Ford, B. (1985), 'The Englishman in Italy', in G. Jackson-Stops (ed.), *The Treasure Houses of Britain: Five Hundred Years of Private Patronage and Art Collecting*, New Haven and London: Yale University Press, pp. 40–49.

Foster, J. (1968), *Alumni Oxonienses*, Nendeln: Kraus Reprint.

Foster, J., Sharp, R. and Wylie, J.A.H. (1988), 'The Royal Hospital of St. Bartholomew, Smithfield: Royalist, Non-Juring, Tory High Church and Jacobite', *Royal Stuart Papers*, 25.

Freedberg, D. (1975), 'The Structure of Byzantine and European Iconoclasm', in A. Bryer and J. Herrin (eds), *Iconoclasm. Papers given at the Ninth Spring Symposium of Byzantine Studies*, Birmingham: Centre for Byzantine Studies, University of Birmingham, pp. 165–77.

Freedberg, D. (1982), 'The Hidden God: Image and Interdiction in the Netherlands in the Sixteenth Century', *Art History*, 5 (2), 133–53.

Freedberg, D. (1989), *The Power of Images. Studies in the History and Theory of Response*, Chicago and London: University of Chicago Press.

Freedberg, S.J. (1971), *Painting in Italy 1500–1600*, Pelican History of Art, Harmondsworth: Penguin.

Freeman, A. (1921), *English Organ Cases*, London: Geo. Aug. Mate & Son.

Friedman, T. (1984), 'James Parmentier in Leeds', *Leeds Art Calendar*, 94, 3–8.

Friedman, T. (2004), *The Georgian Parish Church: 'Monuments to Posterity'*, Reading: Spire Books.

Furtado, P. (1989), 'National Pride in Seventeenth-Century England', in R. Samuel (ed.), *Patriotism: The Making and Unmaking of British National Identity. Volume I: History and Politics*, 3 vols, London and New York: Routledge, pp. 44–56.

Galinou, M. (ed.) (2004), *City Merchants and the Arts 1670–1720*, London: Oblong for the Corporation of London.

Garas, K. (1987), 'Two Unknown Works by James Thornhill', *Burlington Magazine*, 129 (1016), 722–3.

Garlick, K.J. (1974–6), 'A Catalogue of Pictures at Althorp', *Walpole Society*, 45.

Gay, P. (1967–9), *The Enlightenment. An Interpretation*, 2 vols, London: Weidenfeld and Nicolson.

Geertz, C. (1973), *The Interpretation of Cultures*, New York: Basic Books.

Gellner, E. (1998), *Nationalism*, First Published 1997, London: Phoenix.

Gent, L. (1981), *Pictures and Poetry 1560–1620*, Leamington Spa: J. Hall.

Gent, L. (ed.) (1995), *Albion's Classicism: The Visual Arts in Britain 1550–1660*, New Haven and London: Yale University Press.

Gibson, W. (1995), *The Achievement of the Anglican Church, 1689–1800: the confessional state in eighteenth-century England*, Lewiston, NY and Lampeter: Edwin Mellen.

Gibson, W. (2001), *The Church of England 1688–1832. Unity and Accord*, London: Routledge.

Gibson-Wood, C. (1984), 'Jonathan Richardson and the Rationalization of Connoisseurship', *Art History*, 7 (1), 38–56.

Gibson-Wood, C. (1989), 'Jonathan Richardson, Lord Somers's Collection of Drawings, and Early Art-Historical Writing in England', *Journal of the Warburg and Courtauld Institutes*, 52, 167–87.

Gibson-Wood, C. (1993), 'The Political Background to Thornhill's Paintings in St Paul's Cathedral', *Journal of the Warburg and Courtauld Insitutes*, 56, 229–37.

Gibson-Wood, C. (2000), *Jonathan Richardson: Art Theorist of the English Enlightenment*, New Haven and London: Yale University Press.

Gibson-Wood, C. (2002), 'Picture Consumption in London at the End of the Seventeenth Century', *Art Bulletin*, 84 (3), 491–500.

Girouard, M. (1978), *Life in the English Country House. A social and architectural history*, New Haven and London: Yale University Press.

Goldie, M. (1982), 'The Nonjurors, Episcopacy, and the Origins of the Convocation Controversy,' in Eveline Cruickshanks (ed.), *Ideology and Conspiracy: Aspects of Jacobitism, 1689–1759,* Edinburgh: John Donald, pp. 15–35.

Goldie, M. (1991), 'The Theory of Religious Intolerance in Restoration England', in O.P. Grell, J.I. Israel and N. Tyacke (eds), *From Persecution to Toleration. The Glorious Revolution and Religion in England,* Oxford, pp. 331–68.

Goldie, M. (1993), 'Priestcraft and the Birth of Whiggism', in N. Phillipson and Q. Skinner (eds), *Political Discourse in Early Modern Britain,* Cambridge: Cambridge University Press, pp. 209–31.

Goldie, M. and Spurr, J. (1994), 'Politics and the Restoration Parish: Edward Fowler and the Struggle for St Giles Cripplegate', *English Historical Review,* 109 (432), 572–96.

Goodman, D. (1992), 'Public sphere and private life: toward a synthesis of current historiographical approaches to the old regime', *History and Theory,* 31 (1), 1–20.

Graham, C. (1987), 'Moses and Aaron: Two Figures from the Reredos of the Church of St Swithin London Stone', *Transactions of the Ancient Monuments Society,* New Series Vol. 31, 77–87.

Graves, A. (1907), *The Society of Artists of Great Britain, 1760–1791, The Free Society of Artists, 1761–1783: a complete dictionary of contributors and their work from the foundation of the societies to 1791,* London: George Bell.

Graves, A. (1969), *A Dictionary of Artists who have exhibited works in the principal London exhibitions from 1760–1893,* First Published 1901, Bath: Kingsmead Reprints.

Green, A. and Troup, K. (eds) (1999), *The Houses of History. A Critical Reader in 20th Century History and Theory,* Manchester and New York: Manchester University Press.

Green, I.M. (1978), *The Re-Establishment of the Church of England 1660–1663,* Oxford: Oxford University Press.

Green, I.M. (1996), *The Christian's ABC: Catechisms and Catechizing in England c1540–1740,* Oxford: Clarendon Press.

Green, I.M. (2001), *Print and Protestantism in Early Modern England,* Oxford: Oxford University Press.

Green, I.M. and Peters, K. (2002), 'Religious Publishing in England 1640–1695', in J. Barnard and D.F. McKenzie (eds), *The Cambridge History of the Book in Britain,* Vol. IV 1557–1695, Cambridge: Cambridge University Press, pp. 67–93.

Greene, D. (1971), 'The Via Media in an Age of Revolution: Anglicanism in the 18th Century', in P. Hughes and D. Williams eds., *The Varied Pattern: Studies in the 18th Century,* Toronto: A.M. Hakkert, pp. 297–320.

Greenfield, L. (1992), *Nationalism: Five Roads to Modernity,* Cambridge, MA. and London: Harvard University Press.

Gregory, J. (1991), 'Anglicanism and the Arts: Religion, Culture and Politics in the Eighteenth Century', in J. Black and J. Gregory (eds), *Culture, Politics and Society in Britain, 1660–1800*, Manchester and New York: Manchester University Press, pp. 82–109.

Gregory, J. (ed.) (1996), *The Speculum of Archbishop Thomas Secker*, Church of England Record Society, Woodbridge: Boydell Press.

Gregory, J. (1997), 'Christianity and Culture: Religion, the Arts and the Sciences in England, 1660–1800', in J. Black (ed.), *Culture and Society in Britain 1660–1800*, Manchester: Manchester University Press, pp. 102–23.

Gregory, J. (1998), 'The Making of a Protestant Nation: "Success" and "Failure" in England's Long Reformation', in N. Tyake (ed.), *England's Long Reformation, 1500–1800*, London: University College London, pp. 307–33.

Gregory, J. (2000), *Restoration, Reformation and Reform, 1660–1828. Archbishops of Canterbury and their Diocese*, Oxford Historical Monographs (R.R. Davies et al., (eds)), Oxford: Clarendon Press.

Griffiths, A. (ed.) (1996), *Landmarks in Print Collecting. Connoisseurs and Donors at the British Museum since 1753*, London: British Museum Press.

Gross, H. (1990), *Rome in the Age of Enlightenment. The Post-Tridentine Syndrome and the Ancien Regime*, Cambridge Studies in Early Modern History ((eds) J.H. Elliott, O. Hufton and H.G. Koenigsberger), Cambridge: Cambridge University Press.

Gurstein, R. (2000), 'Taste and "the Conversible World" in the Eighteenth Century', *Journal of the History of Ideas*, 61 (2), 203–21.

Gutmann, J. (ed.) (1977), *The Image and the Word: Confrontations in Judaism, Christianity and Islam*, Missoula, MT: Scholars Press for the American Academy of Religion.

Habermas, J. (1989), *The Structural Transformation of the Public Sphere: an inquiry into a cateogry of bourgeois society*, trans. T. Burger with F. Lawrence, Cambridge: Polity.

Hale, J. (1996), *England and the Italian Renaissance*, First Published 1954, London: Harper Collins.

Hall, I. (1993), 'The First Georgian Restoration of Beverley Minster', *Georgian Group*, 13–31.

Hamilton, D.B. and Strier, R. (eds) (1996), *Religion, Literature, and Politics in Post-Reformation England, 1540–1688*, Cambridge: Cambridge University Press.

Hardwick, N. (ed.) (1985), *The Grand Tour: William and John Blathwayt of Dyrham Park 1705–1708*, Bristol: N. Hardwick.

Harley, B. (1994), *Church Ships: A Handbook of Votive and Commemorative Models*, Norwich: Canterbury Press.

Harris, J. (1985), 'Harley, the Patriot Collector', *Apollo*, 122 (283), 198–203.

Harris, J. and Snodin, M. (eds) (1996), *Sir William Chambers: Architect to George III*, New Haven and London: Yale University Press in Association with The Courtauld Gallery.

Harris, R. and Simon, R. (eds) (1997), *Enlightened Self-Interest. The Foundling Hospital and Hogarth*, London: Thomas Coram Foundation for Children.

Harris, T. (1987), *London Crowds in the Reign of Charles II. Propaganda and Politics from the Restoration until the Exclusion Crisis*, Cambridge Studies in Early Modern British History (A. Fletcher et al. (ed.)), Cambridge: Cambridge University Press.

Harris, T. (1993), *Politics under the Later Stuarts. Party Conflict in a Divided Society*, Studies in Modern History ((eds) J. Morrill and D. Cannadine), London and New York: Longman.

Harris, T., Seaward, P. and Goldie, M. (eds) (1990), *The Politics of Religion in Restoration England*, Oxford: Blackwell.

Harrison, P. (1990), *'Religion' and the Religions in the English Enlightenment*, Cambridge: Cambridge University Press.

Harrison, R.H. (1960), 'The Dispersion of Furniture and Fittings Formerly Belonging to the Churches in the City of London', *Transactions of the Ancient Monument Society*, 8, 53–74.

Haskell, F. (1980), *Patrons and Painters: Art and Society in Baroque Italy*, First Published 1963, New Haven and London: Yale University Press.

Haskell, F. (1985), 'The British as Collectors', in G. Jackson-Stops (ed.), *The Treasure Houses of England: Five Hundred Years of Private Patronage and Art Collecting*, New Haven and London: Yale University Press, pp. 50–59.

Haskell, F. (1987a), *Past and Present in Art and Taste: Selected Essays*, New Haven and London: Yale University Press.

Haskell, F. (1987b), 'Gibbon and the History of Art', in F. Haskell, *Past and Present in Art and Taste: Selected Essays*, New Haven and London: Yale University Press, pp. 16–29.

Haskell, F. (1993), *History and Its Images. Art and the Interpretation of the Past*, New Haven and London: Yale University Press.

Haskell, F. and Penny, N. (1981), *Taste and the Antique. The Lure of Classical Sculpture 1500–1900*, New Haven and London: Yale University Press.

Hasler, C. (1980), *The Royal Arms. Its Graphic and Decorative Development*, London: Jupiter Books.

Havens, R.D. (1928), 'Thomas Warton and the Eighteenth-Century Dilemma', *Studies in Philology*, 25, 36–50.

Hay, D. and Rogers, N. (1997), *Eighteenth-Century English Society*, OPUS (C. Butler, R. Evans and J. Skorupski (eds)), Oxford: Oxford University Press.

Haydon, C. (1993), *Anti-Catholicism in Eighteenth-Century England, c.1714–1780*, Manchester: Manchester University Press.

Haydon, C. (1998), '"I Love my King and my Country, but a Roman Catholic I hate": anti-catholicism, xenophobia and national identity in eighteenth-century England', in T. Claydon and C. MacBride (eds), *Protestantism and National Identity, Britain and Ireland, c.1650–c.1850*, Cambridge: Cambridge University Press, pp. 33–52.

Haydon, C. (2000), 'Parliament and Popery in England, 1700–1780', *Parliamentary History*, 19.

Haynes, C. (2001), 'A "natural" exhibitioner: Sir Ashton Lever and his Holophusikon', *British Journal for Eighteenth Century Studies*, 24 (1), 1–13.

Haynes, C. (online August 2005, in print forthcoming), 'Pictures and Popery: the cultural politics of judgement in England 1660–1760', *Historical Research*.

Haynes, C. (2006 (forthcoming)), '"Badge of Superstition" or "mere ornament"? The politics of religious imagery in the late seventeenth century', in J. McElligott (ed.), *Fear, Exclusion and Revolution: Roger Morrice and his Worlds, 1675–1700*, Aldershot: Ashgate.

Hazen, A.T. (1969), *A Catalogue of Horace Walpole's Library*, 3 vols, London and New Haven: Oxford University Press and Harvard.

Hempton, D. (1990), 'Religion in British Society 1740–1790', in J. Black (ed.), *British Politics and Society from Walpole to Pitt 1742–1789*, Basingstoke: Macmillan Education, pp. 201– 21.

Herbert, A.S. (ed.) (1968), *Historical Catalogue of Printed Editions of the English Bible, 1525–1961*, London and New York: Bible Society.

Hetherington, P. (1995), 'The Altarpiece for Wren's Church of St Benet Fink', *Apollo*, 142 (401), 44–6.

Hibbert, C. (1987), *The Grand Tour*, London: Thames Methuen.

Hibbert, C. (1988), *London's Churches*, London: Queen Anne Press.

Hill, C. (1993), *The English Bible and the Seventeenth-Century Revolution*, Harmondsworth: Allen Lane.

Hilles, F.W. and Bloom, H. (eds) (1965), *From Sensibility to Romanticism. Essays Presented to Frederick A. Pottle*, New York: Oxford University Press.

Hodnett, E. (1976), 'Elisha Kirkhall', *Book Collector*, Summer, 195–209.

Holmes, G. (1973), *The Trial of Doctor Sacheverell*, London: Eyre Methuen.

Holmes, G. (1976), 'The Sacheverell Riots', *Past and Present*, 72, 55–85.

Höltgen, K.J. (1984), 'The Reformation of Images and Some Jacobean Writers on Art', in U. Broich, T. Stemmler and G. Stratmann (eds), *Functions of Literature: Essays Presented to Erwin Wolff on his Sixtieth Birthday*, Tubingen: Niemeyer, pp. 119–46.

Honour, H. (1954), 'John Talman and William Kent in Italy', *Connoisseur*, 134, 3–7.

Honour, H. (1958), 'English Patrons and Italian Sculptors', *The Connoisseur*, 141, 220–26.

Hook, J. (1976), *The Baroque Age in England*, London: Phaidon.

Houghton, W.E. (1942), 'The English Virtuoso in the Seventeenth Century', *Journal of the History of Ideas*, 3 (1 & 2), 51–73; 190–219.

Houston, J. (1972), *Cases in the Court of Arches 1660–1913*, London: British Record Society.

Howarth, D. (1985), *Lord Arundel and His Circle*, New Haven and London: Yale University Press.

Howarth, D. (1998), 'Bernini and Britain', in A. Weston-Lewis (ed.), *Effigies and Ecstasies. Roman Baroque Sculpture and Design in the Age of Bernini*, Edinburgh: Trustees of the National Galleries of Scotland, pp. 29–36.

Hughes, P. and Williams, D. (eds) (1971), *The Varied Pattern: Studies in the 18th Century*, Publications of the McMaster University Association for 18th-century Studies, Toronto: A.M. Hakkert.

Hunter, M. (2004), 'The Disquieted Mind in Casuistry and Natural Philosophy: Robert Boyle and Thomas Barlow', in H.E. Braun and E. Vallance (eds), *Contexts of Conscience in Early Modern Europe, 1500–1700*, Basingstoke: Palgrave Macmillan, pp. 82–99.

Hussey, C. (1955), *English Country Houses: Early Georgian 1715–1760*, London: Country Life.

Impey, O. (1977), *Chinoiserie. The Impact of Oriental Styles on Western Art and Decoration*, London: Oxford University Press.

Ingamells, J. (1981), *The English Episcopal Portrait 1559–1835*, London: Paul Mellon Centre for Studies in British Art.

Ingamells, J. (1997), *A Dictionary of British and Irish Travellers in Italy, 1701–1800*, New Haven and London: Yale University Press.

Ingamells, J. and Edgcumbe, J. (eds) (2000), *The Letters of Joshua Reynolds*, New Haven and London: Yale University Press, for the Paul Mellon Centre for Studies in British Art.

Innes, J. (1987), 'Jonathan Clark, Social History and England's "Ancien Regime"', *Past and Present*, 115, 165–200.

Irwin, D. (1997), *Neoclassicism*, London: Phaidon.

Jackson-Stops, G. (ed.) (1985), *The Treasure Houses of Britain: Five Hundred Years of Private Patronage and Art Collecting*, New Haven and London: Yale University Press.

Jackson-Stops, G. and Pipkin, J. (1993), *The English Country House. A Grand Tour*, London: Weidenfeld and Nicolson.

Jacob, M. (1976), *The Newtonians and the English Revolution*, Hassocks: Harvester Press.

Jacob, W.M. (1996), *Lay People and Religion in the Early Eighteenth Century*, Cambridge: Cambridge University Press.

Jacobson, D. (1993), *Chinoiserie*, London: Phaidon.

James, C.W. (1929), *Chief Justice Coke, His Family & Descendants at Holkham*, London: Country Life.

Jardine, N., Secord, J.A. and Spary, E.C. (eds) (1996), *Cultures of Natural History*, Cambridge: Cambridge University Press.

Jasper, R.C.D. (1989), *The Development of the Anglican Liturgy, 1662–1980*, London: SPCK.

Jeffery, P. (1996), *The City Churches of Sir Christopher Wren*, London: Hambledon Press.

Jenkins, I. and Sloan, K. (eds) (1996), *Vases and Volcanoes. Sir William Hamilton and His Collection*, London: British Museum.

Jenkins, S. (2003), 'Power Play: James Brydges, 1st Duke of Chandos, and Sir Robert Walpole. The politics of collecting in the early 18th century', *British Art Journal*, 4 (2), 80–82.

Johns, C.M.S. (1993), *Papal Art and Cultural Politics: Rome in the Age of Clement XI*, Cambridge: Cambridge University Press.

Johns, C.M.S. (2000), 'The Entrepot of Europe: Rome in the Eighteenth Century', in E.P. Bowron and J.J. Rishel (eds), *Art in Rome in the Eighteenth Century*, London and Philadelphia: Merrell in association with Philadelphia Museum of Art, pp. 17–45.

Jordanova, L.J. (1999), *Nature Displayed. Gender, Science and Medicine, 1760–1820*, London: Longman.

Jordanova, L.J. (2000a), *Defining Features: Scientific and Medical Portraits 1660–2000*, London: Reaktion Books.

Jordanova, L.J. (2000b), *History in Practice*, London: Edward Arnold.

Kallich, M. (1971), *Horace Walpole*, New York: Twayne Publishers.

Keene, D.J., Burns, A. and Saint, A. (eds) (2004), *St Paul's: the Cathedral Church of London 604–2004*, Studies in British Art, New Haven and London: Yale University Press.

Kenworthy-Browne, J. (1978), 'Rise and Demise of a Wren Church; the Reredos from St Matthew Friday at Polesden Lacey', *National Trust Yearbook*, 63–74.

Kenyon, J.P. (1972), *The Popish Plot*, London: Heinemann.

Ketton-Cremer, R.W. (1957), *Norfolk Assembly*, London: Faber.

Kidd, C. (1998), 'Protestantism, Constitutionalism and British Identity under the Later Stuarts', in B. Bradshaw and P. Roberts (eds), *British Consciousness and Identity: the Making of Britain, 1533–1707*, Cambridge: Cambridge University Press, pp. 321–42.

Kidd, C. (1999), *British Identities Before Nationalism: Ethnicity and Nationhood in the Atlantic World, 1600–1800*, Cambridge: Cambridge University Press.

Kirkby, A. (ed.) (1996), *From St. James's to St Peter's: Horace Walpole's and Thomas Gray's Letters from the Grand Tour, 1739–1741*, London: Malthouse Press in association with Peter Trigg.

Klein, L.E. (1984–85), 'The Third Earl of Shaftesbury and the Progress of Politeness', *Eighteenth-Century Studies*, 18 (2), 185–214.

Klein, L.E. (1989), 'Liberty, Manners, and Politeness in Early Eighteenth-Century England', *The Historical Journal*, 32 (3), 583–605.

Klein, L.E. (1993), 'Shaftesbury, Politeness and the Politics of Religion', in N. Phillipson and Q. Skinner (eds), *Political Discourse in Early Modern Britain*, Cambridge: Cambridge University Press, pp. 283–301.

Klein, L.E. (1994), *Shaftesbury and the Culture of Politeness: moral discourse and cultural politics in early eighteenth-century England*, Cambridge: Cambridge University Press.

Klein, L.E. (1995a), 'Politeness for plebes. Consumption and Social Identity in Early Eighteenth-Century England', in A. Bermingham and J. Brewer (eds), *The Consumption of Culture 1600–1800. Image, Object, Text*, London: Routledge, pp. 362–82.

Klein, L.E. (1995b), 'Property and Politeness in the Early Eighteenth-Century Whig Moralists. The Case of the *Spectator*', in J. Brewer and S. Staves (eds), *Early Modern Conceptions of Property*, London: Routledge, pp. 221–233.

Klein, L.E. (1995c), 'Gender and the Public/Private Distinction in the Eighteenth Century: Some Questions about Evidence and Analytic Procedure', *Eighteenth-Century Studies*, 29 (1), 97–109.

Klein, L.E. (2002), 'Politeness and the Interpretation of the British Eighteenth Century', *Historical Journal*, 45 (4), 869–98.

Knights, M. (1994), *Politics and Opinion in Crisis, 1678–81*, Cambridge Studies in Early Modern British History ((eds) A. Fletcher, J. Guy and J. Morrill), Cambridge: Cambridge University Press.

Knox, G. (1995), *Antonio Pellegrini 1674–1741*, Oxford: Clarendon Press.

Kohn, H. (1940), 'The Genesis and Character of English Nationalism', *Journal of the History of Ideas*, 1 (1), 69–94.

Krautheimer, R. (1985), *The Rome of Alexander VII, 1655–1667*, Princeton and Guildford: Princeton University Press.

Kriz, E. & Kurz, O. (1979), *Legend, Myth, and Magic in the Image of the Artist. An historical experiment*, New Haven and London: Yale University Press.

Kriz, K.D. (1997), 'The Grand-Tour Forum', *Eighteenth-Century Studies*, 31 (1), 87–9.

Lambert, S. (1987), *The Image Multiplied*, London: Trefoil Books.

Langford, P. (1989), *A Polite and Commercial People. England 1727–1783*, Oxford: Oxford University Press.

Langford, P. (1991), *Public Life and the Propertied Englishman 1689–1798*, Oxford: Oxford University Press.

Langford, P. (2000), *Englishness Identified: Manners and Character, 1650–1850*, Oxford: Oxford University Press.

Lees-Milne, J. (2001), *Earls of Creation. Five Great Patrons of Eighteenth-Century Art*, First Published 1961, Harmondsworth: Penguin.

Lentin, T., Ferguson, J., Furbank, P.N., Hardwick, L. and Hursthouse, R. (1979), *Gibbon's The Decline and Fall of the Roman Empire*, A204: The Enlightenment, Milton Keynes: The Open University.

Leslie, C.R. and Taylor, T. (1865), *Life and Times of Sir Joshua Reynolds: with Notices of Some of his Contemporaries*, II, 2 vols, London: John Murray.

Levey, M. (1964), *The Later Italian Pictures in the Collection of Her Majesty the Queen*, Cambridge: Cambridge University Press.

Levine, J.M. (1981), 'Ancients and Moderns Reconsidered', *Eighteenth-Century Studies*, 15 (1), 72–89.

Levine, J.M. (1987), *Humanism and History*, Ithaca and London: Cornell University Press.

Levine, J.M. (1991), *The Battle of the Books. History and Literature in the Augustan Age*, Ithaca and London: Cornell University Press.

Levine, J.M. (1999), *Between the Ancients and the Moderns: Baroque Culture in Restoration England*, New Haven and London: Yale University Press.

Lewis, L. (1961), *Connoisseurs and Secret Agents in Eighteenth-Century Rome*, London: Chatto & Windus.

Lingo, E. (2002), 'The Greek Manner and a Christian *Canon*: Francois Duquesnoy's *Saint Susanna*', *Art Bulletin*, 84 (1), 65–93.

Lipking, L. (1970), *The Ordering of the Arts in Eighteenth-Century England*, Princeton: Princeton University Press.

Lippincott, L. (1983), *Selling Art in Georgian London: The Rise of Arthur Pond*, New Haven and London: Yale University Press.

Lippincott, L. (1995), 'Expanding on Portraiture. The Market, the Public, and the Hierarchy of Genres in Eighteenth-Century Britain', in A. Bermingham and J. Brewer (eds), *The Consumption of Culture 1600–1800: Image, Object, Text*, London and New York: Routledge, pp. 75–88.

Liversidge, M.J.H. (1980), *William Hogarth's Bristol Altar-Piece*, Bristol: Bristol Branch of the Historical Association.

Liversidge, M.J.H. (1992), 'Prelude to the Baroque: Isaac Fuller at Oxford', *Oxoniensia*, 57, 311–29.

Llewellyn, N. (1999), '"Those Loose and Immodest Pieces": Italian Art and the British Point of View', in S. West (ed.), *Italian Culture in Northern Europe in the Eighteenth Century*, Cambridge: Cambridge University Press, pp. 67–100.

Lyle Jeffrey, D. (ed.) (1992), *A Dictionary of Biblical Tradition in English Literature*, Grand Rapids, MI: William B. Eerdmans.

MacCulloch, D. (1991), 'The Myth of the English Reformation', *Journal of British Studies*, 30, 1–19.

MacCulloch, D. (2004), *Reformation. Europe's House Divided 1490–1700*, London: Penguin.

MacDonald, W. (1976), *The Pantheon*, Cambridge, MA: Harvard University Press.

MacGregor, A. (ed.) (1989), *The Late King's Goods: Collections, Possessions and Patronage of Charles I in the Light of the Commonwealth Sales Inventories*, London and Oxford: A. McAlpine in association with Oxford University Press.

MacGregor, A. (ed.) (1994), *Sir Hans Sloane: Collector, Scientist, Antiquary - Founding Father of the British Museum*, London: British Museum Press.

MacGregor, N. (2000), *Seeing Salvation*, London: BBC Worldwide.

Mannings, D. (2000), *Sir Joshua Reynolds. A Complete Catalogue of his Paintings*, 2 vols, New Haven and London: Published for the Paul Mellon Centre for Studies in British Art by Yale University Press.

Manuel, F. (1959), *The Eighteenth Century Confronts the Gods*, Cambridge, MA Harvard University Press.

Mainwaring, E.W. (1965), *Italian Landscape in Eighteenth-Century England: a study chiefly of the influence of Claude Lorrain and Salvator Rosa on English taste, 1700–1800*, First Published 1925, London: Frank Cass & Co.

Marshall, J. (1985), 'The Ecclesiology of the Latitude-men 1660–1689: Stillingfleet, Tillotson and "Hobbism"', *Journal of Ecclesiastical History*, 36 (3), 407–27.

Martineau, J. and Robison, A. (eds) (1994), *The Glory of Venice. Art in the Eighteenth Century*, London: Royal Academy of Art.

Mason, H. (2004) 'Keate, George (1729–1797)', *Oxford Dictionary of National Biography*, Oxford University Press ; online edition, May 2005 [http://www.oxforddnb.com/ view/article/15217, accessed 24 June 2006].

Mather, F.C. (1985), 'Georgian Churchmanship Reconsidered: Some Variations in Anglican Public Worship 1714–1830', *Journal of Ecclesiastical History*, 36 (2), 255–83.

Matthews, W.R. and Atkins, W.M. (eds) (1957), *A History of St Paul's Cathedral and the Men Associated with It*, London: Phoenix House.

Mayhew, R. (2000), 'William Gilpin and the Latitudinarian Picturesque', *Eighteenth-Century Studies*, 33 (3), 349–66.

McCann, J. (1990–1), 'English Baroque Church Building: Theatres or Law Courts', *Issues (London)*, 1 (2), 4–24.

McGrath, A.E. (1988), *Reformation Thought. An Introduction*, Third, Oxford: Blackwell Publishers.

McKillop, A. (1965), 'Local Attachment and Cosmopolitanism - The Eighteenth-Century Pattern', in F.W. Hilles and H. Bloom (eds), *From Sensibility to Romanticism: Essays Presented to Frederick A. Pottle*, New York: Oxford University Press, pp. 191–217.

McKitterick, D. (ed.) (1995), *The Making of the Wren Library*, Cambridge: Cambridge University Press.

Mead, W.E. (1972), *The Grand Tour in the Eighteenth Century*, First Published 1914, New York: B. Blom.

Merritt, J.F. (1998), 'Puritans, Laudians, and the Phenomenon of Church-Building in Jacobean London', *Historical Journal*, 41 (4), 935–60.

Meyer, A. (1985), 'Wootton at Wimpole', *Apollo*, 122 (283), 212–19.

Meyer, A. (1995), 'Re-dressing Classical Statuary: The Eighteenth-Century "Hand-in-Waistcoat" Portrait', *Art Bulletin*, 77 (1), 45–63.

Meyer, A. (1996), *Apostles in England. Sir James Thornhill and the Legacy of Raphael's Tapestry Cartoons*, New York: Columbia University.

Meyer, J.D. (1976), 'Benjamin West's St Stephen's Altar-Piece: a Study in Late Eighteenth-Century Protestant Church Patronage', *Burlington Magazine*, 118 (882), 634–42.

Micklethwaite, J.T. (1897), *The Ornaments of the Rubric*, Alcuin Club Tracts, 1, London: Longmans, Green and Co.

Middledorf, U. (1957), 'William Kent's Roman Prize in 1713', *Burlington Magazine*, 99 (649), 125.

Miller, D. (1998), 'Nations and Nationalism', in G. Craig (ed.), *Routledge Encyclopaedia of Philosophy*, Vol. 6, London and New York: Routledge, pp. 657–62.

Miller, E. (1995), *From Marcantonio Raimondi to the Postcard: Prints of the Raphael Cartoons*, London: Victoria and Albert Museum.

Miller, J. (1973), *Popery and Politics in England 1660–1688*, Cambridge: Cambridge University Press.

Miller, J. (1986), *Religion in the Popular Prints*, The English Satirical Print 1600–1832 ((ed.) M. Duffy), Cambridge: Chadwyck-Healey.

Miller, P.N. (1993), '"Freethinking' and 'Freedom of Thought' in Eighteenth-Century Britain', *The Historical Journal*, 36 (3), 599–617.

Milton, A. (1995), *Catholic and Reformed: the Roman and Protestant Churches in English Protestant Thought, 1600–1640*, Cambridge: Cambridge University Press.

Monod, P. (1993a), 'Painters and Party Politics in England, 1714–1760', *Eighteenth-Century Studies*, 26 (3), 367–98.

Monod, P. (1993b), *Jacobitism and the English People, 1688–1788*, First Published 1989, Cambridge: Cambridge University Press.

Moore, A. (1985), *Norfolk and the Grand Tour: Eighteenth-Century Travellers Abroad and Their Souvenirs*, Fakenham: Norfolk Museums Service.

Moore, A. (ed.) (1996), *Houghton Hall. The Prime Minister, The Empress and the Heritage*, London: Philip Wilson.

Morrill, J. (1996), 'The British Problem, c.1534–1707', in B. Bradshaw and J. Morrill (eds), *The British Problem, c.1534–1707: State Formation in the Atlantic Archipelago*, Basingstoke: Macmillan, pp. 1–38.

Mowl, T. (1996), *Horace Walpole*, London: John Murray.

Munro Cautley, H. (1949), *Norfolk Churches*, Ipswich: Boydell Press.

Munro Cautley, H. (1974), *Royal Arms and Commandments in Our Churches*, Ipswich: The Boydell Press.

Munslow, A. (2000), *The Routledge Companion to Historical Studies*, London and New York: Routledge.

Murdoch, A. (1998), *British History 1660–1832: National Identity and Local Culture*, Basingstoke: Macmillan.

Murdoch, T. (ed.) (1992), *Boughton House. The English Versailles*, London: Faber and Faber and Christie's.

Murray, P. (1971), *Piranesi and the Grandeur of Ancient Rome*, London: Thames and Hudson.

Murray, P. and Murray, L. (1996), *The Oxford Companion to Christian Art and Architecture*, Oxford: Oxford University Press.

Neff, E.B. (1995), *John Singleton Copley in England*, London: Merrell Holberton.

Nelson, R.S. and Shiff, R. (eds) (1996), *Critical Terms for Art History*, Chicago and London: University of Chicago Press.

New, M. (1978), 'Gibbon, Middleton and the "Barefooted Fryars"', *Notes and Queries*, 223, 51–2.

Newman, G. (1996), 'Nationalism Revisited', *Journal of British Studies*, 35 (1), 118–27.

Newman, G. (1997), *The Rise of English Nationalism: A Cultural History, 1740–1830*, First Published 1987, Basingstoke: Macmillan.

Nisbet, H.B. and Rawson, C. (eds) (1997), *The Cambridge History of Literary Criticism. Volume 4: The Eighteenth Century*, Cambridge: Cambridge University Press.

Nockles, P. (1993), 'Church Parties in the Pre-Tractarian Church of England 1750–1833: the "Orthodox" - Some Problems of Definition', in J. Walsh, C. Haydon and S. Taylor (eds), *The Church of England c.1689–c.1833. From Toleration to Tractarianism*, Cambridge: Cambridge University Press, pp. 334–59.

Nolan, A. (1998), *Public Virtue Display'd: Medicine and Collecting in the Life of Dr Richard Mead (1673–1754)*, MA Dissertation, University of East Anglia.

North, M. and Ormrod, D. (eds) (1998), *Art Markets in Europe, 1400–1800*, Aldershot: Ashgate.

O'Connell, S. (1985), 'Simon Gribelin (1661–1733) Print-Maker and Metal-Engraver', *Print Quarterly*, 2, 27–38.

O'Connell, S. (1988), 'Lord Shaftesbury in Naples, 1711–1713', *Walpole Society*, 53, 149–219.

O'Connell, S. (1999), *The Popular Print in England 1550–1850*, London: British Museum.

Ogden, H.V.S. and Ogden, M.S. (1947), 'A Bibliography of Seventeenth-Century Writings on the Pictorial Arts in English', *Art Bulletin*, 29 (3), 196–201.

Ogilvie, R.M. (1964), *Latin and Greek: a history of the influence of the classics on English life from 1600–1918*, London: Routledge & Kegan Paul.

Olin, M. (1996), 'Gaze', in R.S. Nelson and R. Shiff (eds), *Critical Terms for Art History*, Chicago and London: University of Chicago Press, pp. 208–19.

Oman, C. (1957), *English Church Plate 597–1830*, London: Oxford University Press.

Ostrow, S.F. (1996), *Art and Spirituality in Counter-Reformation Rome: the Sistine and Pauline Chapels in S Maria Maggiore*, Cambridge: Cambridge University Press.

Overton, J.H. (1885), *Life in the English Church (1660–1714)*, London: Longmans, Green & Co.

Pailin, D.A. (1984), *Attitudes to Other Religions. Comparative Religion in Seventeenth & Eighteenth Century Britain*, Manchester: Manchester University Press.

Parry, G. (1981), *The Golden Age Restor'd*, Manchester: Manchester University Press.

Patey, D.L. (1984), *Probability and Literary Form. Philosophic Theory and Literary Practice in the Augustan Age*, Cambridge: Cambridge University Press.

Paulson, R. (1965), *Hogarth's Graphic Works*, 2 vols, London and New Haven: Yale University Press.

Paulson, R. (1975), *Emblem and Expression. Meaning in English Art of the Eighteenth Century*, London: Thames and Hudson.

Paulson, R. (1993), *Hogarth: His Life and Times*, 3 vols, Cambridge: Lutterworth Press.

Pears, I. (1982), 'Patronage and Learning in the Virtuoso Republic: John Talman in Italy, 1709–12', *Oxford Art Journal*, 5 (1), 24–30.

Pears, I. (1988), *The Discovery of Painting. The Growth of Interest in the Arts in England, 1680–1768*, New Haven and London: Yale University Press.

Penny, N. (1978), *Piranesi*, London: Oresko Books.

Perkins, M.A. (1999), *Nation and Word, 1770–1850*, Aldershot: Ashgate.

Pevsner, N. (1993), *The Englishness of English Art*, Harmondsworth: Penguin Books.

Phillimore, R. (1895), *The Ecclesiastical Law of the Church of England*, First Published 1873, 2 vols, London: Sweet and Maxwell.

Phillips, J. (1973), *The Reformation of Images: the Destruction of Art in England 1535–1665*, Berkeley and London: University of California Press.

Phillipson, N. (1993), 'Politics and Politeness in the Reign of Anne and the Early Hanoverians', in J.G.A. Pocock (ed.), *Varieties of British Political Thought, 1500–1800*, Cambridge: Cambridge University Press, pp. 211–45.

Pietrangeli, C. (1983), 'The Discovery of Classical Art in Eighteenth-Century Rome', *Apollo*, 117 (255), 380–91.

Pocock, J. (1975), 'England', in O. Ranum (ed.), *National Consciousness, History and Political Culture in Early-Modern Europe*, Baltimore and London: Johns Hopkins University Press, pp. 98–117.

Pocock, J.G.A. (1981), 'The *Machiavellian Moment* Revisited: A Study in History and Ideology', *Journal of Modern History*, 53 (1), 49–72.

Pocock, J.G.A. (1985), *Virtue, Commerce and History. Essays on Political Thought and History, Chiefly in the Eighteenth Century*, Cambridge: Cambridge University Press.

Pointon, M. (1993), *Hanging the Head: Portraiture and Social Formation in Eighteenth-Century England*, The Paul Mellon Centre for Studies in British Art, New Haven and London: Yale University Press.

Pointon, M. (1997), *Strategies for Showing. Women, Possession, and Representation in English Visual Culture 1665–1800*, Oxford: Oxford University Press.

Pointon, M. (2000), *William Hogarth's Sigismunda in Focus*, London: Tate Publishing.

Pomian, K. (1990), *Collectors and Curiosities: Paris and Venice 1500–1800*, trans. E. Wiles-Portier, Cambridge: Cambridge University Press.

Pope-Hennessey, J. (1950), *The Raphael Cartoons*, London: Victoria and Albert Museum.

Porter, R. (1981), 'The Enlightenment in England', in R. Porter and M. Teich (eds), *The Enlightenment in National Context*, Cambridge: Cambridge University Press, pp. 1–18.

Porter, R. (1995), *Gibbon. Making History*, First Published 1988, London: Phoenix Giants.

Porter, R. (1997), 'The New Eighteenth-Century Social History', in J. Black (ed.), *Culture and Society in Britain 1660–1800*, Manchester and New York: Manchester University Press, pp. 29–50.

Porter, R. (2000), *Enlightenment: Britain and the Creation of the Modern World*, Harmondsworth: Allen Lane.

Porter, R. and Teich, M. (eds.) (1981), *The Enlightenment in National Context*, Cambridge: Cambridge University Press.

Postle, M. (1995), *Sir Joshua Reynolds: the Subject Pictures*, Cambridge: Cambridge University Press.

Prown, J.D. (1997), 'A Course of Antiquities at Rome, 1764', *Eighteenth-Century Studies*, 31 (1), 90–100.

Ramsbottom, J.D. (1992), 'Presbyterians and "Partial Conformity" in the Restoration Church of England', *Journal of Ecclesiastical History*, 43 (2), 249–70.

Randall, G. (1980), *Church Furnishings and Decoration in England and Wales*, London: B.T. Batsford.

Ranum, O. (ed.) (1975), *National Consciousness, History and Political Culture in Early-Modern Europe*, The Johns Hopkins Symposia in Comparative History, Baltimore and London: Johns Hopkins University Press.

Reedy, G. (1985), *The Bible and Reason. Anglicans and Scripture in Late Seventeenth Century England*, Philadelphia: University of Pennsylvania Press.

Rees, A.L. and Borzello, F. (eds) (1986), *The New Art History*, London: Camden Press.

Rensselaer Lee, W. (1940), '*Ut pictura poesis*. The Humanistic Theory of Painting', *Art Bulletin*, 22 (4), 197–269.

Rivers, I. (ed.) (1982), *Books and their Readers in Eighteenth-Century England*, Leicester: Leicester University Press.

Rivers, I. (ed.) (2001), *Books and their Readers in Eighteenth-Century England: new essays*, London and New York: Leicester University Press.

Robertson, C. and Whistler, C. (1997), *Drawings by the Carracci from British Collections*, Oxford: Ashmolean Museum.

Robinson, J.M. (1995a), 'Lordly Chapels', *Country Life*, 189 (49), 72–7.

Robinson, J.M. (1995b), *Treasures of the English Churches*, London: Sinclair-Stevenson.

Roettgen, S. (1993), *Anton Raphael Mengs 1728–1779 and His British Patrons*, London: A. Zwemmer.

Rogers, N. (1989), *Whigs and Cities. Popular Politics in the Age of Walpole and Pitt*, Oxford: Clarendon Press.

Rosenberg, A. (1953), *Sir Richard Blackmore: A Poet and Physician of the Augustan Age*, Lincoln, NE: University of Nebraska Press.

Rosenberg, M. (1995), *Raphael and France. The Artist as Paradigm and Symbol*, Pennsylvania: Pennsylvania State University Press.

Rosenblum, R. (1997), '"Apostles in England": Sir James Thornhill and the legacy of Raphael's cartoons', *Apollo - the International Magazine of the Arts*, 145 (419), 56–7.

Rosenheim, J.M. (1998), *The Emergence of a Ruling Order 1650–1750*, Studies in Modern History, London: Longman.

Rothery (1868), *Rothery's Return of Ecclesiastical Appeals to the High Court of Delegates*, London: House of Commons.

Rowell, G. (ed.) (1986), *Tradition Renewed. The Oxford Movement Conference Papers*, London: Darton, Longman and Todd.

Rubin, P.L. (1995), *Giorgio Vasari: Art and History*, New Haven and London: Yale University Press.

Rupp, E.G. (1986), *Religion in England 1688–1791*, Oxford: Clarendon Press.

Russell, F. (1985), 'A Means to Devotion: Italian Art and the Clerical Connoisseur', *Country Life*, 178 (4607), 1748–51.

Russell, F. (1989), 'The Derby Collection (1721–1735)', *The Walpole Society*, 53, 143–80.

Salerno, L. (1951), 'Seventeenth-Century English Literature on Painting', *Journal of the Warburg and Courtauld Institutes*, 14, 234–58.

Sambrook, J. (1993), *The Eighteenth Century: the Intellectual and Cultural Context of English Literature 1700–1789*, Second Edition, Harlow: Longman.

Samuel, R. (ed.) (1989), *Patriotism: The Making and Unmaking of British National Identity*, 3 vols, London: Routledge.

Saumarez Smith, C. (1988), 'Supply and Demand in English Country House Building 1660–1740', *Oxford Art Journal*, 11 (2), 3–9.

Saumarez Smith, C. (1993), *Eighteenth-Century Decoration. Design and the Domestic Interior in England*, New York: Harry N. Abrams.

Saxl, F. and Wittkower, R. (1948), *British Art and the Mediterranean*, Oxford: Oxford University Press.

Schlereth, T.J. (1977), *The Cosmopolitan Ideal in the Enlightenment Thought: Its Form and Function in the Ideas of Franklin, Hume and Voltaire, 1694–1790*, Notre Dame and London: University of Notre Dame Press.

Scott, J. (1975), *Piranesi*, London and New York: Academy Editions and St. Martin's Press.

Scott, J. (1990), 'England's Troubles: Exhuming the Popish Plot', in T. Harris, P. Seaward and M. Goldie (eds), *The Politics of Religion in Restoration England*, Oxford: Basil Blackwell, pp. 107–31.

Scribner, R., Porter, R. and Teich, M. (eds) (1994), *The Reformation in National Context*, Cambridge: Cambridge University Press.

Searby, P. (1997), *A History of the University of Cambridge. Volume 3*, Cambridge: Cambridge University Press.

Seaward, P. (1991), *The Restoration, 1660–1688*, British History in Perspective, Basingstoke: Macmillan.

Sekora, J. (1977), *Luxury. The Concept in Western Thought from Eden to Smollett*, London and Baltimore: Johns Hopkins University Press.

Sells, A.L. (1964), *The Paradise of Travellers. The Italian Influence on Englishmen in the Seventeenth Century*, London: Allen & Unwin.

Shapiro, B.J. (1983), *Probability and Certainty in Seventeenth-Century England*, Princeton and Guildford: Princeton University Press.

Sharp, R. (1986), 'New Perspectives on the High Church Tradition: Historical Background 1730–1780', in G. Rowell (ed.), *Tradition Renewed. The Oxford Movement Conference Papers*, London: Darton, Longman and Todd, pp. 4–23.

Shearman, J. (1972), *Raphael's Cartoons in the Collection of Her Majesty the Queen and the Tapestries from the Sistine Chapel*, London and New York: Phaidon Press.

Simonsuuri, K. (1979), *Homer's Original Genius. Eighteenth-Century Notions of the Early Greek Epic (1688–1798)*, Cambridge: Cambridge University Press.

Simpson, F. (1951), 'The English Connoisseur and Its Sources', *Burlington Magazine*, 93 (581), 355–6.

Sloan, K. (1996), '"Picture-mad in virtu-land": William Hamilton's Collection of Paintings', in I. Jenkins and K. Sloan (eds), *Vases and Volcanoes. Sir William Hamilton and His Collection*, London: British Museum, pp. 75–92.

Sloan, K. (ed.) (2004), *Enlightenment: discovering the world in the eighteenth century*, London: British Museum Press.

Sloman, S.L. (1991), 'Wade Altarpiece for Bath Abbey: a Reconstruction', *Burlington Magazine*, 133 (1061), 507–10.

Smith, A.D. (1971), *Theories of Nationalism*, London: Duckworth.

Smith, A.D. (1998), *Nationalism and Modernism. A Critical Survey of Recent Theories of Nations and Nationalism*, London and New York: Routledge.

Smith, R. (1989), 'The Achievements of Charles Jennens (1700–1773)', *Music and Letters*, 70 (May), 161–89.

Solkin, D.H. (1986), 'Great Pictures or Great Men? Reynolds, Male Portraiture, and the Power of Art', *Oxford Art Journal*, 9 (2), 42–9.

Solkin, D.H. (1992a), *Painting for Money. The Visual Arts and the Public Sphere in Eighteenth-Century England*, New Haven and London: Yale University Press.

Solkin, D.H. (1992b), 'ReWrighting Shaftesbury: The Air Pump and the Limits of Commercial Humanism', in J. Barrell (ed.), *Painting and the Politics of Culture: New Essays on British Art 1700–1850*, Oxford: Oxford University Press, pp. 73–99.

Solkin, D.H. (ed.) (2001), *Art on the Line: the Royal Academy Exhibitions at Somerset House, 1780–1836*, New Haven and London: Yale University Press.

Sommerville, C.J. (1992), *The Secularization of Early Modern England: from Religious Culture to Religious Faith*, New York: Oxford University Press.

Sommerville, J. (2004), 'Conscience, Law, and Things Indifferent: Arguments on Toleration from the Vestarian Controversy to Hobbes and Locke', in H.E. Braun and E. Vallance (eds), *Contexts of Conscience in Early Modern Europe, 1500–1700*, Basingstoke: Palgrave, pp. 166–79.

Souden, D. (1991), *Wimpole Hall*, London: The National Trust.

Sparrow, J. (1960), 'An Oxford Altar-piece', *Burlington Magazine*, 102, 4–9.

Sparrow, J. (1965), 'Mengs's All Souls Altar-piece: a Further Note', *Burlington Magazine*, 107 (753), 631–2.

Spear, R.E. (1982), *Domenichino*, 2 vols, New Haven and London: Yale University Press.

Spear, R.E. (1997), *The 'Divine' Guido: Religion, Sex, Money and Art in the World of Guido Reni*, New Haven and London: Yale University Press.

Spraggon, J. (2003), *Puritan Iconoclasm during the English Civil War*, Woodbridge: Boydell and Brewer.

Spurr, J. (1988), '"Latitudianarianism" and the Restoration Church', *The Historical Journal*, 31 (1), 61–82.

Spurr, J. (1990a), '"Virtue, Religion and Government": the Anglican Uses of Providence', in T. Harris, P. Seaward and M. Goldie (eds), *The Politics of Religion in Restoration England*, Oxford: Basil Blackwell, pp. 29–47.

Spurr, J. (1990b), 'Schism and the Restoration Church', *Journal of the Ecclesiastical History Society*, 41 (3), 408–24.

Spurr, J. (1991), *The Restoration Church of England 1646–1689*, New Haven and London: Yale University Press.

Spurr, J. (1998), *English Puritanism 1603–1689*, Basingstoke: Macmillan.

Spurr, J. (2002), 'The English "Post-Reformation"?', *The Journal of Modern History*, 74, 101–19.

Stephen, L. (1902), *English Thought in the Eighteenth Century*, First Published 1876, 2 vols, London: Smith, Elder & Co.

Stolnitz, J. (1961–62), 'On the Origins of "Aesthetic Disinterestedness"', *Journal of Aesthetics and Art Criticism*, 20, 131–42.

Stuart, D.M. (1927), *Horace Walpole*, London: Macmillan & Co.

Summers, P. (ed.) (1976), *Norfolk and Suffolk*, Hatchments in Britain, (ed.) P. Summers, London: Phillimore.

Sutherland, L.S. and Mitchell, L.G. (eds) (1986), *The History of the University of Oxford, Volume V: The Eighteenth Century*, Oxford: Clarendon Press.

Swann, M. (2001), *Curiosities and Texts: The Culture of Collecting in Early Modern England*, Material Texts ((eds) R.C. e. al), Philadelphia: University of Pennsylvania Press.

Sykes, N. (1962), *Church and State in England in the Eighteenth Century*, First Published 1934, Hamden, CT: Archon Books.

Symonds, R. (1988), *Alternative Saints. The Post-Reformation British People Commemorated by the Church of England*, Basingstoke: Macmillan.

Taylor, S. (1988), 'Church and Society after the Glorious Revolution', *Historical Journal*, 31 (4), 973–87.

Taylor, S. (1992), 'William Warburton and the Alliance of Church and State', *Journal of Ecclesiastical History*, 43 (2), 271–86.

Taylor, S. (2000), 'Whigs, Tories and Aniclericalism: Ecclesiastical Courts Legislation in 1733', *Parliamentary History*, 19 (3), 329–55.

Thomas, K. (1995), 'English Protestantism and Classical Art', in L. Gent (ed.), *Albion's Classicism: The Visual Arts in Britain 1550–1660*, London and New Haven: Yale University Press, pp. 221–38.

Thompson, A.C. (2002), 'Popery, Politics, and Private Judgement in Early Hanoverian Britain', *Historical Journal*, 45 (2), 333–56.

Thompson, E.P. (1974), 'Patrician Society, Plebeian Culture', *Journal of Social History*, 7 (4), 382–405.

Tillyard, S. (1995), *Aristocrats*, First Published 1994, London: Vintage.

Tindal Hart, A. (1957), 'The Age of Reason, 1660–1831', in W.R. Matthews and W.M. Atkins (eds), *A History of St Paul's Cathedral and the Men Associated With It*, London: Phoenix House, pp. 172–249.

Tinniswood, A. (1989), *A History of Country House Visiting*, Oxford: Basil Blackwell.

Too, Y.L. and Livingstone, N. (eds) (1998), *Pedagogy and Power: rhetorics of classical learning*, Cambridge: Cambridge University Press.

Towner, J. (ed.) (1981), *The English Grand Tour*, Working Paper 79, Birmingham: University of Birmingham Centre for Urban and Regional Studies.

Tumbleson, R.D. (1996), '"Reason and Religion": The Science of Anglicanism', *Journal of the History of Ideas*, 57 (1), 131–56.

Tumbleson, R.D. (1998), *Catholicism in the English Protestant Imagination*, Cambridge: Cambridge University Press.

Tyacke, N. (ed.) (1998), *England's Long Reformation, 1500–1800*, London: UCL Press.

Uglow, J. (1997), *Hogarth. A Life and a World*, London: Faber and Faber.

Vallance, A. (1936), *English Church Screens*, London: B.T. Batsford.

Vallance, E. (2004), 'The Decline of Conscience as a Political Guide: William Higden's View of the English Constitution (1709)', in H.E. Braun and E. Vallance (eds), *Contexts of Conscience in Early Modern Europe, 1500–1700*, Basingstoke: Palgrave Macmillan, pp. 82–99.

Vaughan, W. (1990), 'The Englishness of British Art', Oxford Art Journal, 13 (2), 11–23.

Vaughan, W. (1999), *British Painting: The Golden Age. From Hogarth to Turner*, World of Art, London: Thames and Hudson.

Venn, J. (1922–54), *Alumni Cantabrigienses*, Cambridge: Cambridge University Press.

Vickery, A. (1998), *The Gentleman's Daughter: Women's Lives in Georgian England*, New Haven and London: Yale University Press.

Virgin, P.A. (1989), *The Church in an Age of Negligence 1700–1840*, Cambridge: James Clarke.

von Erffa, H. and Staley, A. (1986), *The Paintings of Benjamin West*, New Haven and London: Yale University Press.

Walsh, J., Haydon, C. and Taylor, S. (eds) (1993), *The Church of England c.1689– c.1833. From Toleration to Tractarianism*, Cambridge: Cambridge University Press.

Walsh, J. and Taylor, S. (1993), 'The Church and Anglicanism in the "Long" Eighteenth Century', in J. Walsh, C. Haydon and S. Taylor (eds), *The Church of England c.1689–c.1833. From Toleration to Tractarianism*, Cambridge: Cambridge University Press, pp. 1–66.

Walsh, M. (1997), 'Biblical Scholarship and Literary Criticism', in H.B. Nisbet and C. Rawson (eds), *The Cambridge History of Literary Criticism. Volume 4: The Eighteenth Century*, Cambridge: Cambridge University Press, pp. 758–77.

Walsham, A. (1999), *Providence in Early-Modern England*, Oxford: Oxford University Press.

Walter, J. (2004), '"Abolishing Superstition with Sedition"? The Politics of Popular Iconoclasm in England 1640–1642', *Past and Present*, (183), 79– 123.

Wardle, J.R. (1899), *Clare College*, University of Cambridge College Histories, London: F.E. Robinson and Co.

Waterhouse, E. (1981), *The Dictionary of British 18th Century Painters*, Woodbridge: Antique Collectors Club.

Waterhouse, E. (1994), *Painting in Britain 1530–1790*, First Published 1953, New Haven and London: Yale University Press.

Waterhouse, E.K. (1952a), 'Paintings from Venice for Seventeenth-Century England', *Italian Studies*, VII, 1–23.

Waterhouse, E.K. (1952b), 'English Painting and France in the Eighteenth Century', *Journal of the Warburg and Courtauld Institutes*, 15, 123.

Watson, F.J.B. (1944), 'On the Early History of Collecting in England', *Burlington Magazine*, 84–5, 223–8.

Watson, F.J.B. (1954), 'A Venetian Settecento Chapel in the English Countryside', *Arte Veneta*, 8, 295–302.

Wayment, H. (1981), 'The East Window of St Margaret's, Westminster', *The Antiquaries Journal*, 61, 292–301.

Weinsheimer, J.C. (1993), *Eighteenth-Century Hermeneutics. Philosophy of Interpretation in England From Locke to Burke*, New Haven and London: Yale University Press.

West, S. (ed.) (1999), *Italian Culture in Northern Europe in the Eighteenth Century*, Cambridge: Cambridge University Press.

Weston-Lewis, A. (ed.) (1998), *Effigies and Ecstasies. Roman Baroque Sculpture and Design in the Age of Bernini*, Edinburgh: Trustees of the National Galleries of Scotland.

Whiffen, M. (1948), *Stuart and Georgian Churches: the Architecture of the Church of England Outside London*, London: B.T. Batsford.

Whinney, M. (1988), *Sculpture in Britain 1530–1830*, First Published 1964, Harmondsworth: Penguin.

Whinney, M.D. and Millar, O. (1957), *English Art 1625–1714*, Oxford: Oxford University Press.

Whistler, C. and Wood, J. (eds) (1988), *Rubens in Oxford. An Exhibition of Drawings from Christ Church and the Ashmolean Museum*, London: P. and D. Colnaghi & Co.

White, C. (ed.) (1983), *Rembrandt in Eighteenth-Century England*, New Haven and London: Yale University Press.

Whitfield, C. (1973), *England and the Seicento*, London: Thomas Agnew and Sons Ltd.

Whyman, S. (1999), *Sociability and Power in Late-Stuart England: The Cultural Worlds of the Verneys 1660–1720*, Oxford: Oxford University Press.

Williams, R. (1983), *Keywords. A Vocabulary of Culture and Society*, London: Fontana.

Williamson, T. (1995), *Polite Landscapes: Gardens and Society in Eighteenth-Century England*, Stroud: Alan Sutton Publishing.

Wilson, M.I. (1984), *William Kent. Architect, Designer, Painter, Gardener, 1685–1748*, London: Routledge & Kegan Paul.

Wilton, A. and Bignamini, I. (eds) (1996), *Grand Tour. The Lure of Italy in the Eighteenth Century*, London: Tate Gallery Publishing.

Wilton-Ely, J. (1978), *The Mind and Art of Giovanni Battista Piranesi*, London: Thames and Hudson.

Wind, E. (1986), *Hume and the Heroic Portrait: Studies in Eighteenth-Century Imagery*, (ed.) J. Anderson, Oxford: Clarendon Press.

Womersley, D. (ed.) (1997), *Edward Gibbon: bicentenary essays*, Studies on Voltaire and the Eighteenth Century 355, Oxford: Voltaire Foundation.

Wood, D. (ed.) (1992), *The Church and the Arts*, Studies in Church History, Vol. 28, Oxford: Blackwell.

Wood, J. (1999), 'Raphael Copies and Exemplary Picture Galleries in Mid Eighteenth-Century London', *Zeitschrift fur Kunstgeschichte*, 62, 394–417.

Woodall, J. (ed.) (1997), *Portraiture: Facing the Subject*, Manchester and New York: Manchester University Press.

Woodforde, C. (1954), *English Stained and Painted Glass*, Oxford: Clarendon Press.

Woodforde, C. (1970), *Stained Glass in Somerset 1250–1830*, First Published 1946, Bath: Kingsmead Reprints.

Woodhead, J.R. (1965), *The Rulers of London 1660–1689. A Biographical Record of the Aldermen and Common Councilmen of the City of London*, London: London & Middlesex Archaeological Society.

Wright, C. (1976), *Old Master Paintings in Britain*, London: Sotheby Parke Bernet.

Wright, S.J. (ed.) (1988), *Parish, Church and People*, London: Hutchinson.

Yates, N. (1986), 'The Condition of Kentish Churches before Victorian Restoration', *Archaeologica Cantiana*, 103, 119–25.

Yates, N. (2000), *Buildings, Faith and Worship*, Revised Edition, Oxford: Clarendon Press.

Yaxley, D. (1995), 'The Houghton Gallery', in A. Longcroft and R. Joby (eds), *East Anglian Studies*, Norwich: Merwood Publishing, pp. 303–10.

Young, B.W. (1998a), 'A History of Variations: the Identity of the Eighteenth-Century Church of England', in T. Claydon and I. McBride (eds), *Protestanism and National Identity. Britain and Ireland, c.1650–c.1850*, Cambridge: Cambridge University Press, pp. 105–28.

Young, B.W. (1998b), *Religion and Enlightenment in Eighteenth-Century England. Theological Debate from Locke to Burke*, Oxford: Clarendon Press.

Young, B.W. (1998c), '"Scepticism in Excess": Gibbon and Eighteenth-Century Christianity', *The Historical Journal*, 41 (1), 179–99.

Young, B.W. (2000), 'Religious History and the Eighteenth-Century Historian', *The Historical Journal*, 43 (3), 849–68.

Young, E. (1976), 'Ricci, Rococo and the English', *Apollo*, 104 (173), 75–6.

Young, E. (1979), 'Vincenzo Damini in England', *Arte Veneta*, 33, 70–78.

Unpublished PhD Theses

Nolan, A. (2002), *Philanthropy and Visual Culture in Mid-Eighteenth Century Britain; the Public Image of the Foundling Hospital*, University of East Anglia.

Osmun, W.R. (1950), *A Study of the Works of Sir James Thornhill*, University of London

Index